The voluntary sector in British social services

FAMILY FUTURES CONSORTIUM LIMITED.
17 NEWINGTON GREEN.LONDON N16 9PU
TELEPHONE & FAX. 0207 241 0503. COMPANY
REGISTRATION NO. 3571649.

A NOT FOR PROFIT ORGANISATION

SOCIAL POLICY IN MODERN BRITAIN

General Editor: Jo Campling

POVERTY AND STATE SUPPORT *Peter Alcock*
HEALTH POLICY AND THE NATIONAL HEALTH SERVICE *Judy Allsop*
THE VOLUNTARY SECTOR IN BRITISH SOCIAL SERVICES *Maria Brenton*
HOUSING AND SOCIAL JUSTICE *Gill Burke*
EDUCATION AS SOCIAL POLICY *Janet Finch*
WORK AND INEQUALITY *Susan Lonsdale*
FOUNDATIONS OF THE WELFARE STATE *Pat Thane*
THE ELDERLY IN MODERN SOCIETY *Anthea Tinker*
SOCIAL RESPONSES TO HANDICAP *Eda Topliss*
THE PERSONAL SOCIAL SERVICES *Adrian Webb and Gerald Wistow*

THE VOLUNTARY SECTOR
IN BRITISH SOCIAL SERVICES

Maria Brenton

LONGMAN
London and New York

LONGMAN GROUP LIMITED
Longman House, Burnt Mill, Harlow
Essex CM20 2JE, England
Associated companies throughout the world

*Published in the United States of America
by Longman Inc., New York*

First published 1985

BRITISH LIBRARY CATALOGUING IN PUBLICATION DATA

Brenton, Maria
 The voluntary sector in British social services.
 1. Charities——Great Britain
 I. Title
 361.7′0941   HV245

ISBN 0-582-29600-5

LIBRARY OF CONGRESS CATALOGING IN PUBLICATION DATA

Brenton, Maria, 1945-
 The voluntary sector in British social services.

 (Social policy in modern Britain)
 Bibliography: p.
 Includes index.
 1. Social service—Great Britain.   2. Voluntarism—
Great Britain.   3. Great Britain—Social policy.
I. Title.   II. Series.
HV245.B768   1985   361.3′7′0941   85-4285
ISBN 0-582-29600-5

Set in 10/11 Linoterm Plantin
Produced by Longman Singapore Publishers (Pte) Ltd.
Printed in Singapore.

CONTENTS

CONTENTS

EDITOR'S PREFACE

This series, written by practising teachers in universities and poly-technics, is produced for students who are required to study social policy and administration, either as social science undergraduates or on the various professional courses. The books provide studies focusing on essential topics in social policy and include new areas of discussion and research, to give students the opportunity to explore ideas and act as a basis of seminar work and further study. Each book combines an analysis of the selected theme, a critical narrative of the main developments and an assessment putting the topic into perspective as defined in the title. The supporting documents and comprehensive bibliography are an important aspect of the series.

Conventional footnotes are avoided and the following system of references is used. A superior numeral in the text refers the reader to the corresponding entry in the list of references at the end of each chapter. A select bibliography is found at the end of the book. A number in square brackets, preceded by 'doc.', e.g. [doc. 6, 8] refers the reader to the corresponding items in the section of documents which follows the main text.

In *The Voluntary Sector in British Social Services*, Maria Brenton takes up a theme which has become increasingly popular in recent years among social policy thinkers and politicians alike. Non-statutory activities and organisations have retained a not inconsiderable role in various of the social services throughout the development of the welfare state. However, it is only since the late 1970s when the institutions of the welfare state reached what many see as a critical turning-point in an unfavourable political and economic climate, that serious questions have been raised about the accepted balance between statutory and voluntary agencies in delivering social services. In this study, the author considers the implications of a return to reliance upon the voluntary sector for the delivery of personal social services – a move advocated, she suggests, more for its potential in reducing the role of the state than for its promise of a more effective system of care. Support for a substitution process, whereby voluntary and informal action would be encouraged to replace much of the current statutory role, is based, she considers, on an uncritical approach to the voluntary sector generally. This is a lack which the present study sets out to remedy by providing as full an account as possible of the functioning of the voluntary sector and its relations with the public sector. For the first time since major studies of the voluntary sector in the 1950s and 1960s, a broad overview is presented which traces both its survival and development in the context of the welfare state and the more recent trends which have paved the way for its current renaissance. The strengths and weaknesses of voluntary organisations are examined by reference to a range of research and other studies which testify to growing interest among academics in the voluntary sector as a subject of enquiry. Special attention is given to growing evidence of a policy shift on the part of successive governments towards encouraging specific voluntary sector activities as a complement or substitute for statutory services. The interpenetration of the two sectors, facilitated by public funds, is seen to raise issues which are both contentious and insufficiently examined.

This book brings together perspectives on the voluntary sector that are scattered among a mass of academic, governmental, semi-official and voluntary sector publications, and harnesses them to an enquiry that is both rigorous and critical. It is a timely study, and one which should prove invaluable to students trying to find their way around a changing subject area that lacks clear boundaries and definitions. Maria Brenton has been active in voluntary agencies in a number of capacities, and has also researched and written about the voluntary social services system in the Netherlands. It has been her experience in this research particularly which has encouraged and informed the detached, questioning approach which is the hallmark of this present volume.

Jo Campling

AUTHOR'S PREFACE

The enormity of the task involved in writing a general study of the voluntary sector in British social services did not strike me forcefully until I attempted it. It is in fact an impossible task – although the term 'voluntary sector' is one that is popularly understood in British society, it does not lend itself to clear definition. Lacking boundaries and uniformly defined structures even when considered solely in the context of the social services, it can encompass much of human life. In two of the countries touched upon in this book, the United States and the Netherlands, use of the term is so broad that it covers forms of association such as trades unions, private universities, the churches and football clubs. We have a narrower understanding, fortunately, but even so the voluntary sector in Britain denotes a mass of small, unstructured and informally constituted groups and activities which lie beyond efforts to quantify or describe them. It was with some relief that I made an early, arbitrary decision to limit my focus in this study to organised forms of voluntary endeavour – for reasons elaborated in Chapter 1. I followed also a definitional convention that has gained strength in recent years, in clearly distinguishing the voluntary sector as I understand it from the 'informal' sector. This book offers a general overview of the organised voluntary sector to students of the social services and sets it in a clear social policy context. While aiming to give a sense of the evolutionary development and growth of voluntary agencies, it takes as a particular focus the new era they encountered in the late 1970s and early 1980s. Accordingly, a major preoccupation of the book lies with the resurgence of support for voluntary social services rather than statutory ones among New Right politicians and among academics. Its dominant, integrating theme concerns the desirability and feasibility of a substantial substitution process whereby the social service roles of the two sectors are radically changed or reversed.

Maria Brenton

ACKNOWLEDGEMENTS

My love and thanks are due first and foremost to Ros Wilkins who has helped carry 'the Albatross' – the invisible subtitle of this book. She has not read a word of it, and probably never will if I know her. Yet, in a very real way she has helped to write it, by supporting me through these past few years and by constantly encouraging progress through such judicious advice as 'you'll do it in the end' and 'never mind – give it up!'

Heartfelt thanks are due also to a number of helpful critics – to Claire Callender and Paul Wilding, who read virtually all the manuscript, and to Sheila Owen-Jones and Paul Lodge who commented on individual chapters and convinced me I will never make a historian. My long-suffering editor, Jo Campling, should get an award for extreme patience in the face of adversity, and I am most grateful for her support and forbearance.

I should like also to record my appreciation of the unfailing helpfulness of Clive Evers and Susan Bates at the National Council for Voluntary Organisations' library in Bedford Square, London. I am grateful too for the reading facilities afforded me by the NCVO.

We are grateful to the following for permission to reproduce copyright material:

Dr Barnardo's for data taken from a table in the *Annual Report 1980/81*; Bedford Square Press of the National Council for Voluntary Organisations for extracts from *Charity Law and Social Justice*, *Charity Law and Voluntary Organisations*, *Social Workers: Their Role and Tasks* (published for the National Institute for Social Work), *Voluntary Sector and Government: A Code for Voluntary Organisations*, *Voluntary Social Services: Financial Resources*; the Controller of Her Majesty's Stationery Office for extracts from *Cmnd Papers 8710* (1952), *3703* (1969), & *The Government and the Voluntary Sector: A Consultative Document*; Croom Helm for extracts from *The Future of Voluntary Organisations*.

To my parents – my mother and the memory of my father

Part One
THE BACKGROUND

Chapter One
INTRODUCTION:
KEY ISSUES

An upsurge of interest in the potential of non-governmental altern-atives to the delivery of social services by the state has been precipi-tated in recent years by changes in the economic and political climate. These changes have not only upturned the growth ethic on which the welfare state has been based for several decades, but have also cast doubt, among all shades of the ideological spectrum, on the way that the welfare state has developed in that time. Reactions on the Right have been pre-eminent, mostly taking the form of a return to a bluntly individualist, self-help philosophy based on rather cold consider-ations of incentives, deterrents and deserts. The Right has also demonstrated a mounting enthusiasm for reprivatisation, or a return of social service functions to the commercial market and the supposed efficiencies of supply-and-demand dynamics and the profit motive. A key element among these trends, one which perhaps represents the 'human face of capitalism' and one which certainly manages, in some of its features, to straddle quite wide political divides, is the rise of support for a much larger role for the voluntary sector. The voluntary sector has, as this study will show, always been with us. It can be seen as a humane, apolitical, small-scale and cheap alternative to our overdeveloped social services, as a means of returning responsibility and freedom to the individual and 'the community' who have become over-dependent on the 'nanny state'. It can also be seen as a route to the transformation of the democratic process, where individuals and groups retrieve a sense of self-determination and begin to participate in the exercise of power. There are both similarities and contradic-tions in these two perspectives, depending on the ideological stance from which they arise. The assumptions in both need unravelling, testing and challenging, through an appraisal of the part at present played in the welfare state by various forms of voluntary social action. A third perspective on the possible resurgence of the voluntary sector, and one to which this book subscribes, involves a more cautious and qualified endorsement of its positive features and a more critical assessment of the negative. It also looks primarily to reform of the statutory system, the careful and reciprocal balancing of functions between the two systems and that of informal care, and the concerted action of both in attacking the wider inequalities of our society.

There are generally two kinds of consideration at work in most debate on the voluntary sector's role in the welfare state – ideological, and operational or practical. On an ideological level, a crucial factor in all arguments for or against voluntarism as a dominant principle for organising a welfare society as opposed to a welfare state, is the value attached to the role and responsibilities of the state. Competing ideologies with regard to the legitimacy and extent of state intervention that have been developed and crystallised largely into party-political positions are the base line for determining both the scale of support for voluntary alternatives to statutory services, and the scale of substitution being proposed. Should we dismantle the statutory social services and replace them with voluntary ones? Should the state provide a basic minimum and leave the rest to be augmented by the voluntary sector? Should the two systems continue side by side, each developing those functions and capacities it seems good at? Normative questions on what the state should or should not do are basic to the advocacy of, to use Stephen Hatch's distinction, either a marginal or an integral role for the voluntary sector.[1]

A further ideological issue, one which has less forceful currency in these times of economic scarcity, concerns the option at the opposite end of the range, that of expanding the public sector to the point where non-government alternatives become redundant. This was the assumption, after all, on which the early welfare state was based and which continues to structure reality in all the major areas of social service, although to a lesser degree in the personal social services. It is still an assumption to which most left-wing politicians are committed, give or take a shift of position here and there in relation to local welfare services and some of the newer forms of voluntary social action. To ask how this 'statist' philosophy was put into effect in the various social services, how far and with what effect, is also to find the crucial departure point for some of the alternative perspectives noted above. It turns discussion to the operational aspects of the welfare state – what people think of its achievements in practical terms and whether they feel that nationalised and municipalised services have worked or not. Practical judgements such as these, amounting at times to disillusionment, are a key to understanding the spread of support for a return to voluntary social action even among those whose political sympathies have hitherto lain in the direction of state collectivism. A corollary of such assessments of the welfare state is the perception of the voluntary sector as an antidote to some of its ills by virtue of the special attributes and qualities of organisations that are non-governmental and voluntary.

What, then, does this collection of positive aspirations and negative reactions amount to? Does it constitute 'an ideology of voluntarism' in any way equivalent to the ideologies defining the role of the state which are the ones we more automatically think of? Webb *et. al.*[2] have noted that 'one of the most interesting features of British post-war social policy is the lack of a coherent theory of voluntary provision: a theory that would specify the role of voluntary organisations in a complex industrialised society which boasts a substantial system of state social services'. Times have moved on apace since this was written and the terms of debate have changed considerably in that it is now quite conceivable that the 'substantial system of state social services' we have learned to take for granted may be progressively dismantled, or at least severely pruned, by being denied the necessary public resources to meet an ever-growing demand. This is the changed reality referred to at the beginning of this chapter and the catalyst to new thinking about the voluntary sector which attempts to put forward a rationale for its assumption of a much more major role. How satisfactory a rationale this proves, and whether it amounts to a coherent theory of voluntarism is an object of enquiry for the present study.

This book asks the following central questions — what role does and should the voluntary sector play in the provision of social services? What are and should be the relative spheres of legitimacy and competence of voluntary and statutory social services? Is there a case, as is being suggested at least at the level of local authority welfare and community services, for a substantial shift away from the present statutory structures towards their partial or even complete replacement by voluntary social action? The theories behind this argument need measuring against what is known about the extent and functioning of the voluntary sector at present and against its estimated capacity for expansion. They also need testing against two possible hypotheses – one is that such a substitution would be based on the straightforward transfer of the resources currently spent on the statutory services, and that it would therefore involve providing services to at least the standards of coverage responsibility, distribution, quality and access met by them. The second, a rather more likely scenario, is that replacement of the statutory services would not be accompanied by the same levels of social expenditure – a situation in which, inevitably, the statutory services could not be directly replaced, like for like, but would be dismantled, and substituted for by provisions of very different, possibly lower, standard. The welfare state as we know it, would not then exist.

Underlying this book's discussion of the voluntary sector in British social services, past, present and future, is a practical, operational question concerning the capacity of the voluntary sector to substitute for the statutory social services, particularly in the field of personal welfare at the local level, where the voluntary sector has never disappeared and so has a head start. Taking the first hypothesis, where substantial resources are transferred, are voluntary social services capable of delivering the goods? Can they meet the kind of social need so far defined by society as requiring a collective response and universally accessible services from, where appropriate, trained or professional personnel? Even if, as might be quite legitimate, they were to redefine this collective response in a way that pre-empted the expensive professional, could they provide a satisfactory level of services without at the same time *losing* the advantages and attributes that make them an attractive proposition from today's standpoint? Questions such as these are implicit in the discussion in the next three chapters of first, the voluntary tradition, where the forerunners of today's statutory services are examined along with their supersession, for the most part, by the state's services they both paved the way for and impeded: second, the survival of the voluntary sector in the field of personal social services to form a 'mixed economy of welfare', as well as the emergence of new forms of voluntary social action from the mid-1960s on. Third, comes an overview of the state of affairs that exists in the voluntary sector today, as far as this can be known, in such matters as its personpower, its geographical and class distribution, and its finances. Attention is focused here on the growing dependence of voluntary organisations on government as a source of finance, with all the risks involved to their independent status and critical voice, threatened either directly by government's selective funding policies or less directly by the operation of an obsolete charity law.

Further implications of the financial relationships cemented between government and voluntary organisations are discussed in Chapters 5 and 6 which give an account of the 'partnerships' fostered by government in certain policy areas, from voluntary sector participation in special employment programmes to the more everyday sharing of social service tasks and planning. The genuine reciprocity of such relationships is questioned, together with the effects of the growing interpenetration between the two sectors that they presage for those fields where government is anxious, for a variety of reasons, to foster an agency role. From the financial and social policies of governments, and the programmes and relationships these engender in the voluntary sector, the book moves on, in Chapter 7, to consider the changing official thought patterns behind them in the Labour and Conservative administrations in power during the period 1974 to the present day, when the economic recession and changing political ideologies brought a new desirability to voluntary alternatives to the statutory social services. In the Treasury-dominated thinking of the early 1980s, is to be found more than a hint of the second hypothesis suggested earlier in this chapter, at least as far as the personal social services are concerned. Ministers urge the reversal of the major/minor roles of state and voluntary sector, place greatest emphasis on informal care and self-help as the front line of welfare provision, and set out to create a climate of reduced expectations of the welfare state and of social expenditure. Fuelled by exhortation and expenditure cuts, this role reversal will, it is hoped, somehow happen of itself, without government's strategy being too clearly revealed by a process of conscious planning and regulation.

Resource scarcity and antipathy to state intervention may supply a motive force for the development of a theory of voluntary provision, but are no substitute for the theory itself. As Chapter 7 shows, ministers have not been slow to borrow ideas from current thinking and writing on the subject of voluntary/statutory sector reversal. There is much to be found in common between their approach and that of the writers classed as 'welfare pluralists' in Chapter 8. Welfare pluralism, where social services are delivered by voluntary agencies and groups rather than by statutory authorities in a process of substitution (the extent of which is left unclear), both goes beyond the Conservative position in one sense and is more restricted than it, in another sense. Although the views of the welfare pluralists vary, they do clearly advocate the deliberate replacement of statutory by voluntary services. They do not, however, go beyond this form of 'dismantling' to liquidate also the state's role as financer of social services – a crucial difference. A further dimension of welfare pluralism explored in this chapter concerns the political ideology of power sharing and popular participative democracy that is both hidden and explicit in the literature on the subject. Finally, Chapters 9 and 10 draw together the data on the voluntary sector supplied in the body of the book, and against this background, attempt to evaluate the proposals, theories and policies emanating from politicans and welfare pluralists alike. Two measuring scales are used to try to assess the utility and desirability of the voluntary welfare systems proposed – first, the experience of countries where a pluriform/voluntary welfare system is the norm, and second, the estimated contribution of a voluntary welfare system to the promotion of a more equitable society.

DEFINITIONS

The discussion so far, in its use of the coverall term 'voluntary', has begged a number of important questions about the definition and use of that term. It has done so designedly in order to highlight the key issues relating to the voluntary sector in British social services, in terms that are familiar and accepted, even if they are also vague and lacking in precision. There is not the intention, in this study, to develop a new vocabulary for voluntary social action along the lines tentatively tried here in Britain[3] and those more in use in the United States, where terms like 'the non-profit sector' or 'the third sector' and the 'not-for-profit organisation' are more common.[4] However, since some stress is laid later in this book on the useful manipulation of terminology by politicians when they wish to fudge issues and evade implications, it is all the more important to define and qualify both the terms and parameters of its discussion of the voluntary sector in relation to social services.

The Wolfenden Committee, in its report on the future of voluntary organisations,[5] made a distinction between the voluntary, the informal, the statutory and the commercial systems for meeting social need. By the informal system is meant a vast range of helping and exchange services between relatives, friends, neighbours, etc. which make up the bulk of caring activities in our society, the hidden part of the iceberg of which the state and voluntary sector services are only a small visible tip. The whole area of informal care is unquantifiable because submerged, but its importance, as Wolfenden noted, must not be overlooked or underestimated. However, if one is talking in terms of collective action for social purposes, of roughly the same order in the voluntary sphere as in the statutory, the one readily substitutable for the other, then discussion must be limited to that which has discernible shape and form. For the purposes of this book, focused as it is on the substitutability of statutory services by voluntary ones, we are talking about organised forms of voluntary action, or

7

voluntary organisations. How then, are we to define voluntary organisations?

A number of writers have attempted to bring together the defining characteristics of a voluntary organisation – not an easy task, and one which defies precision. In a number of early definitions, we find that it is 'initiated and governed by its own members without external control'[6] or, according to Rooff [7], voluntary bodies are those 'which control their own policy, and which depend, in part, at least, upon financial support from voluntary sources'. Generally, Johnson[8] observes, there are four defining criteria to be found in most recent attempts to arrive at a satisfactory definition – method of formation, method of government, method of finance and motive. Hatch's categorisation[9] would appear to contain all these elements and add a measure of precision. Voluntary organisations are defined as: '(i) being organisations, not informal groups; (ii) not established by statute or under statutory authority and not directly controlled by statutory authority; and (iii) not commercial in the sense of being profit-making or (like much of the private sector in health and education) being mainly dependent for their resources on fees and charges paid by private individuals.'

Few recent writers place much emphasis on autonomy through self-finance as a distinguishing characteristic of the voluntary organisation, perhaps in recognition of the growing dependence of voluntary bodies on statutory sources of finance in recent years. What does seem crucial is that financial dependence should not also mean loss of freedom and self-determination. The importance of this factor is underscored by Gladstone[10] when he writes,

> The essence of voluntary action is more a question of independence and autonomy and its fundamental antithesis is statutory action, that is activity carried out under the aegis of local or central government and their associated agencies within the framework of statutory obligations laid down in legislation. By contrast, voluntary action is independent of state control and voluntary organisations are essentially those established and governed by ther own members, without external intervention. Independence, in the sense of self-management, is the hallmark of voluntary action.

Hatch's definition is more cautious, speaking of the absence of 'direct' control by statutory authority, and Webb *et al*.[11] refer to agencies 'which are not directly administered by local or central government' – an even broader criterion, which could presumably include the BBC or the Economic and Social Research Council. These shades of difference illustrate the difficulty of arriving at a totally satisfactory definition in the face of present-day realities. To insist on an absolutely rigorous interpretation of 'independence' or 'control' would eliminate a good number of organisations customarily described as 'voluntary'. Strictly speaking, for instance, the Women's Royal Voluntary Service (WRVS) should not be so classed, for it is wholly dependent on public funds and its director is appointed by government – yet its volunteer members would most probably see it as part of the voluntary sector. The terms 'quasi-autonomous non-governmental organisation' or 'quango' would probably be more appropriate, but this has already been colonised for other more specific uses.

The definition of a voluntary organisation is essentially a statement of an ideal type based on a constellation of features some of which or all of which may be conformed to by voluntary organisations in practice. The key elements of this ideal type are that a body should be a formal organisation, constitutionally separate from government, self-governing, non-profit-*distributing* (as opposed to non-profit-making, as many voluntary bodies raise finance through trading nowadays) and of *public* benefit. This last criterion while not a totally satisfactory way to eliminate public schools or private hospitals which cater for the rich on the whole, is, when thus qualified, at least as adequate as Hatch's final clause, with the advantage of being less wordy. The essence of this definition, as most writers would agree, is contained in the 'self-governing' requirement – a feature that should be a matter for watchful anxiety, given the extent of financial dependence upon government among many organisations that is documented later in this study. If financial dependence also means external intervention in either an active or a passive sense, and there are indications that it does to a significant extent for some organisations, then there must be a point where a body cannot be said to qualify for the title 'voluntary' any longer. It is impossible, however, to specify as a general rule where this point is reached. For the most part, total dependence on public funds is not a dominant feature yet of British voluntary organisations, but if it were to become so, as in the model proposed by welfare pluralists, then it is highly debatable whether we could continue to speak of 'voluntary' organisations, in that a totally publicly funded voluntary sector could hardly be maintained as autonomous and self-governing. The blurring of boundaries between the voluntary and the public is a matter for serious concern and scrutiny, as is evident from the experience of a system rather ahead of us in this

9

regard, that of the United States, which will be discussed in Chapter 9, with reference to a number of writings on the ambiguities involved.[12]

An additional problem in any discussion of voluntary organisations is to distinguish between them and classify what they do. To construct a meaningful typology of voluntary organisations or voluntary social action, one must have an end-point in mind, such as finding out how they differ from the statutory sector in their activities, or to what extent these activities cost money. Such classifications are particularly important for questions of voluntary–statutory role reversal and sub-stitutability. Johnson[13] reviews a number of attempts to devise typo-logies of voluntary social services, ranging from the over-simple to the unnecessarily complex. Too broad a category will have limited uses, such as Morris's simple distinction between voluntary agencies which provide social services and those which provide leisure services.[14] Equally, too narrow and specific a classification will be of little benefit, such as that suggested by Gordon and Babchuk,[15] where their three distinguishing characteristics for voluntary organisations are 'accessibility of membership; the status-defining capacity of the organisation, and the categorisation of its functions as instrumental or expressive'. Johnson comments, 'No single typology is likely to be appropriate for all purposes, and the one selected in particular instances will depend upon the questions that are being asked.'[16]

Given the connection between enthusiasm for expenditure rationing on the part of governments and their interest in the potential of voluntary social services, a typology which highlights the resource bases of voluntary organisations is likely to be of value. The easy conflation of the agency that uses volunteer labour only with the one that depends on paid professional staff is a device frequently utilised by politicians anxious to project the voluntary alternative to statutory social services as financially costless or at least significantly cheaper. A typology that uses the resource base of the voluntary agency as a criterion is that devised by Stephen Hatch[17] where he differentiates between volunteer and mutual aid organisations on the one hand, and 'special agencies' and 'funded charities' on the other. The first cat-egories are distinguished on the basis of the voluntary donation of activity in the first instance, and then by the interests they are promoting – those of the participants themselves (mutual aid) or those of others (volunteer). From the donation of labour power as a resource, Hatch turns to the question of cash resources, distinguish-ing two further types of organisation based on the need to pay staff. The deciding factor here is the source of funds, and Hatch separates agencies dependent on grants ('special' agencies) from those based on donations and charges ('funded' charities). Any classification scheme is in some sense arbitrary, but the second half of this scheme does not seem altogether satisfactory. Why, except that both represent methods of self-financing, are charges linked with donations as a basis for defining a 'funded' charity? Charges, and the more precise contractual obligations connected with them, are surely more closely associated with finance through grants? Grants may be forthcoming from statutory or corporate/philanthropic sources and are rarely unconditional. Hatch acknowledges the ambiguities of his classification scheme, the major problem with which is that it is far from self-explanatory. A further problem with this and any other attempt at a typology is that it is almost impossible to devise categories which are mutually exclusive for the multi-purpose, multiform organisations of the voluntary sector.

A simple typology featured in Johnson's account is that put forward by Murray,[18] who divides voluntary agencies according to function, into caring, pressure-group and self-help organisations. Extending this classification by function, one might suggest the following typology:

- the service-providing function
- the mutual aid function
- the pressure-group function
- the resource function
- the coordinating function

To think in terms of functions lessens but does not eliminate the fundamental difficulty of cross-categorisation of multi-functional agencies. If these functional categories are viewed as ideal types rather than precise descriptions, then total conformity to them will not be expected. It is often possible to pinpoint some major defining function in an organisation, even where there is a blend of activities. When considering the special role of voluntary organisations in the welfare state and the extent to which they may supplement or complement statutory services and how far they could or should substitute for them, the crucial element to identify and classify is what they actually do.

The *service-providing function* typifies those voluntary agencies which supply a direct service to people, in kind or in the form of information, advice and support. It may be delivered by paid employees or professionals, or by voluntary workers. Organisations in this category would be ones like Barnardo's, the Citizens' Advice Bureau, St John's Ambulance Brigade, etc. Of all the categories, this is probably the one requiring most to be broken down into sub-units, as it has the most equivalents in the statutory sector. If one were discussing the replacement of statutory services, for instance, a salient characteristic by which to identify voluntary agencies would be their degree of professionalisation. If one were considering expenditure and cost-cutting, then whether an organisation is formed of volunteers or paid workers is highly relevant. Again, information and advice-giving functions are forms of service that have fewer equivalents in the statutory sector than other kinds of service, and the overall service provision category does not distinguish them.

The *mutual aid function* is about self-help and exchange around a common need or interest. Organised forms of mutual aid would include the Mastectomy Association, the Breakthrough Trust (for the deaf), Cruse (for widows), the National Women's Aid Federation, etc. Essentially, these bodies tend to be unprofessionalised, specialist-interest groups offering their own members mutual support, advice and information and services.

The pressure-group function implies the marshalling of information and argument around some specific cause or group interest and the application of this in some public arena through direct action, campaigning, lobbying and advocacy in order to achieve a desired change. Examples of this type of organisation are the Child Poverty Action Group, the National Council for Civil Liberties, the Disability Alliance.

The *resource function* would seem to provide a useful heading for those voluntary organisations which service other organisations in a particular field of activity or interest, or act as a central catalyst or repository of expertise, information, research, etc. on a specialist subject. Bodies such as the Volunteer Centre, the National Council for Voluntary Organisations (NCVO), the National Children's Bureau and the National Youth Bureau would be included here.

The *coordinating function* covers those umbrella or federative organisations which represent a membership of other voluntary bodies and seek to liaise between them and coordinate their activities, their public relations or their connections with government. There is a thin line between this and the resource category, but there remains a logical distinction. Not all resource agencies are also coordinating bodies and vice versa. Examples of coordinating bodies are the NCVO, the National Federation of Housing Associations, the Association of British Adoption Societies, etc. and the various local and regional councils of social service and guilds of help.

Some organisations fall quite neatly into a particular category by function, most obviously those with relatively discrete objectives. So, for instance, a body like the Spinal Injuries Association is entirely composed of people suffering from spinal damage, who share interests and offer services to each other through the medium of a formal, mutual aid organisation. On the other hand, MIND, the National Association for Mental Health, is an example of an agency which combines a number of functions – service-giving, resource, pressure-group and coordination. It is also a good example of an organisation which has changed its functional emphasis over time.

It is much easier to get an overview of the voluntary sector at national level where organisation is at its most structured and most formal. Many national bodies act as central coordinating and resource agents to a membership of individuals or local organisations, and as their liaison point for government and public relations. They are frequently, with their high profile and public image, equated with the whole of the organisation, but it should be remembered that national bodies like MIND and Age Concern, have behind them large numbers of small, local mental health committees or old people's welfare committees which are autonomous, have a separate identity of their own and perform separate functions in the delivery of services and the raising of funds. They have a fairly loose membership relationship with their headquarters, and may also be far more conservative and less radical. They often also pre-date their national federative structures.

The history of the voluntary sector is a history of small, localised initiatives, sometimes sinking without trace, sometimes growing into bigger, more durable organisations. Chapter 2 offers a brief overview of the origins of today's voluntary sector and statutory sector social services.

NOTES AND REFERENCES

1. HATCH, S., *Outside the State: Voluntary Organisations in Three Towns*. Croom Helm: London, 1980.
2. WEBB, A., DAY, L. and WELLER, D., *Voluntary Social Services: Manpower Resources*. Personal Social Services Council: London, 1976, p. 7.
3. BARKER, A., 'The Erosion of the Public Sector/Private Sector

Model in Social Policy Fields: a Note on Research Needs' (unpublished). SSRC Workshop on the Voluntary Sector in Social Policy, Lancaster University, 1979.

4. WEISBROD, B. A., *The Voluntary Non-Profit Sector*. Lexington Books: Lexington, Mass. 1977; COMMITTEE ON PRIVATE PHLANTHROPY AND PUBLIC NEEDS (FILER COMMITTEE), *Giving in America: Toward a Stronger Voluntary Sector*. Washington, DC, 1975

5. WOLFENDEN COMMITTEE, *The Future of Voluntary Organisations*. Croom Helm: London, 1978.

6. BOURDILLON, A. F. C., *Voluntary Social Services*. Methuen: London, 1945, p. 3.

7. ROOFF, M., *Voluntary Societies and Social Policy*. Routledge & Kegan Paul: London, 1957, p. xiii.

8. JOHNSON, N., *Voluntary Social Services*. Blackwell & Robertson: Oxford, 1981.

9. HATCH, op. cit., p. 15.

10. GLADSTONE, F., *Voluntary Action in a Changing World*. Bedford Square Press: London, 1979, p. 4.

11. WEBB *et al.*, op. cit., p. 11.

12. BRILLIANT, E., 'Private or public: a model of ambiguities', *Social Service Review*, 47 (1973), pp. 384–96; KAHN, A., 'A framework for public–voluntary collaboration in the social services', *The Social Welfare Forum, 1976*, National Conference on Social Welfare. Columbia University Press: Washington, 1977; KAMERMAN, S., 'The new mixed economy of welfare: public and private', *Social Work*, Jan–Feb. (1983), pp. 5–10.

13. JOHNSON, op. cit., pp. 16–22.

14. Quoted in JOHNSON, op. cit., p. 16.

15. Quoted in JOHNSON, op. cit., p. 17.

16. JOHNSON, op. cit., p. 20.

17. HATCH, op. cit.

18. MURRAY, G. J., *Voluntary Organisations and Social Welfare*, Oliver & Boyd: Glasgow, 1969, quoted in Johnson, op. cit., p. 17.

Chapter Two
THE VOLUNTARY TRADITION AND A 'MIXED ECONOMY' OF WELFARE

The pattern of social service provision that exists in Britain today is largely the product of the last four decades of development since the spate of social legislation that followed the Second World War. The major lines of today's health services, education service and the social security system were set between 1944 and 1948, although each area has undergone significant change since. The personal social services responsibilities of the local authorities are a later expansion of those laid down in 1948. Common to all these areas of social service is a strong bias towards state provision, but all of them trace their origin in one way or another to initiatives taken in the past by voluntary and charitable organisations. The public sector 'take-over', occurring at different rates for the various services, was both the result of deliberate policies in the post-war creation of the welfare state and a natural sequence in a long evolutionary process of substitution for voluntary services stretching back into the nineteenth century and beyond. This substitution was never as complete for the local welfare services as for the other areas, and the voluntary tradition survived here either through voluntary organisations retaining separate roles and sources of finance, or, increasingly, through their development of agency relationships with statutory authorities. After briefly reviewing the origins of this process, this chapter considers the post-war development of a 'mixed economy' of welfare in the provision of personal social services, a development which, continuing through the era of Seebohm and large local authority departments, sets the scene for present-day debate about the proper roles of the statutory and voluntary sectors.

FORERUNNERS OF THE PERSONAL SOCIAL SERVICES

Two major impulses discerned by Beveridge behind voluntary social action in the nineteenth century were those of mutual aid and philanthropy.[1] The clearest examples of the former were the working men's Friendly and Cooperative societies set up to meet the income needs of certain contingencies like sickness. These societies blossomed around the middle of the century and were an important means of securing the respectable working man against resources to the statutory Poor Law. Their functions were largely superseded by the entry of the state into the field of social insurance in the twentieth century, and they no longer exist in their original form.[2] The philanthropic tradition, typically manifest in the burgeoning of thousands of small charities set up by individual reformers and churches, particularly after the evangelical revival in the second half of the nineteenth century, is more clearly the forerunner of today's personal social services.[3] The proliferation of charities is evidence of the expansion of the nineteenth-century social conscience combined with social control and patronage of the poor by the wealthy classes, for whom any more radical changes in the distribution of wealth would have been unthinkable. They represent the initiatives which pioneered our social services and did much to alert the legislators of the day to the need for state intervention. On the other hand, because they were essentially non-systematic, capricious, fragmented, uncoordinated and competitive, and because most frequently they were aimed at moral reform and social control more than social need, they proved inadequate to the enormous need that existed. 'Both by its successes and abysmal failures, philanthropy helped to reveal the real outlines of the problem', writes Owen[4] in his account of the transition from charitable to state welfare.

The major input into welfare services, imperfect as they were, in the late nineteenth century, came from voluntary organisations and institutions, and 'the function of the state was to fill the gaps in the network of private charity'.[5] The relationship that should exist between the charities and the public sector, in the form of the statutory Poor Law authorities, was a matter for debate at the time, and this is apparent in the efforts of the Charity Organisation Society to keep the two spheres of activity strictly separate and prevent the 'dole charities' from dispensing relief to those who had a claim on the Poor Law, thus benefiting the ratepayer. The doctrine of mutually exclusive spheres was officially ratified in the Goschen Minute,[6] [doc. 1] advice offered to the London Poor Law Board, by its president, George Goschen, in 1869 in an attempt to prevent duplication and set limits to the exercise of the Poor Law. In their reflections on the Minority Report of the Royal Commission on the Poor Law, Sidney and Beatrice Webb labelled this division of spheres 'the parallel bars' theory of the relationship between state action and voluntary agencies, each having its own appropriate clientele of beneficiaries'.[7] In the Minority Report, they advocated an 'extension ladder' theory, whereby the state should provide a national minimum and the voluntary societies should top it up. This would have the effect of capitalising on voluntary agencies' superiority to public authorities in their capacity to innovate, to give special care to difficult cases and to give expression to religious influence, while minimising the disadvantages of voluntary action which made it unfit to assume responsibility for a large range of problems, namely the uncertainty of its finance, its lack of compulsory powers and its essential discontinuity. They write, 'Here we have a conception, not of "parallel bars" wholly separate and distinct from each other, with a large intervening space of "missed cases", but of an "extension ladder" placed firmly on the foundation of a minimum standard of life, but carrying onward the work of the Public Authorities to far finer shades of physical, moral and spiritual perfection.'[8] In the Webbs' 'extension ladder' model, we find the conviction that voluntary bodies possess inherently superior qualities to those of the public sector for the undertaking of a limited range of supplementary specialist functions, but that they are unfitted, by definition, to be agents of a universal and comprehensive system of services.

Nowhere in this philosophical debate about special roles and separate spheres was it envisaged that the lines should become blurred through the subsidisation from public funds of the activities of the voluntary charities and the consequent transformation of voluntary bodies in some degree or another into agencies of the state. The earliest examples of public subsidy of voluntary bodies are to be found in the field of education in the early nineteenth century. For welfare charities, however, expansion of the agency role, with and without the availability of public funds, came with the gradual assumption by public authorities of more welfare responsibilities in the first decades of the next century. Lloyd George's budget of 1914 included for the first time estimates for grants to organisations active in maternity and child care, provision of home helps and work with the blind. For many voluntary bodies, this development marked a first stage in a process of eventual replacement by statutory forms of provision, as it became clear that the public authorities considered them no longer adequate, even in an agency role, for certain tasks. For some, the agency role and public subsidy, however minor, became a key to survival, supplementing their own charitable revenues and marking out a distinct place for them *vis-á-vis* the statutory sector. A most important ratification of the agency role of voluntary bodies was enshrined in the 1948 National Assistance Act which established the local authority welfare role. This Act, for instance, made the authorities responsible for providing residential care for the elderly. Although the main provision was to be a statutory responsibility, the Act also enabled local authorities to make financial contributions to voluntary agencies for this purpose, and permitted subsidies for voluntary provision of meals and recreation for old people. A Ministry of Health circular at the time stated,

> It will clearly be to the advantage of local authorities to make use of voluntary organisations which are providing satisfactory services, and to coordinate their work with the authorities' own services . . . The more important voluntary agencies concerned with the care of the aged and infirm and with the welfare of handicapped persons have much special knowledge and experience which would be helpful to local authorities in preparing their schemes.[9]

This and other, subsequent legislation, while extending the sphere of statutory intervention, removed barriers inherent in the *ultra vires* principle governing public funds to the use of those funds for non-statutory agencies.[10]

The pioneering, initially innovative role of voluntary social action that was acknowledged by the Webbs has continued to be attributed to voluntary sector activities ever since. Their inability to provide the kind of universally available, basic social services that were eventually seen as necessary, was made the platform for a clear call for a division of responsibilities with the state. The middle-class patronage of voluntary organisations and the concept of charity were to prove less acceptable as democratic rights became more universal, and this stereotype was to linger on beyond the period when it most clearly conformed to reality, to feed suspicion and antipathy towards the voluntary sector. The more importance attached to the need for universal provision, for basic guaranteed levels of service and for legally established rights rather than charity, the more likely the service was to be taken into the public sector entirely. This was the case particularly in the field of social security, education and health, in variable degrees. In the personal social services, as they came to be known, there was not the same rapid rate of development as in the other social services. Consequently there was much more scope for the continued functioning of the voluntary sector, not just in 'topping up' statutory provisions in the way advocated in the Webbs' 'extension ladder' model, but, for a long time, also in providing basic services.

Webb *et al.* have termed the continued coexistence of the public and voluntary sectors in the welfare services after the war a 'mixed economy of welfare'.[11]

THE EARLY WELFARE STATE

Given the relatively low priority attached to the local authority welfare departments which were created in 1948 and their very slow growth in the years following, it is conceivable that welfare services could have remained in the hands of voluntary organisations with the agency relationship sustained as the dominant mode of provision. The agency role had already been established in a minor, *ad hoc* way with public money being made available to some voluntary agencies for purposes which, although they had acquired a public importance, were either not yet important enough, or not suitable, for government to take over. With regard to the role of the state, the functions of financer of services and service deliverer are not necessarily synonymous, but their separability customarily goes unremarked, given the strength of 'the pure doctrine of state welfare' that has formed our perceptions of the welfare state.[12] The state could have taken on a major role in the late 1940s by a conscious decision to assume responsibility only for financing and regulating the social services, leaving their actual delivery to non-governmental bodies. This could have been done on the basis of some kind of contractual, purchase-of-service arrangements or through subsidies. Voluntary organisations could thus have received a new lease of life in many spheres by acting as agents of the state. This happened in the United States and the Netherlands, to name two countries where antagonism to the direct role of the state was strong. There, voluntary organisations as public agents acquired a totally new relationship with the state and, to some extent, an inevitable change of identity. The implications of such incorporation will come up for discussion later in this book.[13]

It is possible, therefore, to imagine a scenario where all the personal social services were delivered by voluntary organisations – financed mostly, as resources became available, by local authorities. This did not happen, but nor did the local authorities acquire a total monopoly. Instead, they built on the major role they had been allocated and consolidated their own position, giving their own services financial priority and leaving voluntary bodies much to their own devices. Paradoxically, this may have ensured a continuing vitality and independence for the voluntary sector which it might otherwise have lost. That voluntary organisations were not utilised as primary deliverers of social services was due to a number of factors. State encroachment on their territory was not a sudden development, but a long and piecemeal process which had begun long before the advent of the welfare state. Local authorities had a long tradition of welfare involvement in the administration of the Poor Law. There was concern, too, that a measure of rationality and coordination be introduced into provisions for vulnerable groups — the children's departments were set up, for instance, on the Curtis Report's recommendation that responsibility for child care be properly established, following the death of a small boy in foster care.[14] One of the major factors explaining the bias towards statutory involvement at this time was, however, the strength of political opposition to voluntary organisations and to charity as a principle of social distribution in the post-war Labour government.

The influence of ideology

Beveridge, the architect of the new social security system, was not keen on the creation of a totally new state apparatus for administering it. He protested that the government had rejected central proposals in his report on *Social Insurance and Allied Services* 'for the use of friendly societies to administer State benefits for sickness and allied purposes to their members',[15] and that in doing this had committed 'the State to setting up a centralised bureaucratic machine'. He commented further, 'whether any such machine can grapple with the fundamental problem of sickness benefit, of reconciling sound finance with sympathy and intimate local handling is uncertain'.[16] Despite the pleas of this supporter of the voluntary principle, the voluntary sector was not seen by the Labour administration after the war as a suitable instrument for its social programmes, whether of social security or welfare services. As Webb *et al*. write,

> A subsidiary but important part of the drive towards statutory social services represented a deliberate move away from voluntary provision not least within the Labour Party. Faith was invested in statutory services as a way of guaranteeing provision that was comprehensive and universal, professional and impartial, and subject to democratic control. The immediate post-war implementation of social policies marked an attempt decisively to move away from social policies that were partial in scope, socially divisive in action, and socially controlling in intent. Voluntary organisations were regarded with not a little suspicion in the process.[17]

While readily acknowledged for their pioneering contribution and their highlighting of social problems, they were also seen as ill-organised, amateur and fragmented and unevenly distributed. With the rapid secularisation of British society between the wars, the voluntary organisations were no longer rooted in significant social groupings in a way that the mass of people could identify with. They were, in a society that continued to be riven with class divides, identified with middle-class patterns of patronage and charity.

For the Labour Party, state socialism in welfare was an integral part of its early commitment to the nationalisation of the major institutions of British society at the end of the war. It was at this stage still imbued with the notion of collective ownership as a means of social trans-formation embodied in the famous Clause Four of its constitution – a principle from which a substantial section of the party, under Gaitskell, Crosland and others, was to depart. In these early days, however, of Fabian socialism, 'The state and its apparatus of admini-stration was to be the instrument of change. Experts would devise and apply a national programme of reform. The public was cast in the role of spectator and consumer, not co-partner.'[18] For collective social goals to be attained, power had to be concentrated in the state. Bevan conveyed something of this philosophy when he asked, in relation to the voluntary hospitals, 'How can the State enter into a contract with a citizen to render service through an autonomous body?'[19] Richard Crossman, reflecting on the early development of the welfare state, remembered 'Philanthropy was to us the odious expression of social oligarchy and churchy bourgeois attitudes. We detested voluntary hospitals maintained by flag days . . .'[20] He continued,

> In the construction of the new social service state we turned our backs on philanthropy and replaced the do-gooder by highly professional administrators and experts. From the 1920s on, the normal left-wing attitude has been opposed to middle-class philanthropy, charity and everything else connected with do-gooding. Those of us who became socialists grew up with the conviction that we must in this point ally ourselves with the professionals and trades unions and discourage voluntary effort particularly since it was bound to reduce the number of jobs available.[21]

A common expectation in those years at the end of the war was that the voluntary sector would just wither away. That this did not happen was a matter of surprise and relief to Crossman, commenting retrospec-tively on his period as Secretary of State for Social Services in the later 1960s. 'One of the things I learned as a minister was the staggering extent of voluntary activity in our welfare state.'[22] 'I am now con-vinced that the Labour Party's opposition to philanthropy and altruism and its determined belief in economic self-interest as the driving dynamic of society has done it grevious harm.'[23] Antagonism towards the voluntary sector was not an entirely uniform sentiment in the Labour Party at any time. We have already noted the basic willingness of the government to accommodate existing voluntary agencies and to exploit their experience, in the 1948 legislation for welfare services. One reasonable explanation for this divergence in the direction of voluntary welfare services is that, in contrast to other social policy areas, the welfare services were not regarded as highly important, nor, at that time, were they regarded as an area requiring professionalism and expertise. The general sentiment with regard to voluntary services was expressed in the 1949 House of Lords debate on 'Voluntary Action for Social Progress' by Lord Pakenham, who said on behalf of the government,

> We have moved far from the era of *laissez-faire*. We have entered what Lord Lindsay and others have called 'the era of the positive state'. But, even at the cost of repetition, I want to make it plain, beyond any shadow of misunderstanding, that, in the view of the Government, democracy without voluntary exertion and voluntary idealism loses its soul . . . We are certain that voluntary social service organisations have a part to play as essential in the future as any they have played in the past, and with the steady development of our social conscience we must look to them as time goes on to put even their own fine records in the shade.[24]

The statutory welfare services

Quite apart from a certain Labour Party distaste for the voluntary principle as a means of delivering the major social services, there were other common assumptions underlying the spate of legislation after the war. It was supposed that the new social programmes of social security, health care, etc. would eliminate Beveridge's Five Giants of Idleness, Squalor, Disease, Ignorance and Want, and would eradicate much of the social need that then existed. The attention paid to the personal welfare services and the setting up of local authority machinery for the welfare of specific categories of the population therefore reflected expectations that their functions would never be more than residual. Aneurin Bevan launched the National Assistance scheme with these words in 1947, 'The House will be aware that in the last few years a number of substantial steps have been taken in transforming and enlarging the social serives . . . However, there will still remain . . . 400,000 persons on outdoor relief, and 50,000 in institutions. There thus remain, after we have bitten into the main body of the Poor Law, these residual categories that have to be provided for . . .'[25]

These residual categories included the blind and the old, and were to become the responsibility of the local welfare departments. The social objectives and methods of these departments in caring for those and other residual categories of social need, were also less easily specified and quantified than in, say, the social security system. All in all, the local welfare services, as a vague category of 'everything else' once the other programmes had been established, were accorded a low priority.

The first fifteen years of the welfare state saw few significant developments in the local welfare services. Their low priority was reflected in their limited organisational and financial resources and the very slow development of professional training and standards of care. The welfare function was split between several local authority departments each of which catered for a limited clientele. These were in no position to compete for scarce resources with the more universal kinds of service such as education, which had greater national priority, nor did they have a professional body to exert leverage on their behalf. The welfare departments provided mainly for the poor and old, relatively powerless groups who were not in a position to press for greater priority. An additional explanation for the neglect of the welfare services was that the extent of social need was disguised and the general belief current that poverty had disappeared in the 1950s spurt of affluence that had upgraded everyone's expectations of life. The welfare services, which started from a comparatively low resource base, remained fairly static and underdeveloped until the mid-1960s. Their share of public expenditure in the decade before 1965 grew from 0.6 to only 0.8 per cent, while health expenditure grew from 9.4 to 10.1 per cent and education grew from 8.8 to 12.4 per cent in that time.[26]

The 1948 legislation was limited in its application, and local authorities were not empowered to supply a total range of services even to the elderly, the blind, the mentally ill and to children, the main groups they existed to serve. There was no comprehensive family care, very little was done for the disabled in general or for other persons who did not fit the legislative categories. While these services fell so far short of the goals of universal access, uniform standards and comprehensive provision that were, ideally at least, applied to the other services, then it is not surprising that scope remained for the continued functioning alongside them of the voluntary organisations which had always provided for the welfare of the elderly, disabled, children, etc. The local statutory departments were in no position to take over the responsibilities of the voluntary sector, especially in the case of expensive residential care – where, for instance, voluntary homes still catered for more than half the children in residential care. Webb *et al.*[27] list 'three major reasons why the apparent shift away from the mixed economy of welfare in the early post-war period has been modified in the intervening years'. To the effects of short-term economic problems and long-term economic strategies, they add the pressures of 'a greater realisation of the scope, vitality and diversity of demands for social services' which forced the original conception of the demand for social services as finite and static to change radically.

The voluntary welfare services

Although the statutory welfare services did not expand to take over or supersede completely the voluntary contribution, there were few compensatory developments among voluntary welfare organisations in this period. They continued to increase in numbers but do not seem to have adopted radically new roles or taken exciting new directions. They seemed, in the words of the Wolfenden Committee[28] 'to have been marking time' in this first fifteen years or so of the welfare state. Why, it might be asked, if the public welfare services were slow in developing, did not the voluntary organisations accelerate their own development and expand to fill a gap for which their long history of social service provision would seem to have fitted them uniquely? Ousted from the spheres of income maintenance, health care and education, they could perhaps have established a near monopoly for the voluntary principle in the personal welfare services, and rendered unnecessary any substantial public involvement in them – at least as far as service delivery was concerned.

Three major reasons may be suggested as to why this did not happen. First, as stated earlier, the dominant assumption in those early years was that social services should be a public responsibility – and a fuller expression of this responsibility was a long-term goal for even the low-priority welfare services. Second, as welfare functions were not politically important in the statutory sphere, so they also lacked a general public support for development by other means. Third, a related and essential point, the voluntary sector could not have expanded without finance. There were two main sources of finance for voluntary organisations – charitable giving and public subsidy. Although charitable funds remained a substantial source of voluntary sector activity, it is unlikely that they could have expanded sufficiently in the years after the war for the voluntary bodies to have developed a total responsibility for the welfare services, even given the limited standards that persisted for some years. It must be remembered that taxation for the major areas of public expenditure was taking an increasing bite out of people's incomes at this time. The Nathan Committee wrote in 1952 that

> Death duties and general taxation have made increasing demands on those who have been the main support of charitable funds in the past; and, until the tradition of charitable giving is more widely accepted, the provision of fresh resources in the future on anything like the same scale as in the past is, to say the least, problematic; while the fall in the value of money has whittled away the value of endowments. It is argued therefore that the use of these should be directed to objects not covered by state provision.[29]

The Nathan Committee clearly saw a continued and viable role for the voluntary sector, discerning in the ambiguities of some of the recent social legislation, Parliament's intention 'that there should be a close partnership between the charitable organisations and the public authorities.[30] The old nineteenth-century theory of the mutual exclusiveness of the two spheres had to disappear, 'but something must take its place if charitable resources which, alone, are clearly inadequate for the tasks confronting them, are to be put to the best use'.[30] The committee, which was set up to review the 'Law and Practice with regard to Charitable Trusts', put a strong emphasis on the 'historic role of charity to pioneer', but it also envisaged that the public sector–voluntary partnership would take other forms. Besides pioneering new types of educational, social and cultural work, the charitable institutions might continue to act as the agent of the public authorities (with the consequent risk of losing much of their freedom of action) and 'fill the gaps' in supplementing the public services. The committee did not follow up their fairly forthright assessment of the limited potential of charitable giving in the future by recommending a wholesale switch to public funding for the voluntary sector. Instead, they suggested rather conservative alterations to the purposes of charitable trusts 'so as to enable them to play the part best suited to them in modern conditions'.[31]

Looking at the experience of countries where voluntary organisations did develop a significant or monopoly role in the provision of social services, it is clear that this could not have been established, and could not have achieved the standards of service considered more and more essential, without substantial support from public funds, directly or indirectly. Given the British bias towards a public sector responsibility, and the pressures on social expenditure which restricted the growth of the statutory welfare services, major support from public funds was not forthcoming, and the agency role of voluntary bodies, while it remained important for them, did not expand significantly. Voluntary organisations continued to play a valuable part precisely because the statutory services were slow in developing. Owen makes the point that 'the intervention of the State extended rather than reversed the long tradition of voluntary effort'[32] in that demand for services was intensified once the local welfare departments were active, beyond their capacity to meet it, making for greater dependence on the voluntary services. The latter did not in the early years, carve out for themselves any distinct and separate functions, but continued, as, for instance, in the various children's societies, to operate parallel services to those developed by the public sector. There were some exceptions to this of course. The National Marriage Guidance Council, formed in 1947, developed a specialist service which has never been widely paralleled in the public sector. The Citizens' Advice Bureaux, started on the eve of the war, continued to provide an advice and information service that has not been supplanted. The Royal National Institute for the Blind has retained a virtual monopoly, based on historic popular support for the provision of services for the blind, and on the development of high levels of expertise. The Samaritans, founded in 1952, fulfilled a need that has never seen any statutory response. All these represent specialised areas where either historical longevity or the peculiar nature of the problem to be met, made the continuation of a voluntary agency role most appropriate.

Writing in 1959, the Younghusband Committee on social workers in the local authority health and welfare services,[33] paid tribute to the contribution of the voluntary sector, and predicted for it a continued and valuable role, a role that it saw as essentially supplementary to the primary responsibility of the statutory sector for social services. It observed that voluntary effort 'is still an integral part of the health and welfare services and is needed now and in future to supplement statutory provision and to undertake work beyond the scope of legislation'.[34]

The committee found in its survey of local authorities that nearly all made use of voluntary organisations, the lowest rates of usage being in Scotland and Wales. The figures for 1956 show that 87 per cent of authorities made use of voluntary agencies for the blind, 83 per cent for the elderly and 70 per cent for the unmarried mother, while for mental health care and family casework, the figures were only 27 and 4 per cent respectively. The figures are fairly meaningless as an index, for the term 'making use of' can mean a minimal or total reliance on voluntary efforts. Non-use could be taken, on the other hand, to mean either that voluntary organisations did not exist for certain specialisms, or that local authorities were reluctant to use them. What the Younghusband data do suggest, however, is that there remained in the mid-1950s, a considerable residue of voluntary agency activity utilised and part financed by local authorities under the auspices of the National Assistance Act.

The Younghusband Committee's major focus was on social workers in the statutory services and their training, and it was from this perspective that they viewed voluntary social action, which they associated with untrained amateurism. Accordingly, they were in no doubt that the main input into welfare services, particularly in the more skilled areas, should be a statutory responsibility.

> We are inclined to agree with the total authority witnesses that these authorities will increasingly take a direct responsibility for providing the services with which we are concerned. This appears to us a logical development of the major changes introduced in 1948. The point has been reached when the larger resources of local and central government are required if the services are to be further developed.[35]

Their local authority evidence demonstrated that more demanding criteria were now being applied to the activities of the voluntary organisations, whose resources and capabilities were often relatively limited. The committee commented, 'This may forecast an extension, and possibly a quickening, of the traditional process by which local authorities take over responsibility for established services which have previously been provided by a voluntary organisation, often on an agency basis.'[36] They foresaw some agencies recognising 'the wisdom of the process of handing over responsibility for an established service' and others resisting this necessity. The committee felt that the most valuable contribution to be made by voluntary bodies would continue to be innovation, pioneering and experimentation, as well as their advantages of flexibility and the personal touch and their important position as a watchdog for citizens over the statutory services. To this end, they felt that local authorities should assist financially, especially in areas like staff training, which had little appeal for voluntary fund raising. Responsibility for monitoring standards in voluntary organisations substantially supported by public funds should rest with the local authorities. All in all, the Younghusband Committee expressed a firm but qualified support for voluntary endeavour, viewing it as a useful back-up to the main-line personal social service provision that could only be guaranteed by the scale and resources of the statutory authorities, which, if they were to follow the report's recommendations, would increasingly be staffed by professionals in the years to come.

Owen, in a study written in 1965,[37] found that the post-war changes, while reversing the roles of the public and the voluntary sector, did not represent an intention to 'establish a statutory monopoly', and that the post-war Labour government 'had proclaimed its adherence to the principle of partnership'. What had resulted, however, was an erratic situation where some voluntary services had never been superseded, where others were left without a function at all, and where the rest had been faced with acute problems of adjustment. He commented, 'There is little evidence of long range thinking in Whitehall or Local Government circles about the future place of voluntary effort in the total welfare scheme, and, indeed, little attempt to define, from the statutory point of view, the function of a voluntary body.'[38] He envisaged that this lack of clarity in the relationship would require constant reassessment by the voluntary bodies and their moving on to new problems. He set out a range of objectives that seemed to be indicated for voluntary organisations:

–to experiment and pioneer
–to supplement qualitatively and quantitatively
–to provide flexibility
–to interpret state services to the ordinary citizen
–to stimulate, restrain and criticise the statutory authorities

Owen was writing at the end of the one and a half decades we have been examining, at a time when the voluntary sector can be said to have been poised on the threshold of new developments. Certainly, his list of objectives for voluntary organisations reflects a new element, one touched on by the Younghusband Committee also. For the 1960s, voluntary bodies were to find a new role, not far removed from the nineteenth-century activities of some of their number in campaigning for social reform and the assumption of social responsibilities by the state, that of catalyst, critic and interpreter of the expanding statutory services. The accent was also placed on those capacities attributed to the voluntary sector which could most readily compensate for the already apparent deficiencies of large-scale, bureaucratised statutory social services.

Before we go on in Chapter 3 to review the new directions in which a partially dispossessed voluntary sector was to develop, a further assessment of the condition of the voluntary sector in the sphere of personal welfare services is offered by the report of the Seebohm Committee on local authority and allied personal social services.[39] From this committee, set up 'to review the organisation and responsibilities of the local authority personal social services in England and Wales, and to consider what changes are desirable to secure an effective family service', we get a useful picture of the state of voluntary social services at the time. The committee's enquiries elicited the fact that in the field of child care, the voluntary organisations were making an essential and substantial contribution; of the 80,000 children in care in 1967, 15,000 were being cared for by voluntary agencies, including some 5000 placed with them by the local authorities. The figures represented a considerable drop from the numbers of children in voluntary sector care a decade previously, but still an obviously important adjunct to the provisions of local authorities. In addition, the committee noted, voluntary bodies were administering 92 approved schools and two remand homes, 'all of them largely financed from public funds', and that more children were placed for adoption with the registered voluntary adoption societies than with the local authorities. With its primary focus on statutory responsibility for children and the problems of the dispersal and fragmentation of this responsibility among several statutory departments, the report has little to say specifically on the place of the voluntary bodies in this field, except to recommend a closer statutory-voluntary partnership, and the increased use of public funds as a means of maintaining and inspecting standards in the voluntary sector.

Where the elderly are concerned, the jurisdictional aspects of care are not such a matter of anxiety to the committee, and, consequently, more attention is paid to the role of voluntary effort. They find evidence here of a considerable input: of the 95,000 elderly people in local authority residential care in 1967, some 11,000 were being housed by voluntary agencies on behalf of the local authorities. In addition, some 43,000 elderly and physically handicapped persons were being housed in registered voluntary and private homes, the majority in voluntary care. In addition to this important input, the committee noted the existence of 7000 social clubs for the elderly, mainly run by voluntary organisations, and over 1500 local old people's welfare committees.

The Seebohm Committee did not seek to mark out separate spheres of statutory/voluntary responsibility in as emphatic a way as Young husband. It is clear that the role of the public authorities had advanced in the intervening years, but perhaps not as quickly nor as completely as Younghusband had expected when it confidently forecast a 'quickening' of the transfer of voluntary services to the local authorities. Reflecting the new developments of the 1960s, both in terms of rising levels of demand and new trends for meeting them, Seebohm gives weight to non-statutory forms of involvement, stating,

> it is increasingly obvious that conventional resources alone are not enough to secure an effective family service. The goodwill and the direct assistance of the community are also needed. We still know comparatively little about how best these might be enlisted and encouraged; of what can or cannot be expected of mutual aid, 'community development', voluntary services or neighbourliness, particularly in urban areas undergoing rapid change.[40]

The committee felt that the new unified departments would be better able to 'adopt a more experimental and exploratory attitude to the stimulation and use of the community's potential contribution to social aid'.[41] It saw this new department, which was to replace the old welfare and children's departments, as part of a wider network of services with which it would need to be coordinated. These included voluntary organisations and volunteers, and the informal exchange of services within geographical and cause-based communities. One of the important functions of voluntary organisations 'should be to ensure a high degree of consumer participation and to help the spontaneous development of neighbourhood interests and activities in meeting needs'.[42] The committee also took on board the growing pressures of the time towards consumer participation in 'the planning, organisation and provision of the social services'. Although it acknowledged that participation could take the form of providing services, or sharing in decision-making, the committee was clearly preoccupied more with the former mode of participation than the latter, and supplied no firm prescriptions for shared decision-making [doc. 2].

Neither the Younghusband nor the Seebohm committees were set up to examine the proper place of voluntary endeavour in the social services, so it is not surprising that they do not spend much time teasing out its precise nature and limits *vis-à-vis* the statutory services. Both confirmed the accepted doctrine of the time, that the main line of social service provision should be a statutory responsibility – one marked out by such standards of professionalism, resource back-up and organisation that only an authority financed from the public purse could be in a position to supply. Both reports carefully avoid negative prescriptions in delineating the proper functions of the voluntary sector, perhaps a pragmatic recognition of the extent of reliance upon voluntary services at the time. They coincide in laying particular stress on the capacity of voluntary organisations to innovate and act as critics of the public services.

CONCLUSION

So far, we have seen that the statutory and voluntary sectors continued to operate in parallel in a 'mixed economy' of welfare, having reversed the original nineteenth- and early twentieth-century relationship whereby the state, as junior partner, acted only to fill the gaps left by voluntary social action. Now, the local authorities carried the major responsibility according to law, and voluntary agencies occupied a secondary, supplementary role, filling the gaps left by the inadequacies of the statutory services and trying to mop up the substantial pools of unmet need that were still to persist. Although often described as a 'partnership', this relationship was neither systematic nor formalised, most often being left to *ad hoc* arrangements or chance. As often as not, the two systems operated entirely separately. The activities of both, we should remind ourselves, represented but the visible tip of a vast hidden iceberg of everyday, ordinary helping and caring services rendered by what is nowadays termed 'the informal care system'. The voluntary sector had, nevertheless, survived to retain a solid if junior role in the provision of social services. In other forms of social and communal action, this era of the late 1960s, when the Seebohm Committee was reviewing the future development of the local authority personal social services, was also a time of new growth for the voluntary sector beyond the service-giving role. It is to this interesting surge of energy and imagination among voluntary groups and organisations from the 1960s into the 1970s that the following chapter now turns.

NOTES AND REFERENCES

1. BEVERIDGE, W., *Voluntary Action*. Allen & Unwin: London, 1948.
2. GOSDEN, P., *Self-help: Voluntary Associations in Nineteenth Century Britain*. Batsford: London, 1973; GILBERT, B., *The Evolution of National Insurance in Great Britain: the Origins of the Welfare State*. M. Joseph: London, 1966; THANE, P., *The Foundations of the Welfare State*. Longman: Harlow, 1982.
3. Some examples from this period are: the YMCA (1844); the

Shaftesbury Homes (1843); the Incorporated Association for Promoting the Welfare of the Blind (1854); Dr Barnardo's Homes (1866); the National Children's Home (1869); the Salvation Army (1865); the Church Army (1882); the NSPCC (1884) and the first Settlement, Toynbee Hall (1884).

4. OWEN, D., *English Philanthropy, 1660–1960*. Harvard University Press: Cambridge, Mass., 1965, p. 597.

5. Ibid., p. 595.

6. GOSCHEN, G., 'Minute to the Twenty-Second Annual Report of the Poor Law Board, 1869–70', cited in WEBB, B and S., *The Prevention of Destitution*. Longman: London, 1912, p. 262.

7. WEBB, B. and S., op. cit., p. 225.

8. Ibid., p. 252.

9. MINISTRY OF HEALTH, *Circular 87/46*, quoted in OWEN, op. cit., p. 547.

10. The doctrine of *ultra vires* means that local government can normally only act within the specific powers granted to it.

11. WEBB, A. *et al.*, *Voluntary Social Services: Manpower Resources*. Personal Social Services Council: London, 1976, p. 5.

12. Ibid.

13. See Chapter 9.

14. MINISTRY OF HEALTH, *Report of the Committee on the Care of Children* (Curtis Report). HMSO: London, 1946.

15. BEVERIDGE, op. cit., p. 82.

16. Ibid.

17. WEBB *et al.*, op. cit., p. 7.

18. HADLEY, R. and HATCH, S., *Social Welfare and the Failure of the State: Centralised Social Services and Participatory Alternatives*. Allen & Unwin: London, 1981, p. 15.

19. WATKIN, B., *The National Health Service: the First Phase. 1948–1974 and after*. Allen & Unwin: London, 1978, p. 18.

20. CROSSMAN, R. H. S., 'The role of the volunteer in the modern social services', Sidney Ball Memorial Lecture 1973, in A.H. Halsey (ed.) *Traditions in Social Policy*. Blackwell: Oxford, 1976, p. 265.

21. Ibid., p. 278.

22. Ibid., p. 274.

23. Ibid., p. 278.

24. HOUSE OF LORDS, *Official Report*, Vol. 163, col. 1119, 1949.

25. BEVAN, A., House of Commons Debate, 24 Nov. 1947, in M. Bruce, (ed.) *The Rise of the Welfare State, English Social Policy 1601–1971*. Weidenfeld & Nicolson: London, 1973, p. 264.

26. CENTRAL STATISTICAL OFFICE (1976), in J.F. Sleeman, *Resources for The Welfare State*. Longman: Harlow, 1979, p. 47.
27. WEBB *et al.*, op. cit., p. 7.
28. WOLFENDEN COMMITTEE, *The Future of Voluntary Organisations*. Croom Helm: London, 1978, p. 20.
29. HMSO, *Report of the Committee on the Law and Practice relating to Charitable Trusts* (Nathan Committee). Cmd. 8710, 1952, p. 149.
30. Ibid., p. 160.
31. Ibid., p. 167.
32. OWEN, op. cit., p. 597.
33. MINISTRY OF HEALTH, *Report of the Working Party on Social Workers in Local Authority Health and Welfare Services*. HMSO: London, 1959.
34. Ibid., para. 152.
35. Ibid., para. 1044.
36. Ibid., para. 1037.
37. OWEN, op. cit.
38. Ibid., p. 543.
39. DEPARTMENT OF HEALTH AND SOCIAL SECURITY, *Report of the Committee on Local Authority and Allied Personal Social Services* (Seebohm Report). HMSO: London, 1969.
40. Ibid., para: 257.
41. Ibid., para. 150.
42. Ibid., para. 451.

Part Two
THE DEVELOPING VOLUNTARY SECTOR

Chapter Three
NEW DIMENSIONS OF VOLUNTARY SOCIAL ACTION

The post-war eclipse of much existing voluntary activity in all the major social services except the personal social services and the slow development within that sphere of the voluntary role was remedied, in a sense, in the wave of change that occurred in the 1960s and which ushered in a new phase for the voluntary sector. The mushrooming of new forms of voluntary organisation and action and the harnessing of energies to new and different causes, testifies to a vibrancy and vigour that gained the attention of policy makers and won the voluntary sector a new place in the welfare state. This chapter seeks to put these developments in their wider context, and to trace the progress of a growing interrelationship between the statutory and voluntary sectors – a relationship which will be more fully documented in the consideration in Chapter 4 of facts, figures and finances relating to voluntary organisations.

The alternative organisations, groups and movements that grew up in the 1960s and 1970s were in many ways the by-product of the public sector welfare system. They were as much a reaction of frustration to the deficiencies, size and inaccessibility of the state welfare apparatus as they were the result of pressures to participate and protest thrown up by a wider process of social and cultural change. They also reflected the emergence and recognition of new social need, such as that produced by the disintegrating effects of slum-clearance policies, or the rising rates of divorce and growing numbers of single-parent families. Many of the pressure-group activities that evolved were aimed at forcing change directly in public policies; many advice and information services were developed to help people find their way around the welfare state; many of the mutual aid and self-help activities that emerged were a signal of gaps in state provision. The welfare state had not met all the expectations it had generated for universal, high-quality and comprehensive provisions. It had not significantly redistributed resources or made much impact on the differential life-chances of the poor, the homeless or other marginal groups. The economy was still relatively buoyant in the late 1960s and so were people's expectations. The forms of voluntary social action that now emerged were not the service-giving supplements to the personal social services that we have discussed in Chapter 2. They were about action and change and criticism – functions noted by both the Younghusband and the Seebohm reports as being unique to the voluntary sector, and transforming its relationship with the statutory authorities.

Much of the impetus for this broadening out and radicalising of the voluntary sector into community action and organisation, protest movements and campaigns, consumer groups and so on, had come from the United States. There, in the 1960s, new anti-poverty and urban renewal strategies were being attempted[1] and all kinds of grass-roots action were taking shape, partly fuelled by civil rights issues and partly by a more general social unrest. This diffusion process resulted in the adoption of new strategies by the British government, strategies which were pale copies of their American counterparts, such as the Community Development Projects, the Urban Renewal Programme, the Educational Priority Areas, etc. The Skeffington Committee was also set up in 1968 to advise on the possibilities for public participation in physical planning processes. All these initiatives released finances for new forms of voluntary action and energies for protest and participation.

The transformation of the voluntary sector, which was a remarkable leap forward in terms of creativity, ingenuity and energy, was also so diverse and multiform that to describe it fully is impossible. The indeterminacy of the label 'voluntary sector' is never more apparent than when stretched to cover the mushrooming of all types and varieties of groups and agencies in this period. Any attempt to classify or quantify all the myriad forms of local voluntary involvement such as action groups, tenants' groups, playgroups, amenity associations, advice centres, consumer cooperatives, good neighbour schemes, resource centres, etc. that developed then and since, is doomed to failure. Groups were born and died often very quickly, with a hardly discernible form. Some were overtly political and hit local and sometimes national headlines; others quietly set about raising voluntary and financial resources to meet new needs in their own way.

It is one of the singularly dynamic qualities of the modern voluntary sector that it is not susceptible to clear definition. This was noted in

Chapter 1, where a rule-of-thumb guideline to the problem was adopted, in that discussion was to be confined to those forms of voluntary action which are organised and thus have some identifiable form or structure. Referring back to the typology by function, developed in that chapter, it might be helpful to fit some of the newer developments into this matrix where possible. The categories listed were those of service-giving, mutual aid, pressure, resource and coordination groups.

It was also noted earlier that organisations at national level are often the most visible manifestations of this mass of localised activity. Without suggesting that the national bodies can be taken to represent all there is to be said about the many local groups that may affiliate to them, it is at least easier to gain a sense of the direction of the 1960s and 1970s changes by reference to the national organisations which emerged at this time. In the service-giving category, a new type of agency was that modelled on organisations in the United States like VISTA (Volunteers in Service to America, a domestic version of the Peace Corps) and the Neighborhood Youth Corps, which sought to channel the energies of young people, who, with soaring birth rates and an emerging youth culture, were beginning to make their presence felt. In Britain, this produced such bodies as the Community Service Volunteers (CSV), founded in 1962; Task Force founded in 1964; the Young Volunteer Force Foundation (later the Community Projects Foundation) started in 1968, and others like the Cyrenians, St Mungo Trust, Outset, Action Space, etc. These bodies recruited and organised young volunteers for specific services to groups like the elderly and the disabled, or for various forms of community work and projects.

Other organisations born at this time to provide services to special groups in the population, and whose local memberships mainly comprise people from these groups and those connected with them, combine a major emphasis on service delivery with public education and some elements of the mutual aid function. Examples of such bodies are the National Schizophrenia Fellowship (1972), the Coeliac Society (1968), the Spina Bifida Association (1966) and the Muscular Dystrophy Society (1959). Not all organisations in this service-giving category are based on membership by consumers, but typically consist of small paid staffs who work for a select target group. Organisations which clearly fall within the mutual aid category that are founded around this time are the Pre-School Playgroups Association (1961), Gingerbread (1970) for single parents, the Spinal Injuries Association (1974) and the National Women's Aid Federation (1975).

Bodies that sprang up in the 1960s to promote the pressure-group function predominantly were Shelter (1966), the National Campaign for the Homeless; the Child Poverty Action Group (1965), set up to fight the cause of family poverty; the Disablement Income Group (DIG), established in 1965 to campaign for a decent income for the disabled and for legislative reform, and the Minority Rights Group, started to fight for specific groups such as travellers, migrant workers, etc. in 1965. A variant on this theme is the coalitions of campaigning organisations centred around a common cause, like the Campaign for the Homeless and Rootless (CHAR), or the Disability Alliance, which combines at least fifty bodies in the field of disability, to press for a comprehensive income scheme from a unified platform. Coalitions such as these have been the product of the diversity, competition and fragmentation that characterise the voluntary sector even within one specialised area of interest. Some campaigning bodies represent the political arm of existing organisations which are seeking to stay within the narrow confines of the Charity Commissioners' interpretations of what constitutes charitable activity, such as the Cobden Trust, an offshoot of the National Council for Civil Liberties. Many established organisations adopted new, more militant and politically acute styles of operating around this period of new developments. For instance, MIND, the National Association for Mental Health, used tactics ranging from court-room advocacy – taking test cases to the European Court of Justice, for example – to expert use of the media.

In the last, intermediary category, where national and local agencies provide resources to, and help coordinate, other organisations, many, such as the councils of social service, have a long history that pre-dates the 1960s and 1970s. Some of the new resource bodies for specific areas that began around this time are the National Children's Bureau (1963), the National Youth Bureau (1964) and the Volunteer Centre (1973).

This brief overview of new developments in these years demonstrates a rich and variegated crop of voluntary bodies at the national level, comparable as evidence of a leap forward in voluntary social action with the nineteenth-century foundations cited earlier. They also represent a clear break with the established, traditional type of voluntary body that had dominated the voluntary sector up until the end of the 1950s. Not that these established voluntary organisations remained impervious to change. An agency like Barnardo's, for instance, radically revised its pattern of work in 1969.[2] Instead of attempting to maintain a nationally available service in the face of all the statutory developments that had gone before and were still expected under the influence of the Seebohm Report, Barnardo's restructured to concentrate its resources and expertise in areas of high need, both geographically and in terms of the most needy and problematic children. Windlesham comments, 'the management and fund-raising functions also underwent radical overhaul. None of this was accomplished without internal friction and dissent, but the result was to reshape a large and deeply rooted voluntary organisation and to redefine its aim in terms of the needs of present day society.'[3] Other long-established agencies were to follow suit, though by no means all – some confining themselves to a catchier change of name or acronym.

Some idea of patterns of growth and development at the local level can be gleaned from a study conducted by Stephen Hatch[4] of voluntary organisations in three towns. In this study he found that 'Although the history of a few existing voluntary organisations in the three towns goes back to the last century, a majority of them have come into being since 1960.'[5] He found, in fact, also that 'nearly 40 per cent of the organisations surveyed in 1978 had come into existence in the preceding eight years'.[6] Hatch was able to identify a number of growth points, indicating the kind of organisations which had come into being in this period. Foremost among them were organisations for people with specific handicaps and diseases, such as the Association for Spina Bifida and Hydrocephalus (1964) or the Epilepsy Action Group (1975) in one of his three towns, 'Anglebridge'. Next in importance came the playgroup movement – 'the largest single addition since 1960 to the number of organisations included in this study'.[7] Other major areas of new growth were in advice and counselling, in neighbourhood organisations, and also in special-need housing, ethnic organisations and environmental organisations.

Hatch found that this period of growth coincided with a rapid expansion of the statutory services, and so 'the two sectors cannot be interpreted as essentially replacements for each other'.[8] How, he asks, can the voluntary sector's growth be accounted for? Partial explanations may be found in factors like simple population growth, or advances in medical science which have ensured the survival of certain handicapped groups. Beyond these, he identifies five types of stimulus to the creation of new voluntary organisations in his survey. 'The type of trigger to which the creation of the largest number of organisations can be attributed are the staff of statutory agencies acting in an official or semi-official capacity.'[9] The rest are: an individual or group organising others around a shared problem to form a mutual aid group; individuals or groups coming together from

[margin handwritten note:] Parallel development of state + of sector.

a philanthropic motive, often in support of a specific cause; groups initiated by local churches, and those 'which represent an outgrowth of existing voluntary organisations'.[10]

In summary, then, Hatch finds two major trends behind the generation of new voluntary organisations – the deliberate intervention of external agencies like the statutory or other voluntary services, and the expression of a consumer movement. Both are the product, he feels, of growing demand and rising expectations associated with the expansion of the statutory services but outstripping their capacity to respond – a point we noted earlier in the writings of Owen,[11] where it was predicted that voluntary agencies would become the beneficiaries of the demand stimulated by statutory social services.

We have reviewed in this section what has amounted to a remarkable transformation and new growth in the voluntary sector, at both national and local level, from the mid-1960s onwards, but more particularly from the early 1970s, a time when, as we shall see in the next section, there was a rapid growth in social expenditure in the statutory sector, and a consequent expansion of the funds available to voluntary organisations. Many of the voluntary agencies and groups active today had their origin in this period of growth.

THE WIDER CONTEXT

The late 1960s and early 1970s saw a growing emphasis in the public sphere on the benefits of organisational reform and enlargement of scale, of planning and budgeting and on the coordination and integration of service provision. The Seebohm Report brought about the unification of the various local authority welfare and children's departments to form a smaller number of large personal social services departments, aimed at incorporating those features and at securing a more effective leverage in the distribution of resources at local level.[12] This reorganisation reinforced the trend towards professional social worker dominance that had been endorsed by both the Younghusband and the Seebohm committees, and had been set in train by developments in the training and organisation of the social work profession. The path was set for a rapid expansion of the hierarchical and administrative structures thought to be necessary for the exercise of the comprehensive and generic responsibilities advocated by Seebohm.

Since the mid-1960s, the hitherto neglected social welfare services had been experiencing a faster rate of growth in expenditure than any other of the major social services, although admittedly from an extremely low starting-point. Their growing importance reflected a deeper awareness of the extent of poverty and of unmet and submerged need for social provisions. The swelling ranks of professional social workers were adding to demand. The community care policies adopted in an effort to deinstitutionalise the health services, especially in the mental health field, were making the provision of comprehensive social services more urgent. The passing of additional legislation such as the 1969 Children and Young Persons Act and the 1970 Chronically Sick and Disabled Persons Act, was to impose new duties on local authorities and, in the case of the latter Act, to stimulate new demand and greater emphasis on rights.

The share of local authority expenditure allocated to the personal social services grew by more than half in the years between 1965 and 1972.[13] Webb comments, 'The first three years of the 1970s were the brief hey-day of the reorganised personal social services' with an annual growth rate of 12 per cent.[14] This boost to the relative importance of the statutory services could not fail to have a 'knock-on' effect on the development of the voluntary sector at local level, and we have already noted some of the effects of this. It is in the early part of the 1970s that new forms of statutory–voluntary relationship of the kind advocated by both Younghusband and Seebohm began to take shape. Webb *et al.*[15] write that the era after Seebohm was 'one of increased financial support from statutory to voluntary agencies, combined with attempts to nurture new initiatives and encourage coordination between existing agencies'.

Just as, during the post-war years, the statutory welfare services' lack of development was more or less paralleled by a similar sluggishness in the voluntary sector, so, from the second half of the 1960s, an expansion of the local authority personal social services was matched by a blossoming in the voluntary sphere. The difference between this and the post-war trends in other services is that it was now recognised that the extent of unmet need far surpassed the capacity of the public services. This new realism threw a different light on the value and potential of the voluntary sector. Both spheres contributed to and benefited from a heightened awareness of social problems, and both gained from a short-lived surge in public expenditure.

The local authority departments were not 'Seebohmised' until 1971, but there were other legislative developments around this time which augmented the resources of many voluntary organisations, and not just in the personal social services field. At central government level, the 1969 Children and Young Persons Act, section 65, gave the

Department of Health and Social Security (DHSS) powers to grant aid to voluntary organisations which were providing residential care under the Act [doc. 3]. The DHSS was also empowered under the 1968 Health Services and Public Health Act, section 64, to subsidise voluntary agencies providing health and social services similar to those provided by the ministry under the Act. The Home Office, under the Criminal Courts Act 1973, was enabled to give money to voluntary bodies supplying probation hostels, working in rehabilitation or conducting research into delinquency. At the level of local government, the 1963 Childrens and Young Persons Act had empowered local authorities to provide assistance to voluntary agencies active in preventive work with children [doc. 4]. Section 65 of the Health Services and Public Health Act 1968 authorised the assistance in cash and kind of voluntary bodies providing services similar to the authority's own in this field. The Local Government Act 1972 gave local authorities power to spend up to the product of a 2p rate in the interests of their area in assisting charitable bodies and other non-profit-making organisations providing a public service. Subsequent legislation gave local authorities a range of powers to subsidise voluntary agencies providing health and social services of various kinds – services for the homeless, and community bus and car schemes, among others. The authorities were enabled to give aid not only in the form of cash, but indirect subsidies in the form of premises, goods and, in some cases, the services of personnel. While these measures dealt with a problem mentioned in Chapter 2, that of the limitations set by the *ultra vires* principle, the powers they granted were discretionary. They have consequently been taken up in only a very uneven way by local authorities, resulting in widely varying levels of financial support for voluntary organisations, as Chapter 4 makes clear.

The growth in public expenditure, the heightened importance of the personal social services and a rising official interest in the potential of the voluntary sector in both major political parties, added impetus to the revival of the voluntary sector. More public money became available, rising from about £2.5 million in central government grants in 1971 to an estimated £20 million in 1975/76.[16] Local authority social services department subsidies to voluntary organisations grew from £2.5 million in 1972/73 to nearly £8 million by 1975/76 – figures thought by Unell[17] to be underestimates.

Quite apart from these financial developments, which boosted voluntary organisations and activities operating outside or parallel to the statutory agencies, there were other interesting developments at this time within the public sphere. These were the growing use of volunteers in the health and social services. Voluntary workers had always been active in hospitals, in prisons and in the probation service to some degree. Use of them now expanded and became the object of official policies, a development recommended for the social services departments by Seebohm, and generally pushed forward for all areas by the publication in 1969 of the unofficial Aves Committee's *Report on the Voluntary Worker in the Social Services*.[18]

The Aves Report

This report was a significant, though non-official, enquiry into the potential of volunteers which acquired a semi-official status by becoming the accepted orthodoxy on the subject. The Aves Committee was set up in 1966 under the auspices of the National Council of Social Service (NCSS) (as it then was) and the National Institute for Social Work Training 'to enquire into the role of voluntary workers in the social services and in particular to consider their need for preparation or training and their relationship with professional social workers'.[18] The report's background in the resurgence of voluntary social action after a long period of decline, has already been documented in this chapter. What made it opportune was a combination of factors – the increased emphasis on the professionalisation of social work, and the developments and reorganisations in the statutory services themselves. The report observes:

> Social services had become more comprehensive and more complex than ever before, and there was increasing realisation of the part that they needed to play. The aims of the services were becoming more explicit; their limitations as well as their potentialities were more clearly realised; shortages of suitably equipped staff were constantly deplored, and there were doubts about the wisdom – even if it had been practicable – of trying to meet all these needs by the use of paid staff.[19]

Making something of a virtue of the difficulty, the Aves Committee did not put forward a precise definition of what constitutes a volunteer, nor did it attempt to estimate the total numbers of volunteers active in the social services. Such research as was available to them demonstrated the existence of voluntary work on a large scale, predominantly, but certainly not exclusively, performed by women, and tending to spring from the higher occupational groups 'better educated, and probably better off, than the average citizen'. The report noted, however, that among the working class, voluntary endeavour was more likely to take the form of informal exchanges of services and mutual aid at the neighbourhood level. A great range of helping activities by volunteers to be found in the statutory health, probation and welfare services was acknowledged in the report, and the committee endorsed the Seebohm Report's recommendation that 'the social service department must become the focal point to which those who wish to give voluntary help can offer their services'.[20] This was already showing signs of increasing – volunteers were being recruited through volunteer bureaux, through the efforts of voluntary services liaison officers here and there in the statutory services, and through voluntary organisations.

There was some resistance among the social work profession to the use of volunteers, and Aves stated: 'We also see a need for social workers to be more aware of the many functions which voluntary workers can perform, and of the potentialities of a partnership between volunteers and professional staff.'[21] The volunteer's contribution was seen as unique, not to be used as a substitute for professional or paid staff but as a means of extending and improving a service. The report makes a number of recommendations [doc. 5] but its major contribution was to focus attention on the possible benefits of a closer integration of the statutory and voluntary sectors in the use by the former, of volunteers. Rather than an exhortation to contract out certain welfare functions to non-statutory organisations, it advocates the reverse – the incorporation of voluntary work within the context of the public services. Webb comments that the Aves Report 'laid the tentative basis for a rehabilitation of volunteer work within the British philosophy of social welfare and indicated the need for an analytical sociology of voluntarism'.[22]

The Aves Report gave rise to new levels of awareness of the value of voluntary workers. One of the most concrete results of its deliberations was the creation, somewhat tardily in 1973, of the Volunteer Centre, a national body that Aves had recommended to serve as 'a focus for all aspects of the work of volunteers in the social services'. This body, under the sponsorship of such figures as Aves and Seebohm, and funded first by trusts and then by central government (the Voluntary Services Unit), expanded to embrace the use of volunteers in hospitals, social services and probation departments and in prisons. It produced numerous studies of good practice in the use made of volunteers,[23] provided guidelines for such contentious issues as the substitution of paid workers by volunteers and strike-breaking by volunteers, promoted the imaginative use of the media in volunteer recruitment, and generally became a catalyst for volunteer involvement in the public services. The 1970s saw a considerable expansion both in the numbers of high-street volunteer bureaux, where unattached volunteers might find placement, and in the appointments of voluntary service coordinators in hospitals, and volunteer and voluntary organisations' liaison officers in social services departments and in the probation service.

The Voluntary Services Unit

In the same year that the Aves Report was published (1969), the Conservative Party who were in opposition set up a working party led by Earl Jellicoe to look at the use of voluntary work by the statutory services. This was the beginning of a quickening of interest in the Conservative Party in what had always been a concern close to its pro-market and individualist ideologies. Windlesham links this working group's preparatory discussions with the appearance in the 1970 Election Manifesto of the following commitment:

> We recognise the important contribution to social welfare that volunteers and voluntary organisations are already making, and we believe there is scope for considerable expansion and development. We are convinced that many of the social problems that now scar society can only be solved through a genuine partnership of effort between statutory and voluntary organisations – between the professional and the volunteer. We will give active support, both financially and legislatively, so that new opportunities may be created in cooperation with the local authorities for all those – and in particular the young people and the retired people – who want to do voluntary work.[24]

Windlesham gives a useful, insider's account of how this electoral commitment was followed up in the Heath administration which came to power in 1970, with the setting up of a ministerial group on voluntary social service with Jellicoe as chairperson. This group was instrumental in eliciting a resource commitment from the government to match its statement of intent. The Prime Minister launched this initiative in late 1971 with a speech to the NCSS, in which he spoke of 'a continuing and developing commitment to the concept of partnership between the Government and the voluntary service movement'.[25] In addition, he announced the government's intention to make available extra finance for departmental expenditure on the voluntary sector for the next financial year.

A further tangible result of this gathering interest in the voluntary sector at central government level in the early 1970s was the setting up of the Voluntary Services Unit (VSU) in 1973, a department of government which was to act as a focal point in government for relations with voluntary organisations. A small coordinating unit for voluntary sector matters had been based in the Cabinet Office under the Labour government of 1964–68, in an attempt to pull together some of the disparate initiatives and lines of communication maintained by a host of separate government departments with a range of voluntary organisations. To strengthen this coordinating function, the Heath administration appointed in 1972, as coordinating minister for voluntary social services, Lord Windlesham, a Minister of State in the Home Office, who had a personal interest in the voluntary sector and was responsible for his department's Community Programmes Department, administering race relations matters, urban aid, and, at the time, the Community Development Projects. This appointment was in fact the resurrection of an old idea, first mooted by Beveridge in the late 1940s, at a most inauspicious time, as we have seen, for the designation of a 'Minister Guardian' for the voluntary services. The Voluntary Social Services Section (VSS), as it was called at first, was opted for from a number of competing alternatives, to fulfil the function of 'a "lead" department which would have coordinating responsibilities and would be expected to take the initiative in fostering voluntary social endeavour, but which would leave the main departmental responsibilities untouched'.[26] The remit of the VSS was to extend to the voluntary sector in general for matters affecting all voluntary bodies. At a future date it would provide financial support for those national bodies with activities spanning all or most of the voluntary sector or falling between the different spending departments' responsibilities. The section remained low priority, for all that it was heralded as evidence of government's enthusiasm for the voluntary sector, in that it neither had a budget of its own nor sufficient political clout in government.[27] Windlesham himself wrote later that

> the effectiveness of the ministerial coordinator was impaired by the fact that he was outside the Cabinet, and so junior to, and not closely in touch with those Ministers in charge of Departments such as Education and Science, and Health and Social Security, which had considerable interests in various forms of voluntary endeavour. The additional funds announced in the Prime Minister's NCSS speech were also under departmental control, and therefore the Home Office Minister of State had little independent power in the all-important matter of grant-aiding particular activities or organisations from public funds.[28]

For some time the VSS remained rather symbolic and ineffectual, administering some Home Office grants to the NCSS for the promotion of volunteer bureaux, and to the Volunteer Centre at its inception. It was, however, some indication, however faint, of the government's interest in the voluntary sector and accumulated some political capital at a time when voluntary activities had taken on a new lease of life. Windlesham stayed with it only briefly, but returned in 1973 when the Prime Minister announced he had decided 'for the first time to give this responsibility to a Cabinet Minister'[29] who would be Windlesham. The VSS was thus upgraded and with it the voluntary sector. It became the Voluntary Services Unit in the Civil Service Department under Windlesham. In addition, it acquired a small budget (under £2 million in 1973) for funding voluntary organisations, which was visibly a token gesture. After the 1974 election, the VSU was returned to the Community Programmes Division of the Home Office under a non-Cabinet minister, where it was to remain, its functions relatively undisturbed by the advent of a Labour government.

The Wolfenden Report on the future of voluntary organisations[30]

In 1974, a committee headed by Lord Wolfenden was set up on the initiative of the Rowntree Memorial Trust, to 'review the role and function of voluntary organisations in the UK over the next twenty-five years'. According to Stephen Hatch[31] who was Senior Research Officer to the committee, it was established in response to the threat that inflation was perceived to represent to the voluntary sector's independence, and as a means of studying the implications for the voluntary sector of the reorganisations of local government and the personal social services. The enquiry was originally conceived in relation to the social services, but this brief was widened to include environmental interests when the Carnegie Trust became its co-sponsor.

The Wolfenden Report noted the existence of four separate 'systems' for meeting social need – the informal, where family, friends and neighbours provide support; the commercial or market system where services are bought; the statutory and the voluntary. It was the committee's view that the informal and the statutory systems are 'the principal means of meeting social needs in our society'[32] [doc. 6]. It saw the role of the voluntary sector as essentially subsidiary to this and the role of the commercial sector, in this context, as rather marginal. The report reviews the positive and negative characteristics of both the statutory and the voluntary sectors and asks what the latter can contribute that will improve on the public services and how it can 'interrelate constructively with the informal and statutory systems'. Its frame of reference concerns 'the strengthening of collective action in meeting important social needs and the maintenance of a pluralistic pattern of institutions'.[33] We shall be enquiring into the political philosophy of the Wolfenden Report later in the discussion in Chapter 8 discussion of welfare pluralism as a theoretical framework for the organising and delivery of social services. Meanwhile, what were the main conclusions and recommendations reached by the Wolfenden Committee?

Wolfenden does not advocate fundamental changes in the central role played by the statutory sector. It sees the state as bearing a main-line responsibility but one that it should increasingly share with the voluntary system. In a sense it asks the state to move over and to give more space to voluntary endeavour, reversing the trend towards expanding the scale of statutory services. The precise lines of this relationship remain unclear, but the voluntary system is seen as contributing to the statutory sphere in three ways. It can extend provisions, improve quality and offer services where the state is not active. In extending services, the voluntary sector could operate by means of innovation, by providing alternatives and therefore offering choice, by attracting all kinds of new resources and by giving direct support to statutory bodies. Improvements in the quality of state provision would be one of the benefits of competition and of the role of voluntary organisations as critics, pressure groups and consumer rights advisers. Where the state does not offer a service, or accords it little priority, the voluntary system can and does take exclusive responsibility.

In relation to the informal system for meeting social need, the committee saw the function of the voluntary system to be essentially supportive, performing three distinct roles. These are the replacement of the informal nework when it cannot cope, or has broken down; offering relief temporarily when necessary, and reinforcing informal caring arrangements through support in the form of encouragement, skill development or material resources.

The committee makes the point that it is not thinking 'simply of a redistribution of activities between the statutory and the voluntary sectors' but 'the development of a new long-term strategy'. This strategy would be the reassessment of what the statutory, voluntary and informal systems might contribute and how they would interrelate. This is likely to point 'to the need for a substantial extension of the last two sectors'. The report thus urges a major reappraisal by government and by the voluntary sector and calls on government in particular to make a new initiative 'based on an explicit recognition of the contribution which the voluntary organisations, both corporately and individually, are in a position to make'.[34]

The expansion of the voluntary sector would depend on a prior expansion of the financial resources available to voluntary organisations. In its section on finance, the committee noted the precarious position of many voluntary organisations dependent upon private giving, a source of finance which had failed to keep up with inflation in recent years. At the time Wolfenden was writing, inflation and, it was thought, public expenditure cuts, were beginning to make inroads into both the statutory and voluntary social services. Wolfenden concluded, 'In thinking about the future we recognise that the voluntary sector will probably not be able to place as much reliance as previously upon private giving. As we are looking for a strengthening of the voluntary sector, lack of money could prove a serious brake.'[35] Examining various alternatives for the voluntary sector in this economic crisis, the committee considered first the possibility of raising money by new devices, but doubted 'whether there is a large pool of untapped resources' and was pessimistic about the potential of more private giving. Secondly it looked at the area of tax concessions, but decided that none of the tax proposals under consideration would help the voluntary sector dramatically. Accordingly, the committee concluded, 'There will therefore have to be greater reliance on statutory funding.'

Noting the strengths of the voluntary system, the report also observed 'these same features mean that there is no guarantee that voluntary effort will necessarily materialise where need is greatest, that standards of service will be maintained, or that the sector as a whole will operate in a coordinated manner'.[36] A further task for the state therefore was to remedy these defects in the voluntary sector – 'local and national government must be ready to take on the task of compensating for deficiencies in the pattern of provision. This means that there must be national and local plans that include voluntary provision, and use the means open to government, including grant-aiding and stimulation of new voluntary bodies, to influence the development of the voluntary sector.'[36]

Some of the new organisations the Wolfenden Committee had in mind formed the main substance of its recommendations. These were 'intermediary bodies' which were intended, at local and national level, to concentrate and centralise a range of functions currently dispersed among a number of organisations. At the local level, the report examines the activities of rural community councils, councils of voluntary service and a small number of area resource centres which have been set up in recent years. From an overview of these bodies, Wolfenden distils out five main functions:

1. Development – the identification of need and the initiation of action to meet it.
2. Services to other organisations – advice, information, practical assistance.
3. Liaison – the exchange of information and opinion between organisations.
4. Representation – articulating views and interests, negotiating with the statutory sector, etc.
5. Direct service to individuals – for example, advice bureaux, adventure playgrounds.

Of this range of functions the committee identified the first four as appropriate for the local intermediary bodies it wished to promote with the aid of public grants attached to the functions, rather than the organisations. The intermediary bodies would help to remedy the problems of uneven distribution and performance, and the duplications and gaps left by uncoordinated voluntary initiatives. They would strengthen the voluntary sector, provide it with an independent voice and make its partnership with the statutory sector less unequal. Because such intermediary functions have little popular appeal for fund raising, the committee advocated funding from central government which would have the added advantage of safeguarding the independence of the intermediary bodies at local level and helping to iron out the widely variable support given by local authorities to voluntary organisations. On a national level, the committee endorsed similar intermediary functions for the National Councils of Social Service, together with the task of servicing the local intermediary bodies. These national bodies would also need increased government support, an estimated £2.5 million extra, in 1978.

The Wolfenden Report was generally well received as a timely contribution to a continuing debate about the role of the voluntary sector, a debate that was to acquire new tones with changes in the political climate subsequently. It was acclaimed as 'a milestone in the history of voluntary organisations since the last war'[37] and as a 'platform for the discussion of the positive role of voluntary organisations in our society'.[38] Possibly its most positive contribution was to underline the mutual importance and interrelatedness of the four main systems for meeting social need – the statutory, voluntary, informal and commercial, and to insist on the need for government to develop a policy with regard to the integration of the first three at least. From the point of view of the voluntary sector, it also served to highlight the great disparities between local authorities in their support – although the report was criticised for failing to point out the major defaulters in this regard.

Whether the Wolfenden Report achieved more than to arouse interest and spark off debate, is a difficult question to answer. Its recommendation of extra government money for intermediary functions (criticised by David Hobman of Age Concern as being too little 'in the face of the Committee's own assessment of the extent and value to society of an independent sector'[39]) was not taken up either by the Labour government of the day or the subsequent Conservative administration. The Callaghan government responded to Wolfenden by setting up an inter-departmental committee to discuss it and by issuing a consultative document[40] [doc. 7] in which it set out certain of its own reactions, and invited those of other interested bodies. In this document, the government stated that while 'it acknowledges the voluntary sector as a fundamental and essential element of society, and fully recognises the need for a greater harmonisation between its policies and those of the voluntary organisations in the provision of services in various fields' it is not convinced 'that there is a need for a long-term strategy, if by this is meant a move towards defining a clear division between the contributions of the voluntary and statutory sectors'.[41] It saw this as a form of centralised planning which could potentially reduce the voluntary sector's flexible response to new problems, and something which the voluntary sector itself would not welcome. The government also made it clear that it could not at this stage give any commitment to the central funding of intermediary bodies. Beyond reiterating its support for the voluntary sector and citing the extent of its direct and indirect assistance to it, the government avoided any major new commitments.

The response from the voluntary sector and from local government to the consultative document[42] was varied and diffuse, and nothing specific has resulted from the exercise. The Conservative government ignored Wolfenden's suggestions on funding for intermediary bodies, and instead announced that the VSU was 'developing three schemes which, while modest in outlay, will . . . yield substantial benefits in assisting the voluntary sector to develop its own resources'.[43] Murray observes: 'The final outcome of Wolfenden, therefore, was a programme of pilot projects, conferences and seminars on voluntary action, a pilot programme of small grants in a number of local areas and the financing of two local charity reviews as a basis for greater collaboration in the use of local resources.'[44]

Wolfenden was also widely criticised in the voluntary sector and elsewhere for its failure to live up to the expectations of its original brief – to assess the likely direction of the voluntary sector over the next twenty-five years. In retrospect, the committee would have done better to have dropped this part of its remit which seemed to commit it to a blueprint that it felt unable to devise and which would probably not have been universally acceptable anyway. Some critics voiced fears that proposals for more government financial support posed a danger to the voluntary sector's capacity to criticise central and local government. Others suggested that it was insufficiently critical – '. . . it was hoped in some quarters that the report would tackle its subject with the sort of critical cutting edge absent from the discussion of the contribution of voluntary effort in the social services. But this expectation was unhappily not fulfilled.'[45] Hatch comments that the report failed to give sufficient attention to the role of the state, particularly in the light of the strains and impending changes in a society where economic growth was faltering.[46] Webb makes a similar point in observing,

> A tough minded analysis of state provision must underpin any analysis of voluntary organisations. The Seebohm Committee did at least refer to the potential dangers, to both sides, of voluntary organisations simply acting as agents of statutory services; Wolfenden did not . . . A limp reference to 'partnership' is not good enough if the ambiguity of state–voluntary relationships is to be clarified and eased by a new and respected philosophy.[47]

CONCLUSION

This chapter has documented the resilience of the voluntary sector in evolving new forms and functions to fit with changing circumstances. This evolution has been achieved both with the help of statutory sources of finance as the personal social services grew in importance, and as official attitudes to voluntary social action became more favourable, and also as a counter-reaction to developments in the statutory sector itself. The service delivery function of the traditional voluntary body was sustained, supplementing public sector provisions, but the real development in the voluntary sector came with the emergence of functions unique to it – those of mutual aid, the provision of information and advice, and the critical, pressure-group function. A basic assumption that underlay the resurgence of voluntary social action in these new forms, and increased attention to it in the public sphere and in the official and unofficial enquiries discussed earlier, continued to be the conviction that it was the task of the state to provide the bulk of

The voluntary sector in British social services

main-line social welfare services, and the role of the voluntary sector
to supplement and complement it, either with more of the same or
with different activities. There was no suggestion, even with the
decline in the economy or the loss of momentum in the personal social
services later, in the mid-1970s, discussed in Chapter 4, that there
should be any radical reversal of these roles. Instead, efforts were
made to integrate the voluntary services more closely in the social
programmes of the state, with central and local government resources
being made available to encourage the formation of a 'partnership'
between the two sectors. A more radical ideological shift towards
reversing the roles in such 'partnerships' and limiting the responsibilities of the state, was to accompany the advent of a Conservative
government on the crest of a rightwards tide, in 1979.

NOTES AND REFERENCES

1. HIGGINS, J., *The Poverty Business*. Blackwell & Robertson:
    Oxford, 1978.
2. WINDLESHAM, D., *Politics in Practice*. Cape: London, 1975, p.
    67.
3. Ibid., pp. 67–8.
4. HATCH, S., *Outside the State*. Croom Helm: London, 1980.
5. Ibid., p. 77.
6. Ibid., p. 82.
7. Ibid., p. 88.
8. Ibid., p. 91.
9. Ibid., p. 92.
10. Ibid., p. 93.
11. OWEN, D., *English Philanthropy, 1660–1960*. Harvard University
    Press: New York, 1965.
12. DEPARTMENT OF HEALTH AND SOCIAL SECURITY, *Report of the
    Committee on Local Authority and Allied Personal Social Services*.
    HMSO: London, 1969.
13. WEBB, A., 'The personal social services', in N. Bosanquet and P.
    Townsend, *Labour and Equality*. Heinemann: London, 1980, pp.
    279–95.
14. Ibid., p. 285.
15. WEBB, A. *et al.*, *Voluntary Social Service Manpower Resources*.
    Personal Social Services Council: London, 1976, p. 7.
16. OWEN, D., House of Commons, 8 July 1975, Hansard, col. 354.
17. UNELL, J., *Voluntary Social Services: Financial Resources*. Bedford
    Square Press: London, 1979, p. 8.

18. AVES COMMITTEE, *Report on the Voluntary Worker in the Social Services*. Bedford Square Press: London, 1969.
19. Ibid., p. 16.
20. DEPARTMENT OF HEALTH AND SOCIAL SECURITY, op. cit., para. 498.
21. AVES COMMITTEE, op. cit., p. 68.
22. WEBB, A., 'Voluntary social action: in search of a policy?' *Journal of Voluntary Action Research*, 18: 1–2 (Jan./Jun. 1979), pp. 8–16.
23. VOLUNTEER CENTRE, Publications department, 29 Lower Kings Road, Berkhamsted, Herts.
24. Quoted in WINDLESHAM, op. cit., p. 46.
25. HEATH, E., Speech to AGM of National Council of Social Service, 1971.
26. ROWE, A., 'Voluntary Services Unit, in K. Jones (ed.), *The Yearbook of Social Policy 1973*. Routledge & Kegan Paul: London, 1974, p. 180.
27. Ibid.
28. WINDLESHAM, op. cit., p. 70.
29. Quoted in ROWE, op. cit., p. 182.
30. WOLFENDEN COMMITTEE, *The Future of Voluntary Organisations*. Croom Helm: London, 1978.
31. HATCH, S., 'The Wolfenden Report on voluntary organisations', in M. Brown and S. Baldwin (eds.), *The Yearbook of Social Policy 1978*. Routledge & Kegan Paul: London, 1979, pp. 101–112.
32. WOLFENDEN COMMITTEE, op. cit., p. 26.
33. Ibid., p. 25.
34. Ibid., p. 74.
35. Ibid., p. 168.
36. Ibid., p. 28.
37. NATIONAL COUNCIL OF SOCIAL SERVICE, *The Future of Voluntary Organisations: NCSS Comments on the Wolfenden Report*, submitted to the government's Inter-departmental Commission, NCSS (undated), p. 1.
38. YOUNG, BARONESS, House of Lords, Jan. 1978, col. 102.
39. HOBMAN, D., 'So much for so little' *Health and Social Services Journal*, 2 Dec. 1977, p. 1644.
40. THE HOME OFFICE, VOLUNTARY SERVICES UNIT, *The Government and the Voluntary Sector. A Consultative Document*. Home Office, 1978.
41. Ibid., p. 11.
42. THE HOME OFFICE, VOLUNTARY SERVICES UNIT, *The Government and the Voluntary Sector. Analysis of the Response to the Consultative*

Document. Home Office, 1981.
43. Ibid., p. ix.
44. MURRAY, N., 'Whatever happened to Wolfenden?', *Community Care*, 8 Apr. 1982, p. 15.
45. SMITH, JEF, *The Times*, 17 Apr. 1978.
46. HATCH, 'The Wolfenden Report'.
47. WEBB, 'Voluntary social action', pp. 13–14.

Chapter Four
FACTS, FIGURES AND FINANCES

Having traced the survival and development of the voluntary sector's contribution to the social services up until the late 1970s, it might be helpful now to draw together such information as is available about the extent and direction of its present-day activities. What do we know in terms of hard data, and what do we not know? No discussion about the proper role of the voluntary sector in the welfare state or about its possible future development can proceed without such questions being asked. The answers can only be culled from a wide variety of different sources – studies that have been made, official reports and statistics, parliamentary answers, the information bulletins of voluntary organisations themselves – as there is no systematic data collection on the voluntary sector, nor could there be in its present state. The information that is available has all kinds of limitations in that it reflects the form in which it was collected and the purposes for which it was collected, as well as the difficulties encountered in gathering data. Consequently, much of what we can gather together about the voluntary sector is expressed in terms of what is measurable and accessible such as the personpower resources of voluntary organisations, or the sources of their finances, the amount of their grants, trends in subsidy policies, reliance on charity, etc. It is to these areas that we now turn, with a note of caution about the reliability of data that are produced by interested parties, such as voluntary organisations or government departments or politicians, who will inevitably be focusing selectively in order to plead a case, win an argument, or create a certain climate of opinion.

FACTS AND FIGURES

Enough has been said in previous chapters about the extreme diffuseness and complexity of the voluntary sector to indicate the near impossibility of quantifying it or estimating the quality of its activities. To talk about the 'voluntary sector' is in itself, although a necessary shorthand, to ascribe a homogeneity and unity to this vast range of activites that is totally artificial and misleading. The voluntary sector's pluriformity and lack of clear boundaries do not lend themselves to the definitions and classifications upon which statistical methods are based. The data available therefore are incomplete and patchy, based either on sample surveys or on studies of localities. Given that a central interest of this book is the voluntary sector's interrelatedness with the statutory sector in the personal social services, we would want from the available research some idea of the comparability of one sector with the other. How does the voluntary sector compare in size, type of activity, numbers and types of personnel, and social and geographical location with local authority social services?

One attempt to answer some of these questions was a study by Webb *et al.*[1] based on a postal survey of a number of voluntary organisations. The data collected are of course well out of date now, but they give us some helpful indications of the size of the voluntary input, and have also been utilised frequently enough in arguments supporting an expanded role for the voluntary sector to merit our consideration. The survey had severe limitations – its very narrow scope was dictated by the fact that the total number of voluntary organisations is not known and therefore there was no way a statistically valid sample could be arrived at. Enquiry was restricted to established voluntary bodies which were national in range, thus omitting new organisations and those at regional or local level which were not branches of national bodies. Webb *et al.* gathered data from forty-four organisations and are careful to stress the unrepresentative nature of their findings which, although considered meaningful within the context of the study, 'are in no sense an accurate representation of the contribution made by the voluntary sector as a whole. Rather, they are indicative of the probable minimum size of the contribution, of the diversity of that contribution, and of the problems faced by the voluntary bodies.'[2] The purpose of the study was to collect data about the personpower resources and training needs of voluntary organisations. The survey established that in 1975 the 44 agencies employed between 13,000 and 15,000 paid staff in four main areas of work – fieldwork, daycare, residential and other. Compared with the equivalent areas of work in local authority social services departments, these figures represented between 15.5 and 18 per cent of total local authority staffs. The proportion of voluntary agency paid staff with relevant qualifications was felt, despite the limitations of the data, to be roughly comparable with that in the statutory sphere with 'at least a hint that more voluntary than statutory residential staff may be qualified', although some doubt may be cast on the comparability of the definitions applied by respondents.

Other general findings were that the voluntary organisations faced staff recruitment problems when unable to match the salary and career opportunities available in the public sector, and that fewer in-service training facilities were available in them. This was considered serious in the light of the range of services they provide, without which 'the statutory sector would face a much heavier demand for service'. The authors listed three basic situations in which local authorities may come to depend upon voluntary agencies as providers of substitute services: 'when new needs are revealed which cannot be immediately met due to temporary resource constraints; when needs are revealed which because of their scale or diversity may never be met by statutory services; and when resource problems cause statutory authorities to default on their basic commitments'.[3] Apart from useful subsidiary data, the major finding of this study was the estimate it produced of the size of the paid workforce in social work and related activities in the voluntary organisations surveyed – the equivalent of nearly one-fifth of such workers in the public sector.

A further source of information on the voluntary sector is the research commissioned by the Wolfenden Committee into the extent and nature of voluntary work in environmental and social services, as opposed to the paid work in social services investigated by Webb *et al*. A survey commissioned from the National Opinion Poll (NOP) in 1976 produced data on voluntary work from which some interesting but crude projections have been made. The survey asked whether people had done voluntary work – 'that is, unpaid work for any organisation or for other people apart from relatives and friends'.[4] Of the representative sample, 15.3 per cent said they had done some voluntary work in the previous year, most of them for a voluntary organisation of some kind, and the time input claimed for the preceding week was 6.1 hours on average. The sheer breadth of the concept 'voluntary work' and the unlikelihood of common definitions being employed among interviewers and respondents, make it necessary to treat these findings very cautiously. There is a danger in such surveys either of recording almost the whole of human life, or registering such a vast range of different activities that the findings are fairly meaningless. The data do not, moreover, tell us anything about the quality of the input reported, only the quantity.

The Wolfenden Report and various other writings by the committee's researchers, go on to gross up these figures to give a yearly estimate for the whole population. Accordingly, they arrive at a total of 16 million person-hours of voluntary work, equivalent to 400,000 full-time workers. As over half the voluntary work reported was connected with welfare activities, in the personal social services sphere this would amount to the equivalent of 260,000 full-time workers. Hatch and Mocroft[5] write, 'Here the voluntary input appears to be larger than that of the paid workers' given that local authority social service departments employed about 200,000 at that time.' They make the qualification, as does the Wolfenden Report, that 'this is a simplified quantitative measure: it takes no account of the skill and training of paid workers, nor the nature of the tasks undertaken or, for example, the large proportion of voluntary effort devoted to fund-raising'. The Wolfenden Report combines this estimate with those for paid workers in voluntary agencies in the Personal Social Services Council (PSSC) study by Webb *et al.*, to conclude that 'in the personal social services the voluntary sector is clearly larger in terms of manpower than the statutory sector'.[6] Later it reiterates that 'the input of the voluntary sector is the greater'[7] despite making it clear in parentheses that the comparison involved does not compare like with like. Hatch writes in a further comment on this input, 'Although much of the voluntary effort goes on jumble sales and other kinds of organisation maintenance, this contribution is not insignificant.'[8] No one would disagree with this conclusion. The wisdom and desirability, however, of comparing such activities with those of the paid staff of local social services departments, is highly questionable. The comparison might be made more cogently with the operations of the Inland Revenue, given that much voluntary work involves fund raising. Wolfenden's conclusion that the voluntary sector's personpower exceeds that of the statutory sector has been much quoted in isolation from the qualifications which originally accompanied it. The dangers of such selective quotation may be easily seen in Mr Patrick Jenkin's evidence to the House of Commons Select Committee on the Social Service in 1979/80, when he referred to the Wolfenden Committee's opinion that 'there was a bigger input to the personal social services from the voluntary sector than there was from the statutory sector'.[9] Combining this judgement with his own estimate of the degree of family support available to those in need, and of the prospect of growth in the voluntary sector, the Secretary of State concluded that help from statutory services 'must be a comparatively small part of the whole' and therefore felt 'able to look to the local authorities to make some savings in this field'. The savings amounted to an intended 7 per cent cut in personal social services expenditure for the following year.

The 1981 General Household Survey enquired into the extent of voluntary work performed by adults in the previous twelve months (unpaid work of service to others besides immediate family and friends[10]) and found that 23 per cent or almost a quarter of the sample had done some, although it is unclear how much. Interestingly, a representative sample survey sponsored in the same year by the Volunteer Centre, found a significantly higher proportion of people involved in voluntary action. This survey found that 44 per cent of the sample had done some voluntary work in the year preceding the enquiry. The survey report itself[11] attempted to explain the discrepancy with other figures by reference to the nature of the questions asked. Compared with the 1976 NOP survey, this survey possibly gave respondents greater scope for refreshing their memories by the use of prompt questions and examples. The finding of 44 per cent represents 'as broad a definition as possible' ranging over education, sport, welfare, health, trade union activities, church activities, membership of local councils, and 'activities that few people would normally think of as volunteering'. Such a broad understanding may have a certain value as long as the temptation is resisted to extrapolate from the figures to produce guesstimates of equivalence to the operations of the social services. There is no suggestion here that the Volunteer Centre has used these generous figures for any other purpose than underlining the prevalence of some kind of voluntary involvement in our society, stressing its value and the need to encourage it. The risk remains, however, that politicians may use certain of the findings to argue a most insubstantial case for the substitution of publicly financed statutory services by voluntary services.

The General Household Survey indicated a slightly greater propensity for women to do voluntary work compared with men, except in the 20–24 and the 75 and over age-groups, where the proportion was higher among men. It also found some variation according to age, but, overall these surveys and Hatch's area studies in three towns[12] do not demonstrate significant differences according to age, sex or hours of paid work. To some extent such findings correct the commonly held stereotype of the female volunteer, but Hatch adds a valuable qualification in the observation that most persons who give *substantial* amounts of their time to voluntary work are women who are not in paid employment. Additionally, most of the voluntary workers who undertake the direct personal care services relevant to 'community care' policies are also women.[13] The major differential relates to social class. 'For both men and women, those in the professional group were more than three times as likely to have done voluntary work as those in the unskilled manual group.'[14] This association with higher socio-economic position has implications for the geographical and class distribution of voluntary work in the personal social services field and for the image of voluntary work as a form of middle-class patronage. Hatch comments that 'the supply of voluntary workers tends to be in inverse proportion to need'.[15] His area studies found, for instance, that the Pre-School Playgroups Association was most prevalent in middle-class suburbs and that local branches of the Child Poverty Action Group are associated not with the presence of poor families, but with the location of universities. This, he comments, suggests that 'social policies relying on voluntary organisations as instruments of policy will be uneven in their impact'.[16] The research conducted for the Wolfenden Committee showed that old county towns like Bath or Exeter had between two and three times as many voluntary organisations' branches as towns in the category 'traditional centres of heavy industry and manufacturing' like Barnsley or Sheffield. Their report described this unevenness of distribution of voluntary activity as one of its greatest weaknesses. 'It is of its essence unplanned and spontaneous, and it will not necessarily of itself allocate its energies in accordance with abstract criteria of need or equity.'[17]

It is clear that the Secretary of State quoted earlier expected growth in the voluntary sector and an increased capacity for voluntary bodies to substitute for statutory personal social services. From the data available on the voluntary sector, however imperfect and incomplete, we now know that voluntary social service capacity does not exist evenly throughout the country nor in the areas of greatest social need. Some voluntary agencies such as the Citizens' Advice Bureaux have distributed their branches rather more evenly in recent years, typically with the aid of substantial support from public funds. We also know that great variations are to be found between one local authority area and another in terms of statutory provision, but this situation, poor as it is, is an improvement on the maldistribution of voluntary bodies. Without specific distributional policies backed by substantial resources on the part of the public authorities, voluntary endeavour is unlikely to be organised according to the principles of territorial or sectional justice. The Wolfenden enquiry noted large variations in the interest and support shown for voluntary agencies by local authorities, some of them giving very little financial aid indeed.

The evidence suggests that where statutory social service priorities were high, so a local authority's support for the voluntary sector was likely to be correspondingly high.

Much of the evidence from Wolfenden and elsewhere suggests that the voluntary sector makes a considerable and valuable input in specific areas of activity. Wolfenden found that voluntary bodies are still providing between 10 and 20 per cent of residential care for children and for the elderly. Most meals on wheels continue to be delivered by voluntary workers, notably from the WRVS, and many clubs and day centres for the elderly and the handicapped are run by churches, settlements and other voluntary agencies. Although this contribution is by no means negligible, it would need to expand considerably to assume the role of substitute provider for the statutory authorities to any significant degree. Those voluntary agencies which have a monopoly in certain areas, such as in the field of advice, information and advocacy, generally achieve this role with substantial statutory assistance. Other valuable areas of voluntary action, such as mutual aid or pressure-group activities, have ther own unique functions and cannot be seen as alternatives to statutory services in the same way as service-providing agencies.

Hadley and Hatch observe that 'for all its virtues, in most localities and most fields the voluntary sector is essentially marginal to the statutory sector, in terms both of financial resources and of the way it is treated by the statutory services'.[18] The following section goes on to review the financial bases of the voluntary sector and the extent of its dependence, as well as the trends shown by that dependence, on the various sources of finance available to voluntary organisations.

THE FINANCES OF THE VOLUNTARY SECTOR

For the great range of activities and organisations that make up the voluntary sector, the question of finance is highly significant. At a very simple level of donating one's time and energy for a few hours a week as an individual, hardly any costs at all may be involved. Once such voluntary work begins to be organised collectively on a large enough scale to ensure effective coverage and adequate provision for a complex range of needs, then resources are required for buildings, for equipment, for administration and a host of other functions. The WRVS, for example, is almost totally composed of volunteers who donate their spare time to running hospital canteens, old people's clubs, meals on wheels services, clothing stores, etc. It also receives one of the largest government grants that goes to any voluntary organisation, as well as local authority grants for local services, and it does not raise any of its own funds. Political statements of recent years have all too frequently contained assumptions that voluntary social services cost nothing, and have also confused relatively sophisticated voluntary organisations which employ paid professional workers with those which rely on unpaid volunteers. Any significant expansion of the voluntary sector's contribution to social service provision or its substitution for parts of the statutory services, particularly if equivalent standards were to be maintained, would be costly and would necessarily require a parallel expansion of the resources available to it. It would also take a considerable time to develop. The Wolfenden Committee were rather pessimistic, as we have seen, about the potential for expansion of voluntary giving as a source of finance in the future, and looked to government to supply a considerable part of the resources needed for augmenting the future role of the voluntary sector.

The increased dependence of voluntary organisations upon public funds that is implied begs certain questions concerning the essential separateness and autonomy of voluntary organisations from the state. If the voluntary sector has a unique function in society which may be regarded as preferable to interventions by the state, is it not compromising this identity by becoming a pensioner of the state? This is a real contemporary problem for voluntary agencies. Can an organisation such as the WRVS, entirely funded from the public purse, its director appointed directly by government, qualify as a voluntary body? Some might classify it as a kind of quango, yet its workforce is almost wholly made up of volunteers, and the organisation itself is, paradoxically, rather more independent of government than many a voluntary agency only partially reliant on government funds. This is a product of its historical roots and its establishment connections more than any other factor – in fact, the WRVS enjoys an immunity from research and investigation by government departments which would dearly like to ask more searching questions about the uses to which its massive grant is put.

Where a voluntary organisation's income comes from and what proportions of its total income derive from which sources, are highly relevant to this vexed question of identity and autonomy, and become all the more so as the pressures of economic recession reduce the availability of resources and the ability to pick and choose financiers. What general picture can we build up, therefore, of the pattern of funding of voluntary agencies? Judith Unell, in a study for the PSSC in 1979,[19] identified five primary sources of finance for voluntary organisations. These are:

1. Government grants, from central and local government.
2. Fees and charges for services, paid on an agency basis by local authorities and by recipients of services.
3. Voluntary giving – subscriptions, donations, legacies, appeals, grants and donations from charitable trusts and other bodies, and affiliation fees from branches.
4. Sales and royalties from trading activities, etc.
5. Investment income.

Efforts to quantify voluntary sector finances precisely suffer from the same difficulties as attempts to specify the numbers and activities of voluntary organisations. Lack of definitions, absence of clear boundaries and inadequate data render precision impossible. Most accounts of the sources of voluntary sector income rely on sample surveys which, although valuable within their limitations, are not statistically representative of the whole voluntary sector. They tend to gather data only from bodies organised at national and regional level, for the good reason that it is at those levels that information is most available and most economically collected.

Unell's study, directed at the personal social services field only, surveyed sixty-five national service-giving organisations in 1975/76. The patterns of revenue revealed are summarised in Table 1. Voluntary giving represents roughly half of total revenues and 'the strongest foundation of voluntary activity' among this small sample. Although this source of income had grown in the five-year period at a faster rate than the rise in the cost of living, it had declined as a proportion of total income.

Table 1. Sources of income of 65 voluntary organisations 1975/76 and 1970/71

Source of income	Year ending 1975/76 % total income	Year ending 1970/71 % total income
Government grants	3.40	4.03
Fees and charges	37.39	30.11
Voluntary giving	47.15	51.38
Sales and royalties	2.60	3.29
Investments	8.07	10.80
Sundry and undifferentiated	0.99	0.39

Source: J. Unell, *Voluntary Social Services: Financial Resources*. Bedford Square Press: London, 1979.

Voluntary sources of income

A substantial income raised from voluntary, non-governmental sources would ideally seem to safeguard those characteristics that make a voluntary organisation voluntary, and to confer on it an essential self-governance and freedom from external interference. The reality is less simple, as the following considerations suggest. First, the very need to raise funds can divert time and energies from an organisation's main purposes and thus reduce its freedom. As the various surveys of voluntary work indicate, a major part of voluntary activity at the individual level is devoted to the raising of funds, and this can be a constant diversion at organisation level too. Additionally, the uncertainties of reliance upon capricious public giving can inhibit development and jeopardise continuity. Large voluntary agencies can and do employ professional fund-raisers to use increasingly sophisticated techniques such as telethons, media appeals, etc. but these represent investments which could fail disastrously given the competitive pull on public sympathies of a sudden earthquake somewhere or a lifeboat tragedy. The competitive attractions of some causes above others are another feature of charitable giving which makes reliance upon it difficult, especially when potential donors are feeling the pinch of inflation or unemployment. When the Health Services Act 1980 gave health authorities the power to raise voluntary funds,[20] there was much concern among voluntary agencies in the health and welfare fields, lest the National Health Service (NHS) appeals cream off funds usually available for other, more routine causes. 'The main objection to the plan', as Nicholas Hinton, NCVO Director, put it, 'is that charities will have to compete with the NHS for the public's money. Not only is there a limit to voluntary giving by the public (witness the recent decline in some of the major charities' income) but the circular gives the NHS an unfair advantage in providing public funds for the start-up costs of NHS fund-raising.'[21] A further DHSS circular[22] was hastily brought out to allay the charities' fears and to instruct health authorities to ensure through wide consultation that volunteers and voluntary organisations' services complementing the work of the NHS were not disadvantaged by NHS fund-raising activities. There are indications that the new fund-raising possibilities have not been widely taken up by health authorities.[23]

Appeals for charitable giving depend upon public sympathy for a particular cause, and public sympathies are notably sentimental. Organisations for children have more appeal than those for the elderly or the mentally ill; respectable causes such as blindness gain much more public support than do 'deviant' groups such as the single homeless, drug addicts or persons with sexual problems. This pattern of giving reflects the dominant values of British society and deep-seated impulses for social control which reinforce conformity and operate according to a hierarchy of 'deservingness' and 'non-deservingness'. Perhaps typical of British sentiment also is the appeal of animals – in 1980/81, the People's Dispensary for Sick Animals received almost as much income from voluntary giving as did the National Society for the Prevention of Cruelty to Children (NSPCC); the Donkey Sanctuary, in the top 200 charities league, received more income from voluntary sources than St Christopher's Hospice for Terminally Ill People.[24] Public sentiment is also fickle – the internal problems or a poor external or media image of a voluntary organisation will swiftly register on the barometer of public giving, as Shelter found to its cost when domestic wrangles in its national headquarters were given wide publicity and its spectacular record as a raiser of funds was overturned by a sharp decline in public giving. Additionally, even when an organisation is relatively successful in attracting funds for its main purpose, it may experience great difficulty in gaining financial support for more mundane but essential functions such as administration, which do not excite the public imagination.

A voluntary organisation which raises substantial sums of money from charity has to meet certain accounting and auditing requirements, the main purpose of which is to protect donors against fraud and the misuse of their money. A registered charity has to conform its activities to the limits set by the Charity Commissioners in their definition of acceptable charitable purposes. In Chapter 5 we shall examine the intricacies of charity law in the context of government fiscal policies towards voluntary organisations. In addition to the requirements of law, voluntary bodies who are beneficiaries of funds from business corporations or philanthropic trusts find that these donors can and do set their own conditions for the receipt of funds. How overt or restrictive such controls may be is a matter for speculation, but it would be an unusual board of management in receipt of such donations or grants which did not make some efforts to avoid offending the susceptibilities of its benefactors. While the large philanthropic trusts such as Rowntree, Carnegie or Leverhulme often do support unorthodox projects, they are themselves the offspring of corporate business empires and their levels of tolerance will inevitably reflect the values dominant within those empires. 'Grantmanship', an art cultivated by any voluntary body which seeks to survive, consists essentially of blending an image of innovatoriness and creativity with the assurance of apolitical respectability and safeness into a basic framework of a trust's known preferences and predilections. The price of conformity to the conservative values of corporate donors and trusts can be social control just as much as dependence upon the largesse of government.

Trends in voluntary giving

Statements from government ministers in the late 1970s and early 1980s generally conveyed the optimistic message to the voluntary sector that it should rely for funds primarily upon voluntary sources of income. Mr Timothy Raison, Home Office Minister responsible for the VSU, said in 1980 that while he recognised that a measure of public support had come to be taken for granted, he nevertheless believed 'that the cornerstone of the voluntary movement is a large degree of independence of the state'.[25] Estimating that at least 70 per cent of charities' income came from non-governmental sources, he expressed faith in the continued potential of voluntary giving. 'I am reluctant to believe that even in these difficult times the great national tradition of generosity towards voluntary causes is drying up or that it is impossible to find new ways of awakening the patent goodwill of our people.' In a later speech, he declared, 'voluntary money and voluntary effort can be the only proper foundations for a vigorous and independent voluntary movement'.[26] Patrick Jenkin echoed this theme in stating that 'the voluntary sector must look largely to the generosity and charity of individuals for financial support'.[27] It was consistent with this expectation of self-reliance that the DHSS initiated in 1980 a scheme whereby government would provide £1 million over the following four years to match, pound for pound, voluntary funds raised to help mentally handicapped children out of hospital into alternative forms of care. The promised £1 million covered capital costs only, leaving voluntary agencies not only to find their half of capital expenditure but also the running costs involved. Criticisms of this initiative centred round the manifest inadequacy of the sums involved and government's political tokenism in failing to implement it until long after it had announced the scheme. It was also clear from the beginning that the scheme was based on optimistic assumptions of the availability of charitable money, and that if its efforts to stimulate this source of funds were successful, it would favour with public money those areas which, already well off, were better placed than poorer areas to raise money directly from the public.

How realistic were government's expectations that substantial pools of charitable resources lay waiting to be tapped for the provision of social services? There are indications from various sources that levels of charitable giving are not keeping pace with the expenditure needs of voluntary agencies at their present levels of operation, let alone those which would be generated by any significant future expansion. Falush[28] noted a general decline in personal donations – fewer households were making donations to charity and these were not keeping up with the rise in disposable income in the five-year period he examined. Company giving had also declined in real terms in the early 1970s, but, together with investment income and public sector income amounted to over half the revenues of general purpose charities in 1975, indicating 'that the sources of charitable incomes have become more indirect and institutionalised'.[29] His main interest was in personal charitable giving, which is of course only a part of the voluntary income of charities. He was, in addition, looking at all charities, in contrast with Unell whose enquiry was limited to some social welfare agencies, which have rather more specialised sources of income. A further pessimistic assessment of the potential for reliance on voluntary giving was offered by the Wolfenden Committee, who concluded 'the failure of private giving to keep pace with inflation is striking'[30] and foresaw a need for greater reliance in the voluntary sector on statutory funding, warning that without such aid, some charities would have to go out of existence. Wolfenden's prognosis was criticised for being too gloomy[31] in that charities managed to hold their own from 1979 to 1980.

Data concerning the income of charities are very sparse. An annual digest of statistics is produced by the Charities Aid Foundation (CAF) which surveys the revenues of the top 200 voluntary organisations which are charities with incomes over £200,000 a year. A large proportion of these operate in the fields of health, personal social services, youth work and care of the elderly, but also included are international aid organisations and animal protection societies. The 1982 edition of the CAF digest conveyed some feeling of alarm in concluding that 'An impression of a sharp decline in the volume of voluntary giving . . . begins to emerge' for the period 1980/81 to 1981/82, that 'There is little evidence that there is any firm financial basis for an expansion of charitable and voluntary effort.'[32] Subsequent years' statistics were to correct this pessimistic assessment as representing 'a temporary interruption of a generally upward trend'.[33]

The fortunes of the richest 200 charities are not a totally satisfactory guide to those of charities much lower on the league table. New methods of raising funds are constantly being devised by charities, large and small, such as trading activities – the Christmas card business and charity shops – and sponsored events of all kinds. The NCVO has explored tentatively the potential of deduction of charitable donations from pay packets. Competition for funds is always increasing, with the yearly addition of some thousands of new charities to the total of roughly 150,000 (some three-quarters of which are inactive). It is understandable that for voluntary agencies providing social services, which are our special concern, a range of sources of finance should be important, among which, government, at central and local level, must figure significantly.

Central government funding of the voluntary sector

Central government grants to the voluntary sector are mostly given on a departmental basis to voluntary agencies operating, usually at national level, in a particular department's field of responsibility. Many departments have financial links with voluntary bodies, and the latter frequently combine grants from a number of different departments for different parts of their work. To give an illustrative example, a glance down the list of voluntary agencies likely to be funded at any one time by the DHSS would find such organisations as the National Children's Home, the Back Pain Association, the Campaign for the Homeless and Rootless, Gingerbread, the Ileostomy Association, the Pre-School Playgroups Association, the Salvation Army and the National Association for Mental Health, among some 200. The general policy towards such subsidies is that they should go to agencies which are seen to supplement and extend the department's own area of interest. 'Where departments have certain statutory responsibilities which must be met from the total amount of money available to them, only limited funds are left over for help to voluntary organisations which are not simply acting on an agency basis to fulfil statutory duties.'[34] The question arises here as to whether there is then any essential difference between voluntary and statutory agencies, or whether the voluntaries have become 'quasi-statutory organisations'. Ball writes, 'A very large proportion of the so-called voluntary sector is simply delivering certain services or values on behalf of the statutory sector, as a glorified sub-contractor. The style and content of these services differ little from those provided directly by the relevant local authority or central government departments. That's why they are best called "quasi-statutory".'[35] The agency role is considered at some length in the discussion in Chapters 5 and 6 of the nature of the 'partnership' between the two sectors.

A special source of government money for the voluntary sector is the VSU, the creation of which was discussed in Chapter 3. This unit's functions may be grouped under four headings: to act as a link between voluntary bodies and government departments; to act as a focal point, through a system of departmental liaison officers, for departmental interests relating to the voluntary sector; to stimulate the use of volunteers and encourage cooperation and coordination among voluntary organisations, and, fourthly, to act as a financier of last resort in Whitehall. This last function involves the subsidy of organisations whose work spans the interests of several departments or which are not the direct responsibility of any one department. Exceptionally, the VSU also funds local innovatory projects 'from which lessons of national relevance can be learned' and provides initial seeding money in areas of high social priority.

The VSU's grants to voluntary organisations in 1980/81 amounted to just over £2¾ million.[36] This total included grants of £500,000 or more to such agencies as the Community Projects Foundation, Community Service Volunteers and the Volunteer Centre, and smaller grants to bodies like Gamblers Anonymous, the National Playing Fields Association, and Task Force. In addition, it administered as grants in aid nearly £750,000 to the NCVO, and almost £4 million to the WRVS. Its largest grants thus go to agencies promoting volunteer work and to organisations providing a resource function for other voluntary bodies.

The sum total of central government grant aid to the voluntary sector represents a crucial and weighty subsidy when viewed from the perspective of struggling voluntary organisations. Although there can be little doubt that the amount of government support has increased in real terms when compared with the subsidies of a decade ago, there can be no certainty about the precise figure it amounts to. Government supplies its own estimates from time to time, usually in the context of ministerial speeches congratulating the government for record levels of support and encouragement to the voluntary sector. Timothy Raison said in a speech in 1981,

> My ministerial colleagues and I have constantly stated our resolve to maintain financial support for the voluntary sector by way of grants in aid. And the facts speak for themselves: if we include substantial contributions made through the Urban Programme, grant aid provided by Central Government in 1980/81 to voluntary bodies in the United Kingdom totalled £124.5 million. This compares with £92 million in 1979/80 – an increase in the order of 35 per cent.[37]

Even when allowing for inflation, this was a real and significant increase. The overall figure should, however, only be taken as an estimate, indicative of the general level of government support, as it is unclear how it was arrived at and precisely what types of funding it includes.[38]

There are no precise figures for the proportion of total voluntary sector income represented by central government finance. As far as individual voluntary organisations are concerned, there are significant variations in the proportions of total income represented by government funds, although here too, firm data are hard to come by. Some agencies receive little or no finance from government, and others rely for their entire income on this source. The operations of the National Association of Citizens' Advice Bureaux (NACAB), of the Community Projects Foundation and of the WRVS are wholly financed by central government. Such organisations as the NCVO, the Volunteer Centre, the National Marriage Guidance Council and MIND, the National Association for Mental Health, depend upon government for around two-thirds of their total incomes. An organisation like Samaritans, on the other hand, raises the major proportion of its income from gifts and legacies, and only one-third of its finances come from government.

In conclusion, then, we can say that government funding of the voluntary sector has increased in real terms in recent years, and that for some voluntary bodies it represents the most important part of their income. We should note, on the other hand, that government grants are in fact spread very thinly over a broad range of activities from the National Trust to Barnardo's to the Scouts Association to the Fluoridation Society. The 1980/81 estimated total of £124.5 million was thus disbursed over some hundreds of organisations, large and small, and as a total sum cannot be taken to indicate very much about the extent of government support in the personal social service field which is the central concern of this book. We know from DHSS and VSU figures that increased funding was available in 1980/81 to voluntary sector social services, but the sums involved were comparatively small parts of the global figure and do not, in any case, represent any reflection of adequacy to the needs being met by voluntary agencies. The total figure of £124.5 million should also be placed in proper perspective. An unknown portion of it only will have gone to voluntary agencies active in the health and personal social services field, and government expenditure for England alone on these services in 1980/81 amounted to over £11,000 million, of which £1600 million was spent by local authorities on personal social services.[39] In contrast to spending on the statutory services, £124.5 million represents a very minor sum indeed and little more than token support from a government claiming to be actively encouraging the expansion of the voluntary sector.

GOVERNMENT FUNDING POLICIES

The policy aspects of government funding for voluntary organisations vary between central departments, but some general patterns may be gleaned from a summary supplied to the Wolfenden enquiry by the VSU. Here, government support is divided into three categories: 'These are where it is considered that voluntary provision is preferable to a statutory service; where the voluntary organisations can provide an alternative to existing statutory provision, providing an element of choice for users of the service concerned; or where a statutory service can be supplemented or extended by voluntary means.'[40] So, for instance, government might support voluntary effort in a situation where a need was small and specialised, or where a case for statutory intervention was insufficiently proven. Equally, for specific groups like drug addicts, alcoholics or the single homeless, the authoritarian image of a statutory service might not be appropriate, or, for some services, such as womens' refuges, statutory structures and attitudes may be quite wrong. A further point relates to the fact that some kinds of service lack popular appeal so that, on the one hand, statutory provision is not viewed as legitimate, and alternative voluntary provision has difficulties gaining financial support, so that a publicly funded voluntary service is a happy compromise. Some kinds of service such as marriage guidance, citizens' advice bureaux and law centres are thought to be more appropriately delivered by non-statutory bodies. It might also be suggested, that, in some instances, less manifest considerations operate behind funding policies. Could it be, we might ask, that subsidies to such organisations as the Pre-School Playgroups Association and the National Marriage Guidance Council represent government's response to middle-class demands for services that are not part of and do not share the stigma of public sector provision? In class terms, each organisation's general ethos, mode of operating and its clientele display a broad middle-class bias which stands in striking contrast to its equivalent in the statutory sector. The local authority day nursery or nursery school is an increasingly rationed resource which tends to be restricted to a single parent, at risk or poor families. The vast majority of working-class couples probably do not have access to any form of marital guidance, but such as is available to them is more likely to be found via the personal social services and the probation service which are used mostly by the poor. To some extent, then, government funding policies towards voluntary organisations may be seen as the tacit operation of a principle of selectivity in certain areas of provision.

The criteria outlined by the VSU on paper are likely to be rather less clear in practice. The Wolfenden Report described the typical departmental stance as reactive, limited to responding or not to voluntary initiatives and requests more or less arbitrarily. In any case, as the VSU account states, choice of which organisations receive funds is restricted in that 'it is more often financial restraints which determine specific departmental policies than general departmental policies which determine the availability of funds'.[41] The duration of grants will also depend on the availability of resources rather than on direct policy considerations. Grants are for the most part given for one year at a time,[42] and their renewal is more likely to depend upon the vicissitudes of public expenditure policies than on departmental monitoring of the activities being financed. The difficulties faced by voluntary agencies wishing to plan for the long term are obvious here.

The VSU paper goes on to relate the conditions under which funds are customarily granted and the extent of government influence or control over the activities of voluntary bodies in receipt of funds. 'The primary determinant must obviously be that the organisation is working to a policy which is in accordance with the department's own policy.'[43] The formal conditions which attach to grants that are small or represent only a small proportion of the voluntary agency's income, are relatively simple – usually some form of annual report and audited accounts. Occasionally, projects are formally monitored, but, for the most part, monitoring is done on an informal basis by the departments concerned. For agencies whose grant constitutes a substantial proportion of total income, the designated status of 'controlled fringe body' applies, and the organisation becomes subject to government location policy and to public sector norms regarding conditions of service and levels of pay. Government departments have used this designation to encourage the dispersal of national headquarters and offices from London, for instance. The VSU itself comments on the possibility that a voluntary body dependent in this way upon government finance may become subject to influence and control.[44] It concludes that this would be marginal, stating that controls beyond those attached to fringe body status are in fact remarkably small, conforming only with the requirements of public accountability. It also expresses concern at the growing tendency for voluntary organisations to turn to statutory sources for funding, with the consequent risk of obscuring their separate identity and losing the advantages of their separateness. The potential danger of government control of voluntary organisations through the medium of its subsidies is a dimension that is explored in the examination in Chapter 5 of the relationships between government and the voluntary sector.

VOLUNTARY SECTOR INCOME AND FISCAL POLICIES

Direct government grants and payments for services are not the only form of public subsidy for voluntary organisations. The importance of fiscal subsidies, where tax exemptions add to income, has been highlighted in recent years by the re-emphasis by social policy writers[45] of Titmuss's 'social division of welfare'. It has been given particular prominence by Frank Field in his insistence on the relevance of tax expenditure as one of a number of hidden welfare states.[46] Tax exemptions or, as Gilbert and Specht describe it, 'money that has "escaped" from the public treasury'[47] are a policy instrument used by governments to confer their blessing on certain sorts of activity and to deny it to others. They can operate as an incentive towards voluntary giving and can bring financial advantage to the donor. For voluntary organisations which are registered charities, tax exemptions add to their income in two ways: they themselves are not subject to direct taxes on income, capital gains and transfers, and to National Insurance surcharge, and they are relieved from 50 per cent of their local authority rates liability at least. In addition, when individuals 'covenant' to pay certain sums of their taxable income over a period of four years to charities, those charities can reclaim from the Inland Revenue the tax paid on that part of the donor's income. There are similar rebates in respect of donations by business firms and industry.

The significance of tax relief as a subsidy to charities becomes apparent from an examination of the sums involved. The full range of tax reliefs is not calculable, but according to one estimate, which included stamp duty, capital transfer tax and the covenant form of tax credits, but not other kinds of tax or rate relief, amounted to over £200 million in 1980/81.[48] It is clear, even though accurate totals are not available, that public revenue forgone in this way in favour of charitable institutions amounts to a not inconsiderable sum and is rather more significant a source of income to voluntary organisations than the sum of central government grants. The Conservative government liberalised some of the existing tax exemptions in its Finance Act 1982, in a fiscal package claimed at the time to be worth an extra £30 million. It should be remembered that the value of fiscal concessions is contingent on successful raising of charitable funds in the first place, although it is also true to say that fiscal incentives could play a significant role in inducing both individual and corporate giving. One area of taxation where charities have not been exempt is that of Value Added Tax. The virtual doubling of VAT occasioned by the post-1979 government's shift to indirect taxation 'placed many charities, for which VAT is one of the largest items of expenditure after salaries, in a position of grave difficulty'.[49] Some of the major charities have mounted an increasingly vocal campaign against the anomalies of this situation.

FUNDING BY LOCAL AUTHORITIES

We established earlier that central government grants are generally available only to national voluntary organisations unless they are mediated through a government body like the Manpower Services Commission or through the local authorities, as in the case of urban aid. The local authorities themselves are a source of finance to local voluntary organisations, and this support can take the form of grants or the payment of fees and charges for the purchase of agreed services, generally in the field of residential care. The dependence of many voluntary agencies on one form of finance or the other is very substantial. Wolfenden's small survey found that organisations like the Shaftesbury Society and Cheshire Homes are dependent for nearly 70 per cent of their income on fees and charges which are mostly derived from local authorities. Precise figures are not available for the whole of the voluntary sector, but there is much that we can learn about the funding relationship between local authorities and voluntary organisations and the trends of recent years.

Local authorities participated in the growth in government support of the voluntary sector manifested in the early 1970s.[50] Their role is particularly apparent in the rise in payment of fees and charges which, according to Unell's small study of service-giving agencies[51] increased at a faster rate than any other source of funds in this period. This led Unell to surmise that voluntary organisations, in the residential field especially, have been increasing their incomes by raising their charges to local authorities, given that the rise cannot be accounted for by higher levels of service, as those in the residential field have remained static or even declined in this period. One of the agencies in her study was Barnardo's, and this organisation's own figures indicate that the trend is continuing, as Table 2 shows. In the decade 1969–80, the proportion of income from local authority maintenance rose from under one-fifth to nearly a half of Barnardo's total income, with a proportional shift in the relative significance of voluntary contributions and legacies. To get some idea of the qualitative changes in residential child care in this period, it should be noted that the numbers of children in care in voluntary homes fell from 7200 to 3800 from 1973 to 1980 – a trend which, according to the head of Barnardo's, 'reflected an increasing view among statutory organisations that they would prefer to make their own provision for residential care, and a considerable increase in foster care and community based alternatives'.[52]

Table 2. Total income of Barnardo's 1969–80

Source	1969 %	1974 %	1980 %
Voluntary contributions	31	21	23
Local authority maintenance	15	19	44
Investment income	9	9	7
Legacies	43	50	

Source: Figures extracted from *Annual Report,* Barnardo's, UK and Eire, 1980/81.

Although Barnardo's shared in this general trend, the agency also changed the nature of its work from the beginning of the 1970s to concentrate on children who are handicapped in various ways – a group who could be expected to cost more per head. Barnardo's also set out to work in closer partnership with local authorities in the areas covered by the agency. This change in direction may partly explain the steadily greater proportion of its income deriving from local authorities. Unell raises the possibility that the steep rise in the proportion of charges as a source of income among voluntary bodies may have been the result of considerable innovation in residential care practice, or may be evidence of their capitalising on a secure source of income, with consequent negative implications for their innovative and pioneering role. The Wolfenden Committee, whose investigations uncovered a similar trend, felt that 'it represents the most significant change in the incomes of the voluntary organisations to which they are relevant'.[53] They also noted that voluntary children's organisations were now following a policy of claiming the full current cost of a child's care from local authorities, and not merely a proportion as formerly. It is likely that voluntary agencies are compensating for the loss of volume in this field of activity as their numbers in residential care decline and the unit costs of their facilities rise accordingly. Whatever the precise mix of causes behind this trend, it is clear that voluntary agencies in the residential field have become increasingly dependent upon fees paid by local authorities. In some cases, this dependence has brought about the closure of voluntary children's homes, as local authorities progressively used their own facilities to full capacity or looked for less costly alternatives. For other voluntary bodies, the result has been the gradual transformation of their relationship with local authorities into a more complete agency one.

As far as grant aid is concerned, many voluntary organisations are also acutely dependent upon local authority support in the form of direct subsidies and grants to match or supplement whatever patchwork of grants they have managed to put together from central government sources, charitable trusts or the commercial world. Local authorities' grant-aiding policies are thus very important, as are the constraining effects of the public expenditure policies of successive governments on local authority finances. Before we go on to enquire into either area, however, some evaluation is necessary of the total impact of local authority grant aid to voluntary organisations. An estimated £22 million formed the sum total of local authority grants to voluntary bodies in the personal social services sector in 1980/81, and £141 million in fees.[54] Compared with local authority spending of £1600 million on the personal social services that year, this sum of money is marginal. Hadley and Hatch write ' . . . in terms of grant aid, support for the voluntary sector amounts to rather trivial sums – even in the case of social service departments it averages only about 2 per cent of the budget, if one ignores fees paid in respect of individuals in residential institutions run by voluntary organisations'.[55]

This estimated average of 2 per cent disguises an extreme variability of practice between individual authorities in their support of the voluntary sector. Wolfenden's illustrative figures show that per capita grant aid ranged from £0.03 in Humberside, to £0.60 in Manchester and £4.69 in the London Borough of Islington (1976/77). A similar pattern was found by the Association of Social Services Directors in its survey of personal social services staffing and activities in 1981.[56] This study contained full information for only just over half of the relevant local authorities. The average amount budgeted for voluntary organisations in 1980/81 for grants *and* fees, was £190,000, but this figure represented a range from a few thousand pounds to £2 million and over. The figures need to be approached with some caution as they hide extreme variations of size and income and levels of social need, as well as differences in the availability of voluntary organisations from one local authority area to another. Nevertheless, they do give an indication of very uneven approaches to the voluntary sector on the part of local government, confirming Wolfenden's earlier findings. Full explanations for such variations would inevitably be complex, but Wolfenden found an association between high per capita spending on statutory social services and more substantial support of voluntary bodies. 'There are very few authorities where one might suspect that grant-aid to voluntary organisations was used as a substitute for local authority social services department expenditure.'[57] Instead, where social services do not appear to have a high priority in the statutory sphere, then their voluntary sector alternatives do not receive high priority either.

As an impression of widespread assaults on local authority social services expenditure in the first year of the Tory government was fostered by the occurrence of some real cuts which did not after all add up to reductions across the board,[58] so, similarly, alarm was voiced about supposed inroads on local authority support for the voluntary sector at this time. Voluntary sector fears stemmed largely from the general climate of resistance to welfare spending, and from isolated cuts by some local authorities. In this early period of the Thatcher government, however, the volume of local authority support for the voluntary sector actually increased.[59]

CONCLUSION

This chapter began with the intention of drawing together such information as is available on the scope and significance of the voluntary sector. The data are imperfect and incomplete, themselves a telling testimony to the diffuseness and variability of the organisations which make up the voluntary sector. The picture that emerges is one of an assortment of types of agency which do indeed tap society's reserves of altruism and make an important contribution to the welfare state. A central theme of this study, however, relates to the feasibility of the voluntary sector replacing the statutory sector to some degree in the provision of personal social services. Asking what is the capacity for such an expansion, in practical terms, we must conclude that the available evidence suggests that it would require a transformation that would be nothing short of miraculous. Voluntary organisations are thinly and unevenly distributed, and where the need is greatest, they do not exist. Should it become a matter of public policy that voluntary agencies should be brought into being by governmental fiat or encouragement? This would be possible to a degree, although perhaps undesirable. The key to any significant expansion would be finance. Although it is possible that Wolfenden's assessment of the potential of continued charitable giving was somewhat pessimistic, what is incontrovertible is that the resources of the vast majority of voluntary social service bodies are altogether too slender for them to carry much more of the burden of meeting social need than they do at present. Any significant expansion of the voluntary sector role would have to be financed by the state. We have seen that public sector support for voluntary organisations, at both central and local government levels, has grown over the period when official interest in the potential of the voluntary sector began to quicken. The sum total of this funding is relatively small and in no way equal to the task of running substantially equivalent services to those of the public sector. There remains the possibility that government could assist the voluntary sector more wholeheartedly – by removing VAT liability, by making individual donations deductible against tax, or by expanding in the direction of purchase of service. The Barclay Report advocated the latter as one possible future option, and a growing interest has been shown recently in the purchase of service arrangements of the United States as a possible model.[60]

The hopes expressed for an expansion and redirection of government funding miss a fundamental point. In the current economic and ideological climate, which has fostered such interest in voluntary services, governments do not look for just an alternative delivery system for social services, but an alternative system of social service finance as well. It appears from an overview of the facts, that current enthusiasms for an expanded voluntary sector are based on an unrealistic expectation both of the voluntary sector and of government.

NOTES AND REFERENCES

1. WEBB, A., DAY, L. and WELLER, D., *Voluntary Social Services: Manpower Resources*. Personal Social Services Council: London, 1976.
2. Ibid., p. 13.
3. Ibid., p. 29.
4. HATCH, S., *Voluntary Work: a Report of a Survey*. Volunteer Centre Occasional Paper: Berkhamstead, 1978, p. 1.
5. HATCH, S. and MOCROFT, I., 'Voluntary workers', *New Society*, 7 Apr. 1977, p. 24.

6. WOLFENDEN COMMITTEE, *The Future of Voluntary Organisations.* Croom Helm: London, 1978, p. 36.

7. Ibid., p. 59.

8. HATCH, S., 'The voluntary sector, a larger role?', in E. M. Goldberg and S. Hatch, (eds) *A New Look at the Personal Social Services.* Policy Studies Institute: London, 1981, p. 68.

9. HOUSE OF COMMONS SOCIAL SERVICES COMMITTEE, *Report on the Social Services, 1979/80.* HMSO: London, Q. 195.

10. GENERAL HOUSEHOLD SURVEY 1981, in *Social Trends 1984*, No. 14. HMSO.

11 HUMBLE, S., *Voluntary Action in the 1980's: a Summary of the Findings of a National Survey.* Volunteer Centre: Berkhamsted, 1982.

12. HATCH, S., *Outside the State.* Croom Helm: London, 1980.

13. HATCH, 'The voluntary sector', p. 70.

14. GENERAL HOUSEHOLD SURVEY, op. cit., p. 153.

15. HATCH, 'The voluntary sector.'

16. HATCH and MOCROFT, op. cit., p. 24.

17. WOLFENDEN COMMITTEE, op. cit., p. 58.

18. HADLEY, R. and HATCH, S., *Social Welfare and the Failure of the State: Centralised Social Services and Participatory Alternatives.* Allen & Unwin: London, 1981, pp. 96–7.

19 UNELL, J., *Vountary Social Services: Financial Resources.* NCSS/PSSC: London, 1979.

20. DEPARTMENT OF HEALTH AND SOCIAL SECURITY, HC (80) 11.

21. *Guardian*, 18 Feb. 1981.

22. DEPARTMENT OF HEALTH AND SOCIAL SECURITY, HC(80)11, part ii.

23. 'Health authorities ignore new powers to raise cash.' *Voluntary Action*, NCVO, Spring 1982, p. 2.

24. CHARITIES AID FOUNDATION, *Charity Statistics 1980–81.* CAF: Tonbridge.

25. RAISON, T., Speech to the Voluntary Movement Group, Jan. 1980.

26. Ibid.

27. JENKIN, P., Speech to the Central Council for Jewish Social Services, Oct. 1980.

28. FALUSH, P., 'Trends in the finance of British charities', *National Westminster Bank Quarterly Review*, May 1977, pp. 32–44.

29. Ibid.

30. WOLFENDEN COMMITTEE, op. cit., p. 166.

31. *The Economist*, 26 Dec. 1981.
32. CHARITIES AID FOUNDATION, *Charity Statistics 1981-82*. CAF: Tonbridge 1982, pp. 7-8.
33. CHARITIES AID FOUNDATION, *Charity Statistics 1982-83*. CAF: Tonbridge 1983, p. 1.
34. WOLFENDEN COMMITTEE, op. cit., Appendix 4.
35. BALL, C., 'Whatever happened to voluntary bodies?' *Community Care*, 22 Feb. 1979, pp. 26-7.
36. Hansard, 6 Mar. 1981, Written Answers, 216-9.
37. RAISON, T., Speech to AGM Northampton Council of Voluntary Service. July 1981.
38. See CHARITIES AID FOUNDATION (1983) for discussion on the difficulties of defining and measuring central government grants.
39. *Social Trends, 1982*, No. 12.
40. WOLFENDEN COMMITTEE, op. cit., Appendix 4.
41. Ibid.
42. The DHSS announced a change of policy in 1984, setting grants on a two- to three-year basis, to give greater stability to voluntary agencies. House of Commons, 28 Feb. 1984, Hansard, cols 131-2.
43. WOLFENDEN COMMITTEE, op. cit., Appendix 4.
44. Ibid.
45. For example, REDDIN, M., 'Occupation, welfare and social division', in C. Jones, and J. Stevenson (eds), *The Year Book of Social Policy in Britain 1980-81*. Routledge & Kegan Paul: London, 1982, pp. 130-53.
46. FIELD, F., *Inequality in Britain: Freedom, Welfare and the State*. Fontana: London, 1981.
47. GILBERT, N. and SPECHT, H., *Dimensions of Social Welfare Policy*. Prentice-Hall: New Jersey, 1974, p. 147.
48. NCVO Information service, Oct. 1981.
49. NCVO, *Fiscal Working Party 1980*. NCVO: London, Section 2:1.
50. WOLFENDEN COMMITTEE, op. cit.
51. UNELL, op. cit.
52. *Community Care*, 27 May 1982.
53. WOLFENDEN COMMITTEE, op. cit., Appendix 6D.
54. CHARITIES AID FOUNDATION, op. cit. (1983).
55. HADLEY and HATCH, op. cit., p. 97.
56. ASSOCIATION OF DIRECTORS OF SOCIAL SERVICES, *Personal Social Services Expenditure and Resources*. ADSS: Newcastle, 1981.
57. WOLFENDEN COMMITTEE, op. cit., Appendix 6D.

58. WEBB, A. and WISTOW, G., *Whither the Welfare State?* RIPA: London, 1982.
59. HOUSE OF COMMONS, 11 May 1982, Hansard.
60. UTTING, B., 'Personal care by government purchase: lessons from the American experience', *Social Work Service*, 31 (Autumn 1982); LANNING, H., *Government and the Voluntary Sector in the USA*. NCVO: London, 1981; JUDGE, K., 'The public purchase of private care', *Policy and Politics*, Vol. 10, No. 4 (1982).

Part Three
VOLUNTARY – STATUTORY PARTNERSHIP

Chapter Five

VOLUNTARY SECTOR RELATIONS WITH GOVERNMENT
– A PARTNERSHIP?

Chapter 4 documented some of the financial relationships that exist between different levels of government and the voluntary sector. It observed that government subsidy of voluntary enterprise has grown steadily since the beginning of the 1970s, but that this still amounts to only a relatively minor expenditure compared with government's spending on the social services generally. Seen from the perspective of the voluntary organisations, these comparatively insignificant sums of money have figured increasingly as an important source of growth in the voluntary sector, one upon which voluntary agencies have become more and more heavily dependent. Dependency does not rest all on one side, however, for this financial relationship also disguises the extent of increased dependence of government on the voluntary sector. The 'partnership' that results is a means by which governments work out their own purposes through the agency of non-government bodies, just as much as a means whereby voluntary bodies secure their own futures. The present chapter will seek to enlarge upon the growing interpenetration of the statutory and voluntary sectors at the national level in recent years. In the first half it will reflect on the implications for the voluntary sector of its closer relationship with central government, in terms of its potential impact upon public policy and the limits set on this by virtue of the control associated with government funding policies and the constrictions of the Charity Law. The second part of the chapter will examine the specific examples of collaboration and interpenetration between the two sectors that may be seen in the government funding programmes directed at unemployment and inner-city problems in recent years.

THE 'PARTNERSHIP' IN BROAD TERMS

The notion of partnership implies some kind of reciprocity that is not necessarily an equal relationship but at least confers upon even a junior partner a measure of separate autonomy and influence. It also supposes convergence of interest and a certain consensus of values. Whether the term appropriately describes the various relationships between government and voluntary bodies where it is employed is open to question. There is a sharing of tasks, based on transfers of funds in one direction and of voluntary sector energies in the other, but this exchange does not necessarily have the positive, active attributes of a partnership as it is usually understood. It might be suggested that, for very many voluntary organisations who go, cap in hand, to statutory sources for funds, who live with the annual insecurity of bidding for grants vulnerable to cuts, and who have to trim their activities to their funder's priorities, the notion of a partnership may ring a little hollow. Even where mutual relations are excellent, voluntary organisations may never exercise any real influence upon funding priorities or upon the totality of activities and services to which they contribute.

It is clear that central government departments view the relationship as a 'partnership'. For example, the 1977 DHSS priorities guidelines *The Way Forward*,[1] stressing the value of voluntary effort in the health and personal social services, cited the newly launched Good Neighbour Scheme as a model of the kind of partnership it wished to see replicated generally. It viewed partnership with the voluntary sector as essentially a collaborative relationship where 'voluntary organisations and the health and personal social services at national and local levels must plan and work together'.[2] The idea that voluntary organisations should be drawn into the processes of planning and policy determination by health and social services authorities is probably wishful thinking rather than a positive DHSS guideline for action. As we shall see, the reality of statutory–voluntary relationships is far removed on the whole from this kind of collaboration. Consultation, which at its best implies a different order of reciprocity and influence, is a far from universal habit among the various statutory authorities which liaise with voluntary organisations. Even where consultation is a strong feature, it is of course bedevilled by the difficulties of identifying authoritative and representative voices from among the myriad voluntary agencies and groups with which a public authority has to deal. The participative ideal is however a significant element in the thinking of the proponents of welfare pluralism whose work we shall be discussing in Chapter 8. They see the incorporation of voluntary groups and organisations into statutory decision-making as a necessary remedy for the shortcomings of the representative democratic system, and the funding of their activities as a valuable diversification in the face of large-scale public services dominated by bureaucrats and professionals. Whatever the merits of these arguments, we should look into what is known about existing relationships between the two sectors, to ask what kind of mutuality is currently evident.

At central government level, although departmental policies towards the voluntary sector do not, as we have noted, betray any particular unity or coherence of approach, there is a fairly well-established tradition of *ad hoc* consultation of some of the larger national voluntary agencies. This is patchy and sometimes more tokenistic than real, but has been boosted by the pro-voluntarist policies of recent years. Among the established specialist bodies, the institutionalisation of a range of pressurising and lobbying functions has built up their potential as sources of advice and expertise for government. Many have their own research and information departments, and some even conduct research on behalf of government. A national body specialising in one consumer group or in a specific cause can make its own weighty representations directly or indirectly when new or changed legislation is under discussion or when policies are under review by such bodies as Parliamentary Select Committees. The priming and briefing of a lobby of sympathetic Members of Parliament is a recognised part of the parliamentary process, one which although never reaching the dimensions of similar lobbying in the United States, has featured increasingly in recent years.[3]

The stimulation of public debate and the formation of public opinion through use of the media has become a standard activity of the national voluntary organisations. Governments themselves often use and encourage such interest groups to raise certain issues in order to create a favourable political climate and to demonstrate popular demand and pressure on government for the enactment of measures politicians would like on the agenda. Bodies like Mencap[4] and Radar[5] were able to exercise some slight influence upon the content of the Education Act 1981.[6] Views and evidence submitted by MIND alongside energetic public campaigning, consumer rights advocacy and judicious use of the media, exercised a considerable influence on the revision of the 1959 Mental Health Act.[7] The adoption and fostering societies had a major impact on the form taken by the Children Act 1975. More recently, the Family Rights Group has sought to amend certain features of the legislation governing the rights of children and their natural parents.[8] Influential consultative and lobbying roles may coexist with a separateness and independence of stance and critical voice unwelcome to government, but there is no doubt that an implicit collaborative partnership exists at times between central government, its officials and the national voluntary organisations, which both parties exploit to their advantage. It is often difficult to make a clear distinction between the effects of the national organisations' independent lobbying and pressurising tactics, and those of their formal consultations invited by government. It is also impossible, as with any form of participation where the participants hold such unequal power, to make any accurate assessment of the impact of such consultations.

Examples of an active partnership at national level where the relationship with government is perhaps more explicit are to be found in the promotion by government of certain policies through the agency of voluntary organisations. We noted earlier in the section on public finance, that central departments mostly finance voluntary activities that conform to departmental policies and objectives. Traditionally, departmental relationships with the voluntary sector have been mainly reactive, responding or not to requests for funds but not springing from positive initiatives on the part of governments, inviting a voluntary sector response. However, this has changed to some extent in recent years, and one can see a close conformity amounting to interdependence at times, between governmental preoccupations and policy initiatives and the pattern of voluntary sector activity. Where finance is made available, voluntary bodies very easily become agents of government. In this symbiotic type of relationship, one may discern a factor which the sceptic might describe as 'the bandwagon effect' where voluntary organisations energetically subscribe to the policies upon which finance is currently contingent. Government social policies characteristically exhibit *ad hoc* and short-term enthusiasms and 'we must be seen to be doing something' political reflexes. Voluntary bodies, trading on a reputation for flexibility and innovation, and short of money, tack and turn expertly in relation to them. Governments value these capacities for flexibility and innovatoriness more highly than any other partly because they add an instant task-force capability to the cumbersome machinery of government in a way that rapidly accumulates instant political capital for relatively small financial outlays, particularly for policies which governments are not too keen on. There may be other factors involved, such as a government's wish to distance itself from certain groups or functions, or the desire to bypass potentially uncooperative interests such as local authorities or trade unions.

A variety of social problems, periodic public outcries, policy trends

and fashionable political dogmas have been reflected in the availability to voluntary agencies of new sources of public money. Developments in penal policy such as the Community Service Order,
found, in the early 1970s, a readiness by voluntary bodies to become
vehicles of public policy in supplying opportunities for 'voluntary'
activity by offenders. Intermediate Treatment, never adequately
funded as the preventive or alternative form of juvenile care it was
supposed to represent, also became a source of funds for participating
agencies. If racial strife blows up in deprived inner-city areas, instant
panaceas become available through adjusted funding policies for
ethnic voluntary groups, disguising to an extent the damaging consequences of longer-term official neglect. If an urgent demonstration of
government concern is required to placate mounting criticism of
youth unemployment levels, without at the same time seeming to be
establishing permanent structures which would give the lie to the
alleged transience of the problem, funds are disbursed to the voluntary sector. Voluntary organisations, for their part, become increasingly adept in the fine art of grantmanship, changing direction or
sprouting new projects to fit the label attached to whatever grants are
available, with all the dangers of incorporation into government
purposes, political manipulation and loss of real independence and
critical faculty. As one observer has written,

> voluntary organisations have, over the past decade, so hocked them-
> selves to state money that their right even to be called voluntary has
> been called into question. Many have trimmed their services in order to
> pick up government financial breezes while others have become almost
> indistinguishable in their service delivery from state or local govern-
> ment provision. Yet others have flourished like hot house plants under
> the protective glass of government urban or regional policies – all
> manner of local organisations, special interest groups, ethnic organ-
> isations, community schemes have flowered in the government's
> window box – ample evidence to the voter of the benign and caring face
> of the state.[9]

An additional consequence of increased dependence on government
subsidy and on the 'bandwagon' factor is of course the heightened
vulnerability of voluntary organisations to changes and lurches in
policy. 'The funding business is as fashion conscious as Oxford
Street', wrote one commentator,[10] ruefully observing the non-
availability of funds for black youths who do not fall into the
'alienated' category. Voluntary schemes which opportunistically link
government subsidies available for specific and manifest purposes
such as relieving unemployment, to their own latent objectives of

delivering services to vulnerable groups, can find the benefits to their customers unhealthily and precariously dependent upon changing trends in official employment policies which do not in any way take them into account.

To highlight the volatile nature of much voluntary agency activity in certain fields is perhaps to do no more than to underscore the fact of their growing dependence upon government. The actions of governments are inherently political and therefore changeable and vacillating, but this is not meant to suggest that their policies must always be viewed with absolute scepticism. A conspiracy theory of welfare which would see social policies as primarily and deliberately directed towards such objectives as social control or electoral advantage, would, in the complex and messy world of politics, represent only a partial explanation for specific measures. Government programmes such as the inner-city initiatives or the mass of special employment programmes to which the second part of this chapter will refer, can be justly criticised for lacking a thoroughgoing structural analysis of social and economic problems and a radical strategy, and also for being inadequately resourced to meet even their own short-term aims. Inasmuch as they serve as substitutes for effective solutions they may be viewed sceptically, and voluntary sector participation within them associated with tokenism. This being said, it must also be acknowledged that even partial measures to relieve socio-economic problems can have immediate beneficial effects for some people. Similarly, voluntary bodies which reach out for available finance where they can get it, should not perhaps be too strongly criticised. There are also many encouraging examples of voluntary enterprise in the field of job creation, self-help employment schemes, development of cooperatives and the employment of ex-offenders, which make a substantial and worthwhile contribution to both inner-city life and employment opportunities. For such initiatives, the aims of government subsidy policies and the uses to which grants are put, coincide. However, in relation to the general point being made above, it is right to question the nature of voluntary agencies' relationships with government bodies and the extent and consequences of their reliance on statutory sources of finance.

A final general point relevant to the nature of such relationships is a phenomenon familiar in the world of business – 'interlocking directorships'. Underlying the connecting links of subsidy and consultation, most particularly at the national level, but not unknown at local level also, is the constantly circulating membership of voluntary agency management boards, chairpersons' or treasurers' positions, of a relatively small number of people who move easily between public, private and voluntary spheres, gaining the ear of a minister or official here, dropping a word there, sustaining relationships of mutual benefit. We have already noted the association of voluntary agency distribution and of voluntary work with higher social class,[11] but there are no studies as far as this writer is aware, of the composition and cross-cutting memberships of the boards and management committees of national or local voluntary agencies. Such a study might afford an illuminating insight into the nature and extent of a closed circle of social, political and economic connections where 'the old school tie' or its equivalent confers on certain individuals a disproportionately powerful role and privilege both domestically in controlling the agency's policies, and externally in its relations with government bodies, trusts or big business. Apart from the sponsorship of their royal or at least titled figureheads, many of the large, more establishment-oriented voluntary organisations seek out and coopt influential persons on to their boards of directors who are influential by virtue of their social positions and titles, their previous official positions, their membership of government-sponsored bodies, their success in high finance, etc. and their connections in official and political circles. This 'circulation of élites' where individuals wear a succession of hats, *may* serve the interests of some voluntary agencies very well. It might, on the other hand, be challenged by those who value democratic participation by memberships, by clients and consumers or by staff, or by those who resist the dominance and conservatism of the establishment's world view. The competitive rating of less 'respectable', anti-establishment or more working-class types of organisation in the bids for funds also ranks low in comparison.

Besides the advantages conferred on some of the more privileged agencies by this form of interpentration between the sectors, there are undoubtedly benefits for government departments in this system of communication and influence, providing as it does a conveniently informal means of exercising a reverse influence upon the priorities and activities of the voluntary bodies concerned. Is there, however, evidence of more extensive and formal control by government of the behaviour of recipients of its voluntary sector subsidies? The VSU's evidence to the Wolfenden Committee (Ch. 4) suggested that government control and influence in this respect is 'marginal'. There is also the question of the Charity Law. The following sections will examine the links between government funding and control generally and the exercise of the Charity Act in particular.

GOVERNMENT FUNDING AND GOVERNMENT CONTROL

We have already noted the increased dependence of voluntary agencies on government as a source of funds, a dependence which carries with it the risk of loss of identity, multiple changes of direction and loss of independent voice. Enough has perhaps been said to suggest that the very shape of the voluntary sector may be subtly changing according to official priorities, for those activities and organisations which do not fit such priorities fail to win funds, and, unless they can find resources elsewhere, will not survive. Generally, the worst casualties here will tend to be newer, less orthodox or respectable and working-class groups. At the crucial level of funding policy, then, given all that Chapter 4 had to say on the shrinkage of voluntary sources of funds, it must be acknowledged that government control and influence over the future development of the voluntary sector is more than 'marginal', and that for some kinds of agency it can be decisive.

If we look at the actual funding relationship with individual agencies, how much direct control is there and how real and effective is it? It is likely, if we look at control in this specific sense, that for most voluntary organisations the VSU's description of controls extending beyond the requirements of public accountability as 'marginal' is fully accurate. It stands to reason that they will not be excessive, given the relatively diminutive nature of the amounts involved from government's point of view, and given the importance to government of the voluntary body's freedom from red tape and its flexibility. A common-sense judgement would also suggest that for government departments to monitor very closely the activities of every one of the hundreds of agencies subsidised would be both impracticable and almost impossible. Given that those bodies which do not conform to government policies do not receive funds in the first place, what happens to those which do and then fall foul of government in some way? Quite possibly, large numbers of agencies manage to retain a sizeable area of discretion in the uses to which they put their funds and in how they direct their activities. The important factor here would be managing to avoid attracting attention to themselves, for it is evident that government control can be promptly mobilised when political pressure or media exposure call into question its support of a specific organisation. In some cases, it must be said, such intervention would be entirely justified, as where a charity is fraudulently using its funds or mistreating its charges. The loudest clamour for such intervention, however, arises generally where recipients of public funds adopt a political stance unacceptable to the government of the day. There was an outcry in 1980, for instance, from those who opposed the line taken by MIND, in relation to certain occurrences at the secure psychiatric hospital, Broadmoor, directed at persuading the DHSS to cut its grant to the agency. In the event, this was not done, but it was a near thing. The Secretary of State at the time addressed the question posed by government subsidy of pressure-group activity when he asked, 'How far is it right that authorities should finance their own critics?' Dismissing the complaints against MIND, he nevertheless went on to say, 'if there is a body which is simply concerned to campaign vociferously for or against certain policies, then I think public authorities should be very slow to spend money on supporting them'.[12] Warning that voluntary bodies wishing to be free from the constraint of acting responsibly, especially in relation to government, 'would be much better advised not to accept public grants', he declared 'It would be a very sad day for this country if it was thought that the Government was trying to silence its critics by cutting off public funds.'

That the political climate had changed in this respect a year or two later was a point made by a *Voluntary Action* editorial[13] calling attention to the 'steady erosion' of the freedom and independence of voluntary organisations under the Conservative government of Mrs Thatcher. A forceful example of the greater readiness of government to use its powers over purse-strings to discipline voluntary agencies was supplied in April 1983 by the Consumer Affairs' Minister's suspension of half of the £6 million grants paid by his department to NACAB. The grant to NACAB was to be placed on a six-monthly basis and its financial management investigated because of allegations of improper political activity among its employees, notably the personal status of one of its local organisers, Joan Ruddock, as chair-person of the Campaign for Nuclear Disarmament (CND). In the event, this attack was shown to be unfounded and the finances not only restored but shown to be insufficient, to the political chagrin of the minister concerned, yet the incident itself provided an instructive insight into government attitudes to the freedom of the voluntary sector.[14] Further examples of a new government restrictiveness can be seen in a Home Office requirement (1983) to the Community Projects Foundation to control the 'political' activities of its staff; the switch of Manpower Services Commission (MSC) funding away from community arts groups and unemployment centres to forms of activity less critical of government policies, and the termination of grant to the Sheffield Centre for the Unemployed after its members took part in a demonstration against unemployment.[15] Additionally, the National Youth Bureau (90 per cent funded by government) was required by the Department of Education and Science to become a comparatively silent quango after criticising government policies.[16]

Earlier acceptance of the campaigning and critical activities of grant-aided voluntary agencies as long as these remained subsidiary to their main functions, seemed to have given way to a more abrasive and controlling *political* line. Addressing the NCVO Annual General Meeting in 1983, the minister for the VSU observed, 'There will be times when the aims of a particular voluntary body and our aims will not coincide. If the body concerned is in receipt of public funds, then the more strident its voice, the noisier its style of campaigning, the closer it comes to striking party political attitudes, the more likely we are to receive complaints from the public, the more difficult it is going to be to justify the government funding.'[17] Shortly afterwards, the NCVO issued a *Declaration on Government Influence on Voluntary Organisations*[18] to its members, which articulated the concern expressed by many regarding 'what they perceive to be certain signs of growing influence, sometimes interference, by government (national and local) on the proper conduct of their roles'. The declaration listed examples of complaints which included government departments' insensitivity to the aims and needs of voluntary agencies themselves when using them to implement departmental priorities, riding roughshod over their own priorities; the uncoordinated impact of different government programmes 'both on the character and management of voluntary bodies'; Whitehall's neglect of 'the overhead costs and managerial strain imposed by suddenly expanded government-sponsored programmes'; strings attached to grants improperly and diminishing voluntary agency independence; 'attempts by government to use voluntary bodies as tools in a systematic redrawing of the now traditional frontiers between statutory and private services', seen as an ideologically motivated involvement of those agencies; the substitution of short-term central funds for long-term local authority funds, and discrimination against voluntary agencies on suspect political grounds.

The NCVO did not, wisely, align itself with this list of concerns, but presented for discussion a code of principles for dealing with the government[19] [doc. 8]. This urged voluntary bodies to assess carefully the extent of desirable dependence upon government, to make a distinction between 'arm's length' financial support which would justify broad measures of accountability but not interference in policy, and the kind of contractual relationship based on specific services paid for, which should have forms and degree of accountability written into the contract. The declaration included a strong statement of the rights of voluntary bodies which are charities to 'exercise their freedom to advocate changes or continuity in public policy, programmes and law to the extent that this is judged to serve the aims and objectives of the body'. This was linked with firm advice to voluntary agencies to safeguard their charitable status, and to avoid involvement with the electoral process and party politics. The significance of the definition of unacceptable *political* activity as that which is connected with taking sides in the electoral process will become clearer in the following section where the interpretation of the Charity Act's limits to 'political' activities on the part of registered charities is seen to be a matter for great contention.

CHARITABLE STATUS AND CONTROL

As we saw in Chapter 4, because public subsidy in the form of tax concessions and rate relief, as well as charitable income in the form of grants from charitable trusts, are only available to bodies which qualify as charities, the conditions for qualifying for this status are very important. Present-day organisations which wish to be registered as charities and avail themselves of these benefits have to conform to requirements which owe more to the seventeenth-century origins of the Charity Law than to contemporary needs and circumstances. According to Gladstone, 'No English statute has ever attempted to give a fundamental definition of the legal meaning of charity.'[20] What constitutes charity depends on a list of 'charitable purposes' attached to a statute of 1601. This statute was redefined in the nineteenth-century [doc. 9] when charitable purposes were grouped into four categories: the relief of poverty, the advancement of education, the advancement of religion and 'other purposes beneficial to the community'.[21] Gladstone comments that the latter category does not apply to just any beneficial purposes, but those which have been established as such by precedent. The lack of any clear definition of charity and of charitable purposes in the law throws the burden of clarification on to case law and the Charity Commission, the official body responsible for registering charities and supervising their conformity to the Charity Law. Unsurprisingly, in the operation of such an archaic law, there is much room for confusion, anachronism and inconsistency, as well as conservatism.

In the context of our previous outline of the voluntary sector's relationship with its government 'partners' we can understand that the restrictiveness of the Charity Law's interpretation has been subject to mounting criticism over the years, as organisations have been refused registration, have had it removed from them or have been compelled to curb their activities under the threat of losing their charitable status. At the very least, this criticism centres on the failure of the Charity Commission to move with the times and to adapt to the changing forms of social action and organisation that have evolved in recent years. As a consequence, there are certain forms of activity and certain types of organisation which do not qualify. The charitable purpose of relieving poverty, for instance, is so narrowly interpreted that a function like the relief of unemployment *per se* does not come within the scope of the law, even though it might be thought to be intimately connected with the state of poverty.[22] It would be accepted as a charitable purpose only if specifically directed towards the poor, in which case the orientation to unemployment becomes subsidiary to the main objective of relieving poverty.

Because the concept of charity is understood in terms of patronage or a benefactor–beneficiary relationship, it cannot be extended to the efforts of people to help themselves. Charitable status is not therefore available to such modern forms of social action and mutual aid as a tenants' association, a food cooperative, a claimants' union, etc. 'At root, charity law is a profoundly political law, enshrining a view of poverty and altruism that reinforces the dependency of the poor. There are those who give and those who receive.'[23] It is no coincidence that these forms of social action are typically working-class forms. A more fundamental criticism of the workings of the charity legislation can be directed at the political bias permeating the selective interpretations which confer charitable status on organisations and activities higher up the socio-economic scale which may be equally geared to self-help but in a form that is more acceptable to the Charity Commission. For instance, it should be noted that professional associations can be charities, and fee-paying schools and fee-paying medical clinics may also be registered as charitable.[24] The Charity Law works in these cases to protect and perpetuate privilege, while it denies the benefit of public subsidy to infinitely more needy groups and organisations.

A further instance of the restrictive and obsolescent nature of the Charity Law is its application to social change strategies. In a nutshell, any activity which is directed at changing structures or attitudes through direct action, pressure or public education, is deemed to be political and therefore non-charitable. To relieve the effects of poverty is permissible, but to endeavour to bring about social change to eliminate poverty is not. A Charity Commissioner is quoted by Gladstone as saying: 'The role of the charity is to bind up the wounds of society. This is what they get their fiscal privileges for. To build up a new society is for someone else.'[25] To work to eliminate injustice is not a charitable purpose, nor is to promote peace or racial harmony, nor to campaign to change a law.[26]

So, for instance, Amnesty International, which takes up the cause of forgotten prisoners of conscience, cannot have charitable status. War on Want, the Third World aid agency, has frequently been in conflict with the Charity Commissioners over its efforts in 'bringing pressure to bear on government to procure a change in policies, practices and administration'.[27] The law thus acts as a powerful force to preserve the status quo and to constrain attempts to change society and its values. Paradoxically, although charitable status is denied to a straightforward campaigning organisation or pressure group, it is permitted to many bodies who employ political lobbying methods as a subsidiary part of their activities. Gladstone explains this in saying: 'this does not mean that a charity cannot seek changes in the law or in administration or even to advance human rights. It can – provided that it does so as a *means* to a non-political end: and provided that end is a charitable purpose and among those specified by the charity's trust deed.'[28] In this way, certain pressurising and promotional activities are allowed, as long as they are not party political, to such charities as the Child Poverty Action Group, the National Council for Civil Liberties, Age Concern and MIND, all of which have, through lobbying and public education, striven to make an impact on the legislative process and on government policies. As Gladstone notes, the *style* of such political activities is held to be crucial by the Charity Commission – 'a "reasoned memorandum" is acceptable but a public demonstration is not. It should be done in a seemly way.'[29] [doc. 10] These major charities have to tread a very careful path. MIND had to make a case to its critics for its membership of a voluntary agency group, the Unemployment Alliance, aimed at increasing public awareness of the evils of unemployment, by carefully tracing a connection between its main concern with mental health and the effects of unemployment.

The unwillingness of government to change the law was restated by Timothy Raison in a speech in 1981. Noting that charities can in fact 'pursue political activities provided they are ancillary to their charitable purposes and kept in due subordination to them', he defined the proper limits of such an activity as 'providing it does not take the form of campaigning for (or against) change'.[30] No clearer statement of the law's bias towards the status quo could be made, and supporting the status quo is, in Ben Whitaker's words, 'itself a political attitude'.[31] Whitaker, commenting on the absurdity of preventing a charity from trying to remove the cause of the problems it exists to relieve, goes on to say: 'I think it should not only be the right but also the positive duty of charities in a number of fields to act as political pressure groups, and that legislation is overdue to end the present widespread uncertainty about this.'[32] [doc. 11]

There has been clamour for the reform of Charity Law for some years. The Charity Law Reform Committee in 1975, the House of Commons Expenditure Committee report in 1975, and the report of the Goodman Committee on Charity Law and Voluntary Organisations in 1976, have all recommended at least some changes to the present law, the Charity Law of 1960, which itself did not reflect all the reforms recommended by the Nathan Committee in 1952.[33] Most suggested reforms are of a fairly conservative nature, involving minor modifications of the boundaries of permissible activity. The Charity Law Reform Committee proposed, however, the extension of the privileges of charities to a new form of political organisation, the Non-Profit-Distributing Organisation, but this proposal has not been taken up. One of the most trenchant critics of the Charity Law is Ben Whitaker, author of a minority report in the Goodman Committee report.[34] Strongly critical of the channelling through the charity legislation of a disproportionate public subsidy to institutions which cater only for a privileged élite 'at the expense of democratically determined programmes – many of which we see today are badly short of finance', Whitaker's suggested remedy for this subsidy of the rich by the less well off is the concentration of tax relief primarily on deprivation and the disadvantaged, and state subsidy of charities 'as independent critics of established thinking and programmes'. While there is not universal agreement with the various proposals for reform, there is widespread feeling among voluntary organisations that some reform is long overdue, and the NCVO has mounted a campaign for reform. Governments have so far not responded positively.

Now that we have explored general aspects of the voluntary sector–governmental relationship, and some of the conflicts between independence and control that characterise this relationship despite the fact that in many instances it is definitively described as a 'partnership', it would be useful to look at examples of this partnership in practice at central and local level. Among central government programmes, an area that has demonstrated a mounting level of interpenetration between the two sectors in recent years is the range of employment projects financed and sponsored by MSC and the DHSS among others.

VOLUNTARY SECTOR INVOLVEMENT IN EMPLOYMENT PROGRAMMES

The network of programmes initiated by government in the last few years as unemployment crept up past 3 million and the problems of long-term and youth unemployment became progressively more serious, is untidy, complex and cumbersomely bureaucratic, more a demonstration of official ad-hoccery and political image management than a coherent strategy. Voluntary organisations have been drawn into these programmes in two principal ways: they, like statutory and private agencies, entered the business of making work aimed at simply occupying people and preserving their work habits or at providing skill enhancement or training of some kind. To some extent they have also concentrated on the creation of small numbers of new jobs. Secondly, they have been called on at frequent intervals to supply opportunities for the unemployed to work 'voluntarily'. Either way, the voluntary sector has focused particularly upon the young, especially disadvantaged youth from minority ethnic groups, and on groups with specific disadvantages like disability or a criminal record, whose chances of employment in the open market are negligible.

Temporary employment projects

One of the earliest programmes, and one which was wholly entrusted to a voluntary body, was Community Industry, set up as a temporary measure in 1972 under the auspices of the National Association of Youth Clubs. This programme 'aims to help socially and personally disadvantaged young people prepare for permanent employment by providing them with practical work of community benefit'.[35] Directed primarily at 16 and 17 year-olds, the scheme has provided some thousands of places yearly, employing the youngsters on a wage in small teams on community projects and workshops and in placements in social service institutions. It is financed by the Department of Employment as part of its MSC-administered programmes for the young unemployed.

The Job Creation Programme (JCP) (1975–78) was set up to 'provide worthwhile temporary employment for people who would otherwise be unemployed on projects which seem to provide community benefit'. Administered by the MSC, it was sponsored at local level by local authorities, who were the major participants, by private employers and by voluntary organisations (who received about 35 per cent of the total budget). Although, undoubtedly, voluntary sector participation made positive contributions within the limitations of the scheme, there are some indications that voluntary bodies were at times unready or unsuited for the responsibilities they undertook. F. Ridley, chairperson of a Merseyside JCP, comments that many of the community work projects offered 'ill-defined activities unrelated to any future form of employment'[36] and that 'the training element was limited'. Such criticisms might also justly have been levelled at the other participants, but clearly some of them arose from the fact that many local voluntary agencies and groups lack sophistication and experience. Reliance on community work and on minor environmental projects was partly a result of trade union opposition to the threat of undercutting regular jobs, but Ridley also felt that a difficulty of the scheme was the fact that it was short of sponsors and lacked the resources for inducing sponsors to mount more desirable projects. 'Voluntary organisations', he comments, also 'had a natural inclination to offer projects that would promote their own goals rather than start from the problems of the unemployed.'[37] Voluntary agencies were in a difficult position within this programme because MSC-provided overhead expenses were rather limited, and also because they lacked, particularly in more deprived areas, technical expertise, the experience of managing a workforce and skill in keeping accurate financial records. The latter problems have been given greater attention by the MSC since the Job Creation Project, although it must be said that the administrative regulations and procedures surrounding its employment initiatives have attained a complexity of daunting proportions for even the most sophisticated voluntary agency, and the MSC's oversight of its schemes has frequently been criticised for being over-controlling.

The JCP was replaced in 1978 following the Holland Report,[38] by the new Special Programmes for the unemployed. These comprised a bewildering array of constantly changing acronyms, testimony to a stream of policy changes and switches of programme goals. The Youth Opportunities Programme (YOP) provided work experience for disadvantaged young persons for an average twenty-three weeks, a type of experience which has been variously criticised for its substitution of the jobs of adult workers, for its often custodial nature and its lack of a genuine training component, as well as its declining success in returning youngsters to anywhere more hopeful than the dole queue. Voluntary agencies, especially councils of voluntary service, typically employed about 10 per cent of all YOP places, mostly in community service and project-based work experience. Some of these places were of very high quality, providing socially useful and personally satisfying temporary jobs or basic vocational skills. In 1983 YOP was replaced by the Youth Training Scheme (YTS), a programme with somewhat different terms. Voluntary bodies, expected to maintain the same level of involvement in the YTS as in YOP, were severely critical of some aspects of the new scheme, particularly its potentially compulsory features linked to the withdrawal of eligibility for supplementary benefits, but they nevertheless participated in providing community-based places, information technology centres and training workshops for youngsters on the scheme. Voluntary agencies, with local authorities, sponsored some 89,000 places for the YTS in 1983/84,[39] but, by the end of this period were abruptly faced with massive cutbacks imposed on community projects by the MSC and the necessity to make redundant considerable numbers of support staff and to wind up many projects. The MSC's turnabout, which caused great consternation among voluntary organisations dependent upon it as a source of funds, was caused by a shortfall in the numbers of recruits to the employer-based parts of the YTS scheme and by the government's growing emphasis on more direct forms of work experience.[40]

Other programmes, such as the Community Programme (CP), aimed at providing work for unemployed adults that is 'of some community benefit', represent the latest in a series of abrupt policy changes on the part of the MSC. The CP was much criticised by voluntary agencies at its inception for its restrictiveness, low wage rates, limited training resources and complexity. The voluntary sector itself, although expected to sponsor roughly one-third of CP places, had little influence on the overall shape of the programme, its conditions or priorities. While many encouragingly critical voices were raised among voluntary organisations on this and other aspects of MSC policy, some agencies, such as Community Task Force, rapidly became 100 per cent dependent upon finance from MSC programmes, devoting their total energies to working for the MSC. The capacity of such client agencies for maintaining an independent, critical stance in relation to government must clearly be limited.

Voluntary work programmes for the unemployed

The Special Programmes providing various kinds of paid 'make-work' for the unemployed sketched out in the preceding paragraphs had their origins under a Labour government and were continued, albeit with variations, by the post-1979 Thatcher administration. A confusing series of initiatives were subsequently to draw voluntary organisations into 'partnership' with government in providing opportunities for *voluntary* work by the unemployed. These bore the unmistakable hallmark of the individualism of the New Right. It was entirely in keeping with its self-help philosophy that the new government should regard the opportunity to donate one's labour as a heaven-sent solution for the offensive problem of subsidised idleness represented by dependence on social security benefits. One of the stumbling blocks to this kind of volunteering was the availability for work requirement for benefit eligibility and the earnings limit which restricted even the small amounts of money volunteers might be able to earn. In 1982, the DHSS eased the regulations to allow claimants to earn up to £2.00 a day, to work voluntarily in their own occupation provided it is for a charity, local authority or health authority, and to give those claimants working on voluntary projects a twenty-four hour exemption from the availability for work requirement, extended to up to sixteen days for those away from home.

Examples of government-initiated volunteer programmes for the unemployed, again dependent upon private sector, local authority and voluntary organisations' sponsorship, were the Voluntary Projects Programme (VPP) and the Opportunities for Volunteering Programme, following each other in rapid succession in 1982. The VPP was run by the MSC and it made available £8 million for 1982–83 for the recruitment of unemployed people to adult education schemes and to community activity. These voluntary activities were required to be of benefit in relation to training or to obtaining work, and each recruit was to be taken on for one year. The parallel DHSS scheme, Opportunities for Volunteering, was restricted to voluntary organisations and to activities related to the health and social services. It was intended to develop opportunities for unemployed people to undertake voluntary work, to expand voluntary work in the health and social services, and to spend the money in ways which would produce long-term benefits. The latter objective might be described as an example of extreme DHSS optimism as the sum of money available was only £3.3 million in 1982/83 and £5 million in 1983/84. Unusually the DHSS passed over the money to the voluntary sector to disburse. Two-thirds of it was allocated by fifteen specialist organisations, such as CSV, BASSAC, Age Concern and Barnardo's, and the rest, a general fund, was distributed by a consortium of seven national voluntary organisations administered from the NCVO. Opportunities for Volunteering represents, according to its NCVO coordinator,[41] 'the first opportunity for national voluntary organisations to be directly involved in awarding and administering grants on behalf of the government'. Such a distributive function may well enjoy certain advantages over the disbursement of funds by the DHSS directly. It has also produced a valuable spin-off in the stimulus it presents for greater cooperation and coordination among national and local voluntary organisations participating. It presents a curious precedent, however, as a form of direct privatisation of control over public funds, and the dividing lines between statutory and voluntary partners become rather blurred as the national voluntary organisations assume the role of administrative agent for government.

Comment

The plethora of paid and voluntary work schemes and projects mounted by voluntary organisations on the basis of government-initiated policies and government-provided finance is evidence of a degree of interdependence between the two sectors which, for all its short-term positive aspects, must be viewed with concern. Some anxiety should arise from a consideration of the nature of the programmes themselves, and, it should be said, there is a fair amount of disquiet here and there in the voluntary sector about its identification with government policies designed to soften the effects of its broad economic strategy and to distract attention from the harsh realities of long-term unemployment which will continue when individual programmes have come and gone. Voluntary organisations continue to express doubts as to the desirability of cementing a firm association between volunteering and unemployment, particularly as such agencies as the Volunteer Centre have spent considerable energies stressing the importance of keeping clear distinctions between paid employment and volunteering. There is concern lest voluntary work become tarred with the same stigma as unemployment in the public mind, as well as a more fundamental scepticism regarding the desirability of promoting voluntary work as a solution to the problems of the unemployed. The voluntary sector easily becomes prey, moreover, to extreme proposals which verge on transforming what is essentially voluntary and altruistic activity into a kind of compulsory service, much beloved of those who have long lamented the passing of the character-building rigours of national service in the armed forces. Just such a proposal was that promulgated by Youthcall, in May 1981, when various pillars of the voluntary sector such as Anthony Steen

(Conservative MP and founder of Task Force) and Alec Dickson (founder of CSV) got together to launch the idea of a national community service scheme for all young people, an idea which 'could be philosophically, politically and economically attractive'. It is not clear whether the scheme was designed to be compulsory or optional, but there are obviously inherent risks of the former, especially when questions of supplementary benefit eligibility are closely related. To their credit, many voluntary organisations rejected Youthcall and attacked such proposals as 'do-goodery gone mad', offering no answer to the problems of youth unemployment. 'If they are to be voluntary then they will end up as a dustbin activity for under-achievers.'[42]

June 1981 saw the launching of a counter-attack in the form of an Unemployment Alliance of nine national voluntary organisations 'to draw attention to the poverty, demoralisation and family stress being experienced in particular by the long-term unemployed'. One of the objects of the Alliance was to dispose of the notion that 'voluntarism was a soft option to be set up as a panacea for all social ills'. 'It is not the job', declared Tony Smythe, then director of MIND, 'of voluntary organisations just to provide services and support without looking at the structural problems which cause need.'[43]

Quite apart from the at times disquieting features evident in voluntary sector participation in the actual programmes of government, what is the nature of the relationship between the two sectors that it promotes? In Chapter 1 we held that a voluntary organisation's independence of government is a defining characteristic on which its identity relies, and the source of many of its more distinctive attributes. The transformation of voluntary bodies into agencies for public programmes in the way described above may be a good thing and serve very many useful purposes, but there is no denying that it inevitably has repercussions for the separateness of their identity and for their independence. This incorporation of the voluntary organisation into the orbit of government has implications for the central arguments of welfare pluralism which we will be considering in Chapter 8. With regard to the partnerships established, one positive consequence of the closer relationships they generate might counterbalance some of the losses involved, if indeed they are regarded as losses. This is the emergence of the voluntary participants as partners in the full sense alluded to earlier, whereby they enjoy status and influence in either programme planning or consultation. There seems to have been little sign of such a quid pro quo in the employment programmes we have considered – voluntary organisations have acquired little or no effective voice in the content and direction or implementation of the programmes they help to bring about. Indeed, a rather plaintive and revealing reflection of this lack of influence or autonomy was contained in the NCVO's 'Agenda for Action', a list of twelve points for action by whatever government was to win the June 1983 general election. Point eleven urged government to 'consult voluntary bodies on those official programmes, MSC employment initiatives for example, in which they are expected to take part *before* the programmes are determined'.[44]

THE VOLUNTARY SECTOR AND INNER-CITY POLICIES

The Urban Programme announced in 1968 by Home Secretary James Callaghan, was set up to direct positive discrimination towards areas of severe social deprivation where poverty, unemployment, housing stress and poor social services amounted to 'conditions of special social need'. It was intended to 'arrest, in so far as it is possible by financial means, and reverse the downward spiral which afflicts many of these areas'. One of its manifest aims was not designedly to stimulate growth in the voluntary sector, but this was to be a considerable by-product of the programme and its successors. The financing of voluntary as well as statutory sector projects was, however, always part of the scheme, and local authorities were asked by a later, Conservative government, in 1971, to give them greater emphasis. Thereafter, the voluntary share of the Urban Programme grew steadily, and, in its first decade, 24.5 per cent of total expenditure went to projects run by voluntary organisations and community groups.[45]

The Traditional Urban Programme (TUP) had in these early years a service orientation based on a social pathology approach to urban deprivation. This approach later gave way, under the impact of accumulating research evidence, to a stress on the economic decline of inner-city life and the need for a mixture of social, economic and environmental measures to counteract it. The White Paper, *Policy for the Inner Cities*[46] subsequently augmented the traditional programme with what became known as the 'Enhanced' Inner City Programme, through which a more total and comprehensive approach might be directed, along with more funds, to selected areas. These were designated as Partnership and Programme areas, where special relationships were to be established between central and local government. The White Paper contained a strong emphasis on the involvement of local people in urban renewal 'both as a necessary means to the regeneration of the inner areas and as an end in its own right'.[47] It stressed the need 'to harness the good will and energies of tenants' and residents' associations, local councils of social service, settlements and charities, and more informal groups such as pensioners' clubs . . . Public policy should aim to stimulate voluntary effort and help voluntary bodies to play a constructive role.'[48] [doc. 12] The formal concept of partnership specified relationships between the two levels of government, but ministers made clear in successive speeches that they understood the notion in a wider sense, to extend to a partnership between government, local industry, voluntary and community groups and local residents [doc. 13]. It was envisaged that local people and voluntary and community groups would be consulted in identifying problems and in drawing up the programme, but that they would not be represented at the Partnership committees running the programme.

The Programme, in its traditional and enhanced versions, had three principal aims. These were intended as a supplement to mainstream economic and social programmes but also 'clearly intended to change agency attitudes and organisational practices, through the "bending" of the existing main programmes'.[49] Accordingly, it was envisaged that it would: (a) 'encourage local authorities to tackle special problems requiring the coordinated efforts of several local authority departments and/or other agencies; (b) encourage innovation leading to the adaptation of the main programmes; and (c) unlock community initiative'.[50]

Resources were to be made available through the local authorities for initiatives which were essentially either experimental or filling a need that would not otherwise be met. Projects were to function as short-term, pump-priming exercises which would, if proved worth while, eventually transfer to more permanent funding from local authorities and other sources. Examples of the kind of projects funded include the following: information and advice centres, under-fives projects, good neighbour schemes, volunteer bureaux, women's centres and refuges, victim support schemes, home insulation for the elderly, community farms and community workshops, advice services for small businesses, skill-training, anti-vandalism campaigns and landscaping. This selection reflects the social, economic and environmental strands of TUP, but exaggerates the ratios of each to the other. In fact, 96.4 per cent of all voluntary TUP projects in 1982 came under the social category.[51]

Several thousands of voluntary projects were generated by the urban renewal programme. The major voluntary involvement has always been in the TUP, where it was increased as a matter of policy to just over half of all TUP projects, spending just under half of the funds. As voluntary participation did not figure so highly in the 'Enhanced' programmes, the voluntary sector's share of total funding was about one-fifth. Amounting to only a small amount of money in terms of public expenditure, this has represented for voluntary organisations a 'much welcomed injection of life blood'.[52] For government, it has presented a visible sign of its continued commitment to a policy of encouraging voluntary initiatives. Much that is positive and useful and also genuinely creative at times, sprang from this reinvigoration of voluntary enterprise, but it must be doubted whether the combined urban programmes themselves have contributed much of lasting value to the original purpose of regenerating the inner city.

Comment

Much criticism has been levelled at the Urban Programme, essentially for failing to take a structural approach to structural problems and for its inadequate resource levels. The policy itself has to be measured against its effective sabotage by a deteriorating economic situation, with rising levels of unemployment resulting from deliberate government strategies, and by government economic and public expenditure policies which actually worsened the plight of the inner cities. Further criticisms have centred on the fact that many local authorities used urban aid money as a substitute for their regular expenditures. Williams comments that the Urban Aid Programme 'has tended not to be regarded by local authorities as an opportunity for piloting new community initiatives, but as a flexible, piecemeal subsidy programme, suitable for tackling "gaps" in mainstream programmes experiencing severe resources constraints'.[53] The concept of planning has frequently been sacrificed to a scramble for money which has rarely been based on worked-out and coordinated local strategies. Local authorities and voluntary bodies have been at fault here, but a fundamental difficulty for the voluntary sector hws been the absence of clear criteria for their participation, and the lack of specific finances for the researching and preparation of bids for funds. A certain opportunism on the part of voluntary organisations has been an inevitable consequence of the uncertainties and lack of continuity deriving from the programme's stress on demonstration and experiment which has meant the abrupt termination at times for time-expired projects banking on renewal.

If we leave the substantive issues connected with the programme and turn to our initial interest in the nature of the relationship it forged between the voluntary and the statutory sectors, we find the client-status of voluntary organisations a rather more significant by-product than their emergence as collaborative partners. Dependence upon statutory sources of income to the degree experienced by many voluntary bodies in the Urban as in the Unemployment Programmes must lead similarly to some blurring of their separateness and independence. Was there some compensatory exchange in this more intimate relationship which has given substance to the notion of partnership? Consultation of the voluntary sector and its involvement in the planning process had, as we noted earlier, been an important part of the rhetoric of the White Paper and of subsequent government statements. Although advocated, however, it was not required for successful local authority applications for funding. The exhortation had not, according to Williams, 'been accompanied by central guidance on its interpretation, and the extent of local authority discretion, both in project sponsorship and in working out means of incorporating community views, has meant that attitudinal factors and prior experience have critically influenced the scope for voluntary sector involvement'.[54] There were some exceptional attempts at joint planning and consultation, as in the London Borough of Islington, where, for a time, genuine attempts were made to build up a local participatory system encouraging the involvement of urban-aided voluntary groups and bodies.[55] Where consultation did take place, criticism was often voiced that it was exclusively directed towards the established and well-organised voluntary agency, as was, consequently, much of the funding. 'What rankled most as far as the residents were concerned was the way the voluntary sector, and in particular the big community based professional organisations, managed successfully to put themselves forward as the true representatives of the "poor and deprived" and of "the community", while in reality the majority were run in a paternalist manner by charismatic individuals and were completely unaccountable to the local people.'[56] The unrepresentativeness of the voluntary sector emerges here, along with its diversity and fragmentation. In practical terms, it is difficult for officials to identify spokespersons and representative points of view, and, in political terms, their legitimacy can be challenged from within the representative political system.[57]

Secondly, a point raised by Williams in his study of the inner-city Partnership in Manchester, consultation and planning have been impeded by the diversity and lack of a unified perspective in the voluntary sector. Organisations focus on their own individual interests to the exclusion of a broader strategy of coalition and co-ordination with other bodies, and have 'tended to see Partnership largely in terms or providing "new" resources rather than as a focus for wider participation in the local policy environment'.[58] According to this study, the local authority established hegemony over the Partnership arrangements very early on, appealing to the notion of 'public accountability' to deny legitimacy to voluntary sector and community involvement in real decision-making, and to confine it to a public relations-oriented consultative role. The balance of power was heavily biased in favour of the authority on whose sponsorship access to funds depended. Voluntary agencies were not entirely powerless, Williams points out, as they were needed in the Partnership, but what influence they had was undoubtedly eroded by their resource dependence and their lack of internal cohesion. Williams quotes from a Council of Voluntary Service report, the following indictment: 'The voluntary sector, indefinable and fluctuating, cannot establish any thorough-going, democratic structure to represent it, control it or whatever.'[59] The allocation of Partnership funds remained almost wholly under authority influence, geared to the priorities of mainstream statutory departments and accompanied by strict controls. Williams comments, 'Partnership experience, whilst undoubtedly facilitating opportunities for enhancing contact between the voluntary and statutory sectors, has provided little evidence of any significant influence either over Programme content or implementation.'[60]

We asked earlier if a certain absorption of voluntary agencies into the statutory sector might have been balanced by compensatory gains in participation in the planning and decision-making processes of the Urban Programme. Did they become partners in the Partnership schemes? The indications are that they did not. Incorporated by public authorities when this suits their purposes, dismissed as unrepresentative when it does not, voluntary bodies are prey to all the tensions and conflicts inherent in the clash between a directly participative model of democracy and the representative model which elected authorities exist to defend. The fragmentation and conflicting sectional interests of the voluntary sector do not fit well with the rational bureaucracy of the local authority. The unequal distribution of power, where one partner controls the resources and the other is almost totally dependent, is the major impediment – a lesson learned many times now in such programmes as the Community Development Projects and, in the United States, in the failure of 'maximum feasible participation' in the War on Poverty.

CONCLUSION

This chapter has explored several dimensions of the relationships between the voluntary sector and government, ranging from the broad issues of autonomy and control raised by growing financial dependence, to more specific considerations of the roles played by voluntary bodies at local level in the nationally funded programmes for employment and the inner cities. It is clear that much of the great impetus behind voluntary sector activities in recent years has come from the availability of public funds, without which many imaginative and creative ventures would not have got off the ground. Yet the relationships engendered between the two spheres through finance, whether they retain a mutual distance or become incorporative, are fraught with all kinds of difficulties emanating from the very nature of the two sectors involved. To an extent, the problems faced by government, national or local, are a measure of the wide gulf that exists in the electoral system between governors and governed, where public authorities claim a legitimacy which excludes the organisations and groups set up voluntarily by various of their electors. The voluntary sector, on the other hand, is so diverse and diffused and unrepresentative, that public authorities must inevitably make arbitrary decisions and alliances. It is evident from the preceding pages that the interface between government and the voluntary sector comprises a vast mixture of conflicting motives, interests and goals on both sides. Voluntary organisations and groups cope with their need for public money often by walking a precarious tightrope between becoming agents or puppets of government and thus losing their identity and independence and setting themselves up as adversaries and critics so stridently as to disqualify themselves from funding. There is no doubt that in the voluntary sector itself there is considerable disquiet about the dangers of growing financial dependence upon government, particularly in an ideological climate where the rhetoric of 'partnership' is a euphemism for a radical transformation of the established patterns of responsibility in the welfare state.

NOTES AND REFERENCES

1. DEPARTMENT OF HEALTH AND SOCIAL SECURITY, *Priorities in the Health and Social Services: the Way Forward.* HMSO: 1977.
2. Ibid., para. 2:11.
3. ALDERMAN, G., *Pressure Groups in Britain.* Longman: Harlow, 1984; FIELD, F., *Poverty and Politics: the Inside Story of the CPAG Campaigns in the 1970's.* Heinemann: London, 1982; MARSH, D.,

Pressure Politics – Interest Groups in Britain. Junction Books: London, 1984.

4. National Association for Mentally Handicapped Children and Adults.
5. Royal Association for Disability and Rehabilitation.
6. *The Listener*, 19 Nov. 1981.
7. BINGLEY, W., 'How the MIND people made their mark', *Voluntary Action*, NCVO, Winter 1983, pp. 16–17.
8. Childcare Bill 1982.
9. 'Friendly Satellites.' *Community Care*, 27 Sept. 1979, p. 1.
10. MACKIE, L., 'Are blacks getting the cash?' *Voluntary Action*, NCVO, Summer 1981, pp. 6–7.
11. See Chapter 4.
12. JENKIN, P., *DHSS Press Release*, 80/150, 13 June 1980.
13. 'The myth of freedom.' *Voluntary Action*, NCVO, Summer 1983, p. 1.
14. LONEY, M., 'Pulling the reins tighter,' *Voluntary Action*, NCVO, Summer 1983, p. 6.
15. Ibid.
16. *Guardian*, 4 Feb. 1984.
17. WADDINGTON, D., Speech to NCVO AGM, quoted in *Guardian*, op. cit.
18. NATIONAL COUNCIL FOR VOLUNTARY ORGANISATIONS, *NCVO Declaration on Government Influence on Voluntary Organisations*. NCVO: London, Nov. 1983.
19. NATIONAL COUNCIL FOR VOLUNTARY ORGANISATIONS, *Relations between Voluntary Sector and Government: A Code for Voluntary Organisations*. NVCO: London, March 1984.
20. GLADSTONE, F., *Charity Law and Social Justice*. Bedford Square Press: London, 1982, p. 46.
21. Ibid., pp. 48–9.
22. Ibid.
23. 'Killing a campaign with kindness.' *Voluntary Action*, NCVO, Winter 1982, p. 1.
24. GLADSTONE, *Charity Law*, p. 88.
25. Ibid., p. 75.
26. GLADSTONE, F., 'Political activity: how far can charities go?', *Voluntary Action*, NCVO, Autumn 1982, pp. 13–15.
27. 'Uncharitable thoughts.' *Voluntary Action*, NCVO, Autumn 1982, p. 4.
28. GLADSTONE, *Charity Law*, p. 102.
29. GLADSTONE, 'Political activity'. p. 14.

30. RAISON, T., Speech to Northampton Council of Voluntary Service AGM, 10 July 1981.
31. WHITTAKER, B., 'Time to reform the Charity Law?', *Voluntary Action*, NCVO, Winter 1979, p. 4.
32. Ibid.
33. HMSO, *Report of the Committee on the Law and Practice Relating to Charitable Trusts (Nathan Report)*, Cmd 8710. 1952.
34. GOODMAN COMMISSION, *Chartiy Law and Voluntary Organisations*. Bedford Square Press: London, 1976.
35. MANPOWER SERVICES COMMISSION, *Annual Report, 1980–81*.
36. RIDLEY, F., 'Job Creation Programme: administrative problems of implementation', *Public Administration*, Autumn 1980, pp. 261–85.
37. Ibid.
38. MANPOWER SERVICES COMMISSION, *Young People and Work: Report on the Feasibility of a New Programme of Opportunities for Unemployed Young People*. 1977.
39. *Voluntary Action*, Longman, April 1984, p. 9.
40. C. ST. JOHN-BROOKS, 'Riding the MSC roller-coaster.' *Voluntary Action*, Longman, May 1984, pp. 7–8.
41. C. SMITH, 'Funding the five thousand'. *Voluntary Action*, NCVO, Spring 1983, p. 27.
42. NATIONAL COUNCIL FOR YOUTH SERVICES, *Community Care*, 21 May 1981.
43. *Community Care*, 4 June 1981.
44. NATIONAL COUNCIL FOR VOLUNTARY ORGANISATIONS, *Information Service*, 94, June 1983.
45. NATIONAL COUNCIL FOR VOLUNTARY ORGANISATIONS, *The Traditional Urban Programme*. NCVO: London, 1978.
46. DEPARTMENT OF THE ENVIRONMENT, *Policy for the Inner Cities*, Cmnd 6845. HMSO: London, 1977.
47. Ibid., para. 34.
48. Ibid., para. 35.
49. WILLIAMS, G., *Inner City Policy: A Partnership with the Voluntary Sector?*, NCVO Occasional Paper. Bedford Square Press: London, 1983, p. 22.
50. DEPARTMENT OF THE ENVIRONMENT, *The Urban Programme*, Circular 18 (Aug. 1978).
51. DEPARTMENT OF THE ENVIRONMENT, *The Urban Programme*, Circular 22 (June 1982).
52. CLARKE, C., 'People in Partnership'. *Voluntary Action*, NCVO, Spring 1981, pp. 23–5.

53. WILLIAMS, op. cit., p. 20.
54. Ibid., pp. 32–3.
55. HATCH, S. and MOCROFT, I., *Components of Welfare*. Bedford Square Press: London, 1983.
56. SHARRON, H., 'The souring of the Partnership', *Voluntary Action*, NCVO, Winter 1981, pp. 18–20.
57. HATCH and MOCROFT, op. cit.
58. WILLIAMS, op. cit., p. 70.
59. Ibid.
60. Ibid.

Chapter Six

'PARTNERSHIP' AND LOCAL SOCIAL SERVICES

Moving away from enquiry into the nature of the voluntary–statutory partnership contained in some of the major national programmes, a number of which have, of course, been concerned with relationships at local level, let us now survey the interaction of the two sectors in local authority social services. Central government has to a limited extent encouraged the development of a fuller concept of partnership in local services. We noted earlier that DHSS guidelines in the 1977 policy document *The Way Forward* envisaged a form of collaboration between the voluntary sector and the local authorities which included voluntary participation in planning those services. The ministry continued to encourage this kind of partnership in a new community care initiative in early 1983. After consultation with some national voluntary organisations, the DHSS set in motion a process whereby the contribution made at local level by voluntary bodies to the health and social services should be reflected by their membership of joint consultative committees, the statutory bodies set up to advise health and local authorities on mutual cooperation and on the planning and provision of joint services. Voluntary agencies had long been participants in the joint-funded projects themselves, but had no formal role in the planning process. This was to be amended by a provision in the Health and Social Services and Social Security Adjudications Bill, 1983. The joint finance arrangements were expanded and extended with the aid of a small extra injection of central funds, and a government circular[1] asked local authorites to arrange meetings with voluntary bodies to discuss a joint approach. It encouraged the joint care planning teams to take into consideration the potential contribution of voluntary organisations, and advised the latter to discuss proposals for community care with local social services departments and district health authorities at an early stage.

This move certainly added an impetus to the involvement in a more concrete way of the voluntary sector in local joint planning processes, an involvement that potentially accorded voluntary organisation a new status in relation to the statutory authorities. The fact that it was to be based on a statutory requirement, not made permissive, showed the strength of DHSS attachment to the voluntary role and, perhaps, a realistic acknowledgement of the lack of voluntary organisation participation in local statutory policy-making generally. The joint-financed projects have always amounted to only a relatively small part of local social services operations, but it might be that once sufficient experience had been gained through them of the potential benefits of partnership between the two sectors, they might represent an entering wedge which would facilitate progress in wider areas of social services responsibility.

A significant conclusion reached by the Wolfenden Committee in reviewing the relationship between voluntary and statutory bodies, was that it is at the local level that voluntary sector involvement in public policy-making is at its weakest. It commented upon the extreme variability of local authority support for voluntary organisations, and the lack of explicit policies for relations with them. 'Central government . . . officially accepts the principle of partnership with the voluntary sector though there may be criticisms of the application of this principle in practice. It is different in local government.'[2] Wolfenden had found some exceptions, where local authorities did consult the voluntary sector, where active policies were pursued of cooption of voluntary representatives on to statutory committees and where the local authorities were represented on the management boards of voluntary agencies. In general, however, the notion of an active partnership in local level policy-making seems unrealised. Formidable obstacles to it may be found in the indifference or antagonism of some local authorities, especially to their critics, and the fragmentation of the voluntary sector itself, along with its natural suspicions of local government infringements upon its freedom of action and independence.

PARTNERSHIPS IN ADOPTION

An illustrative case of the limitations of the concept of partnership in practice is the relationship between local authority social services departments and the voluntary adoption societies. Adoption services are old and established and highly professionalised, more particularly among voluntary organisations whose services for children preceded the entry of statutory authorities into this area and continued to operate in parallel to them. There is a long tradition of reciprocity at least in operational terms between the two sectors, with voluntary agencies often providing services for local authorities which lacked their own, and being paid at least part of the cost from public funds. Such relations have not characteristically been close and harmonious, nor have local authorities universally acknowledged any explicit form of partnership. This has been true in children's services generally, but especially so in the field of adoption. Referring to local authority and voluntary adoption services after the 1958 Adoption Act, Stone writes, 'Consultation between them was comparatively rare and there can have been few instances of joint planning. In some cases, it must be feared, the voluntary and statutory services viewed each other with suspicion and saw themselves as being in competition as to who could provide the better or more extensive or more considerate services.'[3] These attitudes began to change with the changing ideas that flowed from research studies and writings in recent years, and with a growing self-scrutiny and adaptation by voluntary organisations. The concept of a partnership between the two sectors was given legislative force in the requirement of the 1975 Children Act that local authorities be responsible for the provision of a comprehensive statutory adoption service either directly or indirectly through the agency of approved voluntary bodies.

The 1975 Act had two important objectives – that adoption should be integrated with other services for families and children, and that the statutory adoption service should be provided as 'a planned partnership between statutory and voluntary authorities'. In an anticipatory memorandum in 1979,[4] the DHSS expressed concern about the unevenness stemming from low levels of collaboration between the two sectors, and the under-use by statutory authorities of the adoption societies' services. It stressed that coordination of the activities of different agencies is of the utmost importance where children are concerned. Some preliminary initiatives had been taken in this respect in the voluntary sector, in the setting up of the Adoption Resource Exchange (later to become part of the British Association for Adoption and Fostering) where a number of local authorities and voluntary agencies work together 'on a basis of equal partnership, working to agreed standards and accepting each other's casework, recording and decisions'.[5] Additionally, some voluntary bodies anticipated the implementation of the Act by taking the initiative in joint planning with local authorities. The DHSS memorandum envisaged a substantial role for approved voluntary adoption agencies in the provision of a comprehensive service. It was expected that they would specialise with particular groups, such as parents and children from certain religious or ethnic backgrounds; that they would offer specialist services such as counselling, and that they would test out new practices in the adoption process. The memorandum recommended the institution of procedures to facilitate the joint planning process necessary for a comprehensive service, and urged local authorities to make realistic financial provision for the substantial role to be played by voluntary organisations. It was hoped that joint planning would pave the way for inter-agency cooperation and joint action in a number of areas such as home-finding for children with special needs, coordination of recruitment and selection policies, participation in resource-exchanges, formal arrangements for responsibility in inter-agency placement work, pooling of residential facilities, provision of specialist services and training resources, as well as arrangements for cross-representation on case committees.

Many of these recommendations reflected the best of existing practice in those areas where a productive statutory–voluntary partnership had already been worked out. In advocating their extension and replication nationally, the DHSS was aiming to compensate for the poor relations which had existed historically, and to design a close-knit partnership, based on statute, which was perhaps unique in the field of personal social services. The full implementation of the Act was delayed for some time, however, leading to great uncertainty among voluntary agencies, a number of which have gone out of existence in recent years. Section four of the Act, requiring voluntary adoption agencies to be approved by local authorities, came into force in 1982. Whether the centrally mandated partnership between them will come to fruition in the very full and collaborative sense intended, to remove decades of mutual distrust, remains to be seen.

Even though the ingredients of partnership spelled out by the DHSS have remained at the level of intention rather than achievement nationally, they do contain a number of interesting acknowledgements. Viewed in terms of our general interest in the kinds of relationship that exist or might exist between the two sectors, here we see an explicit recognition that voluntary organisations have a special expertise and experience in a certain area, adoption. Their separate contribution is considered one that not only should be encouraged, but integrated within a comprehensive whole alongside a more mainstream set of services supplied by the statutory authorities. The overall coverage responsibility, authority and resources of the latter appear as the necessary counterpoint to those features of the voluntary sector which would make a coordinated and complete service based upon it difficult or perhaps impossible. The integration desired for the voluntary agencies is not just as a specialist delivery system filling in gaps but as a participant in joint planning and decision-making. The balancing out of positives and negatives in the ideal partnership sketched in by this DHSS memorandum may prove a useful model. We should note, however, that it applies to that part of the voluntary sector which is organised formally and reliant on professionals, where a tradition of expertise has been developed, and where financial support is already derived substantially from the public sector but is augmented by private giving in a cause where public sympathies are easily tapped.

PATCH SYSTEMS AND A WIDER PARTNERSHIP

A further example of the development of a partnership in an operational sense, where the different systems work closely together in the provision of local social services, is the patch system. This involves the deconcentration of local authority social services from their large area offices to smaller administrative areas and even neighbourhoods. It is a form of decentralisation that has attracted interest at central government level particularly for its potential blending of the statutory and voluntary services with informal care networks. The necessity of interlocking these care systems at local level had been stressed in the Seebohm Report where its authors wrote: 'We are not suggesting that "welfare through community" is an alternative to the social services, but that it is complementary and inextricably interwoven.'[6] Similarly, as we noted earlier, the Wolfenden Committee acknowledged the importance of the informal system, observed that its relationship with the statutory and voluntary systems of social care is largely haphazard, and recommended 'more systematic evaluations of these inter-relationships' and the development of policies 'which more consistently and deliberately support the informal system'.[7]

Patch systems became fashionable in the late 1970s, at a time when the political and economic climate was changing towards greater emphasis on limiting public expenditure and on expanding self-help. This coincided with a trend among social planners and theorists that stressed a 'small is beautiful' philosophy in reaction against some of the large-scale reorganisations of the earlier part of the decade. In *Going Local*,[8] Roger Hadley and Morag McGrath collect accounts of seven patch schemes which show a good deal of internal variation but also share an orientation to a small geographical patch. They were aimed at establishing links between local statutory and voluntary organisations, at recruiting volunteers to community care, and to trying 'to interweave the team's service with other systems of care on the patch, formal and informal'.[9]

The patch systems documented here and elsewhere are a conscious attempt by the statutory authorities who have initiated them to formalise a working partnership with the other forms of care. There is little suggestion that real or significant control over policy or overall social service budgets has shifted in the process from the statutory authorities to their patch-based voluntary and informal sector partners. The patch systems were taken up with some enthusiasm in the DHSS, and ministerial blessing was given to the launch of *Going Local* as part of the ministry's encouragement of 'the importance of the voluntary sector, the role of the family, of friends and of neighbours, and of partnerships between social service departments and these informal caring networks'.[10]

INTERMEDIARY VOLUNTARY BODIES AT LOCAL LEVEL

One of the key recommendations of the Wolfenden Report concerned the committee's hope that the voluntary sector would in future work in a close and more equal partnership than hitherto with the statutory authorities carrying the major responsibility for social services. The report ended with an appeal to government 'as the central strategic makers of social policy' to 'take urgently the initiative in working out, with the variety of agencies which are now operating in this field, a collaborative social plan which will make the optimum and maximum use of resources'.[11] We have already noted a range of hopeful collaborative developments at local level encouraged by central government departments in certain fields of activity and specialist areas. In terms of the comprehensive and general responsibility for social services that exists at the level of the local authority, Wolfenden placed great faith in the partnership possibilities of a key multi-purpose voluntary agency, the 'intermediary body'. This body, typically on the model of existing rural community councils (RCCs) and councils of voluntary service (CVSs), was seen to be ideally placed to encourage local authorities to make policies including and promoting voluntary sector input, and to coordinate and develop voluntary organisations so that a more equal partnership might exist between the two sectors. As we noted earlier, Wolfenden recommended that these local umbrella bodies should receive much of their finance from central government so that they would feel more secure and retain more independence of local government.

In a sense, the Wolfenden Committee had to come up with a major development which would resemble some kind of tangible programme and show results emanating from its deliberations, in the same way that governments have to find symbolic initiatives to sustain an image. The notion of the intermediary body as a catalyst for pluralist developments was fairly predictable, given the already existing prototypes, but it remained for the post-Wolfenden era to ascertain their potential for the developmental, supportive and representative roles projected for them. Little response was forthcoming from government to the suggestion that it find new money for these functions. Some VSU money was made available to the NCVO to employ a few additional staff to promote the development of the CVSs. The NCVO itself raised a small sum of money to 'develop a cooperative partnership with local authorities', and promoted the idea of local development and resource agencies for voluntary bodies in each local authority area. It made specific plea for central matching grants for this purpose (some £5.5 million in 1983) in its 'Agenda for Action', a twelve-point programme for government, prior to the June 1983 general election. The final exhortation on this agenda was addressed to government 'to encourage partnership between local authorities and voluntary organisations'.

If the role of the voluntary sector was going to expand in the way Wolfenden hoped, and if there was going to be meaningful voluntary sector participation in local authority planning of social services and policy-making, the local intermediate body was a logical target for development. Only a single, multi-purpose body, which could draw together the many disparate and specialist interests of local voluntary agencies and represent their views, could hope to make an authoritative and sizeable impact upon statutory policy-making. It would also have to possess the expertise and resources for that participation to be meaningful.

Statutory–voluntary collaboration

A further initiative which sprang from the Wolfenden vision of local intermediary bodies performing a range of functions in relation to both the voluntary and the statutory sectors, was a research enquiry mounted by the NCVO and funded by the Leverhulme Trust.[12] This was a feasibility study of a small number of CVSs and RCCs in different parts of the country. The study specifically took as its terms of reference the two major premises of the Wolfenden Committee's 'scenario' of voluntary–statutory relationships. These were 'the need to decrease statutory dominance and a corresponding development of a pluralist approach'. Although Wolfenden spoke of a collaborative social plan only in general terms and in relation to central government, the Leverhulme study's starting-point was the notion of a *local* statutory–voluntary collaboration in planning. Its object was 'to examine the extent to which intermediary bodies participate in the planning of services at local level; and, second, to produce guidelines on voluntary sector participation of use throughout the country'.[13]

The Leverhulme study's profile of this type of intermediary body reflects a useful picture of the variability of the voluntary sector in general. The thirty-six RCCs were, in 1980, partly funded by the Development Commission, partly from local authority and voluntary resources, and had, on the whole, a more substantial income than the CVSs. They were occupied in rural development work; each employed at least one full-time paid officer, and most had between four and eight paid staff. The CVSs, on the other hand, of which there are some 200, were more likely to be dependent upon voluntary or part-time staff, with only 60 per cent having a full-time general secretary. Having to patch together an income from diverse sources such as the local authorities, the Urban Aid Programme, MSC grants or DHSS student training programmes, as well as from a host of voluntary sources, the CVSs have a much less secure financial base that the RCCs, with over half of them operating on total budgets that amount to no more than one or two full-time salaries. Dependence upon statutory funding was a major feature, the research sample showing a range from 12 per cent of total income from statutory sources to 97 per cent.

The picture that emerges of this intermediary body is that of a multi-purpose agency which is loosely constructed and internally fragmented, holding together in a non-representative capacity a variety of bodies which have their own separate activities and constituencies, as well as their own separate lines of communication with statutory authorities. Its own activities do not exhibit any internal consistency necessarily, nor is there an easily discernible orientation to the range of intermediary functions listed by Wolfenden. Its financial dependence upon statutory sources and the insecurity of its funds is seen by the researchers to contribute to an essential conservatism and to consensus politics. This has the effect of minimising its role as a critic, of inhibiting development and of discouraging involvement with new or radical forms of voluntary action. Most of the bodies are too small and under-resourced to do much about organising the voluntary sector or collaborating with the statutory sector in planning and policy-making. The study comments, 'The notion of a pluralist planning partnership between the statutory and voluntary sectors is not one which guides present practice, nor is it yet accepted as the vision which will guide future practice.'[14] The researchers suggest further reasons for this apparent failure to realise a closer partnership in this regard. Among them are, 'lack of clarity in both sectors concerning the proper role of the voluntary sector within the context of a (statutorily controlled) welfare state, lack of commitment on both sides to the pluralist vision, local statutory defensiveness, lack of consistent central government policy'.[15]

Although the Leverhulme study produced a pessimistic picture of current practice among the intermediary CVSs and RCCs in the functions identified by Wolfenden as development, servicing, co-ordination and representation, the authors did not feel that this invalidated the original Wolfenden vision of a more pluralistic welfare state with the intermediary body playing a central role. They make a number of recommendations for change, advocating in the first place the systematic alteration of central government policy towards the promotion of statutory–voluntary partnerships by means of legislative and financial inducements. This, they felt, would need to be paralleled by a change in attitude on the part of local authorities towards a greater commitment to a genuine partnership, as well as a change in heart among both national and local intermediary bodies. At local level, voluntary agencies would need to be educated in participation in the policy process and to acquire 'the capacity for informed policy input'. The local intermediary body would facilitate such changes. This kind of transformation is seen by the authors as being necessarily founded on the availability of central government funding.

Government response

Both the Leverhulme and the Wolfenden reports advocated the promotion of a mixed economy of welfare where voluntary enterprise would advance and statutory involvement decrease to the point where a more 'pluralist' partnership might evolve. This could only happen, it was felt, through an injection of new resources from central government so that voluntary agencies' freedom and flexibility should be preserved, especially in relation to local government. There are a number of issues for scrutiny here, not least the assumption that the promotion of voluntarism is a government responsibility and that it is both logical and feasible for central government to assume the task of extending local democracy and participation. The expectation of new funds also runs counter to a major strand of government thinking in recent years, that voluntary services are a substitute for public expenditure, not just a different delivery system using public funds. For the present, however, let us consider the actual response of government to the ideas concerning intermediary bodies contained in the two enquiries.

The Wolfenden Report influenced the prevailing climate of opinion towards the voluntary sector and its partnership with the statutory sector, but it had little greater impact in concrete terms. Beyond the unprecedented consultative exercise in relation to the report, carried on from its predecessor, the post-1979 government was in the difficult position of needing some earnest sign of its support for the voluntary sector without compromising its ideological position with regard to limiting public expenditure. Accordingly, the Voluntary Services Unit, in line with its role as flag-bearer heralding official enthusiasm for voluntarism, set up a number of small initiatives. The first were half a dozen tiny pilot projects, explicitly linked to one of the four intermediary functions identified by Wolfenden – that of development – and which represented government's only response to that committee's call for statutorily funded intermediary bodies and functions. The other initiatives were a very small grants programme to stimulate self-help in six areas, and the funding of two local charity reviews to explore alternative methods of charitable funding such as community chests and the rationalisation of charitable trusts. Described as 'a particularly limp Home Office initiative',[16] this collection of schemes met with some fierce criticism, mostly focused on the miniscule amounts of money involved, 'the ambiguity of political motivation'[17] and their being 'little more than a token response to the scale of need'.[18]

THE BARCLAY REPORT AND LOCAL PARTNERSHIP

Having reviewed some aspects of local voluntary–statutory relationships, what conclusions can we reach? First of all, we must accept the evidence of the Wolfenden enquiry and the Leverhulme study that generally the notion of a formal and conscious partnership between local authorities and voluntary organisations is still a fiction. Even where the services they provide are closely related, or where individuals from the different care systems actually work together, as in the spreading number of patch schemes, there is little sign as yet of voluntary agencies emerging as full participants in planning and policy-making and so gaining equality of status with their local authority 'partners'. The intermediary bodies, viewed by Wolfenden as ideally placed, once upgraded and financed, for such collaboration in the making of comprehensive plans, were found by Leverhulme to operate at a level far removed from this aspiration. The finance necessary for this enhancement of their role has not been forthcoming from central government as both reports proposed, and it is unlikely that it will be provided by local authorities except in some exceptional cases.

What does emerge from this review is a gathering body of opinion that supports this understanding of partnership, at least as an ideal to be striven for. Indeed it is for the local level of the direct provision of services, where, as we have seen, such involvement is at its weakest, that prescriptions concerning the voluntary sector's role are being most clearly worked out. We noted that legislative force has been given to the inclusion of the voluntary sector in the committees responsible for joint care projects, and that prescriptions for statutory–voluntary partnership in adoption services await full legislative enactment. It is possible to distil from the growing number of prescriptions, certain key elements for a collaborative local statutory-voluntary partnership. These include the recognition, primarily by statutory authorities, but also by voluntary organisations, of the total environment of service provision and activity in which each contributes a part. Following this comes acknowledgement of the value of coordinating the activities of each sector through review and forward planning jointly operated by representatives of both, so as to make the best use of resources and meet need most effectively. All these elements are contained in the appraisal of social work and the voluntary sector conducted by the Barclay Committee enquiry entitled *Social Workers: Their Role and Tasks*.[19]

The Barclay Report was widely expected, in its own words, 'to endorse a view that statutory provision should be cut back and the work done in the voluntary sector expanded'. It did not fulfil this expectation but instead placed a heavy emphasis on the potential complementarity of the two sectors. 'We do not feel there is any "proper" proportional division of work between the two sectors, but it has become clear to us that the two sectors need each other if any comprehensive social caring is to be developed or maintained.'[20] Their review of criticisms of the functioning of both sectors led the committee to the conclusion 'that the characteristic deficiencies of one sector could to a considerable extent be compensated by the characteristic strengths of the other – but only if each sees the other as a complementary service, and if both work together to plan a partnership which is mutually reinforcing'.[21] It was fully in accord with the

Barclay Report's orientation to what it termed 'community social work' where personal social services should develop a much closer partnership with the informal networks of local citizens and their existing coping mechanisms, that it should also view as essential the establishment of close links with voluntary organisations. The report is careful to distinguish between voluntary agencies and informal care networks and to stress the importance of the whole spectrum of care.

In assessing the nature of the partnership between the two sectors, the report finds that 'The voluntary sector is potentially an equal partner with the statutory in the planning and provision of services.'[22] The committee shares the view taken by Wolfenden and other reports of the current state of the relationship between local authorities and voluntary organisations: 'in our view, the relationship to date between the two sectors could seldom be described as a genuine partnership. It sometimes resembles rather that between statutory master and voluntary servant.'[23] For a genuine partnership to be established, a philosophical revolution would be required of local authorities accustomed to making their own internal plans and decisions before involving voluntary agencies and hidebound by a restrictive understanding of the mandate of public authority and the limitations of public accountability. A similar change in thinking is called for from the voluntary sector, although Barclay's main focus seems to concentrate on the statutory sector's responsibility for widening out the concept and practice of social responsibility. This preoccupation is logical, given the statutory social services department's central responsibilities and control over resources. Barclay criticises these departments for sometimes keeping tasks and roles to themselves, to the detriment of voluntary agencies and possibly to the detriment of client groups involved. The report urges a total approach to local services in which 'a rationale for the distribution of roles and tasks is essential'.

Barclay saw a future for partnership between the two sectors if certain measures are taken. It places greatest stress on the necessity of joint planning and joint analysis of needs, although this point is then somewhat weakened by a recommendation for consultative and collaborative machinery 'which will allow decision making to be at the very least fully informed by (and consideration given to how it might in some circumstances be shared by) not only formal voluntary organisations but also local self-help groups and other parts of the caring networks'.[24] There is surely a crucial difference between voluntary agencies submitting their views, and being actively involved as partners in the statutory decision-making process. Ancillary suggestions made by Barclay include the clarification by local authorities of their grant-making processes, the mutual secondment of staff, joint research, common training programmes, etc. and the use of written agreements or even contracts, possibly on the United States model of 'purchase of service contracting' to make explicit the nature and terms of the partnerships entered into between voluntary bodies and local authorities [docs. 14 and 15].

The Barclay Report did not have a great deal to say on the voluntary sector as such. We have already noted that it has made what may be regarded as two major contributions to thinking in this field. The first is that it did not accept the philosophy prevailing in government circles at the time regarding the desirability of substitution of statutory services by voluntary, and maintained its own independent line on community social work. Its second positive contribution was its view of the essential worth and efficacy of the voluntary sector in the context of a total system of provision where the latter's good and bad points might articulate with those of the statutory sector in a genuine collaborative partnership. On the negative side, it might be suggested that while Barclay gave some attention to the thorny issues of accountability and the equitable distribution of resources – both major impediments to the integrating of voluntary services with those of the public sector – it failed to develop or resolve them satisfactorily. Of the even more serious obstacle of the resource starvation and insecurity of the voluntary sector *vis-à-vis* the public sector, it made no mention at all. Lastly, beyond drawing clear distinctions between four categories of social care – informal carers, mutual aid groups, volunteers and formal voluntary organisations – Barclay did not question the nature of the relationship of the formal voluntary sector to the rest of its categories. In arguing from its concern with involving the 'community' of ordinary citizens in social service to the notion of partnership between voluntary agencies and the statutory sector, it assumes an identity between voluntary organisations and groups and the wider 'community' which ought not to be taken for granted. Voluntary organisations, mutual aid groups, etc. may frequently constitute 'the only significant public'[25] on certain issues, or the only easily identifiable sources of non-statutory activity and opinion which a local authority can plan with, but the nature of their relationship with the wider public, their representativeness and their accountability all require questioning at depth when they are being viewed as partners in public processes on the ground that they are the 'community's' voice.

CONCLUSION

The understanding of 'partnership' as a collaborative relationship between local authorities and local voluntary organisations through which each carries a joint responsibility for planning, policy-making and implementation as part of a whole, and where voluntary agencies enjoy parity of status and influence, is one that exists more in theory than in reality. The reality is that in most areas, with a few exceptions, the two sectors operate as if they were entirely separate. The responsibility for this divide lies mainly with statutory authorities, for it is they who have the task of planning and providing comprehensive service provision and meeting the needs of their localities. The question might be asked at this juncture – why is it important that the voluntary sector should be admitted into a genuine partnership with local authorities? We know that although voluntary organisations make a significant, if variable, contribution to social care, they are in fact marginal to the functioning of the average social services department. It is not surprising that they do not have a more major role in decision-making. This answer would have proved perfectly satisfactory some years ago, but no longer suffices in the changed ideolocal and economic climate of today.

We have already remarked on the way relationships in practice tend to lag behind the theoretical ideals on which the prescription of collaborative partnership is based. The expansion of the voluntary sector is also the awaited product of the changing ideas of politicians, social policy writers, officials, the personnel of voluntary organisations themselves. To some extent, as we have seen in Chapters 4 and 5, there *had* been an expansion in voluntary sector support and activity. Their statutorily provided finances have grown and voluntary organisations have been incorporated into one government programme after another. It cannot be said, however, that they have yet attained the kind of weight and status, roughly comparable to that of the statutory providers of mainstream social services, which would entitle them to be accepted as full participants in social planning processes. That there exists a growing body of opinion which believes that their role *should* expand to take on a much more significant and extensive part of the provisions of the welfare state, is the reason why the concept of statutory–voluntary sector partnership has been developed ahead of the reality it prescribes. The following chapters examine this changing pattern of thought and the values underlying it in the writings of politicians from recent governments. The terms of debate on the role of the voluntary sector have fundamentally changed with changes in the fortunes of the economy and with the related

swings in political opinion which have ushered in successive governments dedicated to rolling back the frontiers of the state and redis-
covering the nineteenth-century values of mutual aid and philanthropy.

NOTES AND REFERENCES

1. DEPARTMENT OF HEALTH AND SOCIAL SECURITY, *Health Service
   Developments, Care in the Community and Joint Finance*, HC(83)6.
2. WOLFENDEN COMMITTEE, *The Future of Voluntary Organisations*.
   Croom Helm: London, 1978, p. 85.
3. STONE, M., 'The changing role of voluntary agencies in
   adoption', *NCVO Briefing*, March 1982.
4. DEPARTMENT OF HEALTH AND SOCIAL SECURITY, *The Statutory
   Adoption Service, A Memorandum of Guidance* (Draft circular,
   April 1979).
5. STONE, op. cit.
6. DEPARTMENT OF HEALTH AND SOCIAL SECURITY, *Report of the
   Committee on Local Authority and Allied Personal Social Services*.
   HMSO: London 1969, para. 483.
7. WOLFENDEN COMMITTEE, op. cit., p. 23.
8. HADLEY, R. and MCGRATH, M., *Going Local: Neighbourhood Social
   Services*. NCVO Occasional Paper. Bedford Square Press:
   London, 1980.
9. Ibid., p. 13.
10. JENKIN, P., DHSS Press Release, 10 Feb. 1981.
11. WOLFENDEN COMMITTEE, op. cit., p. 193.
12. LEAT, D., SMOLKA, G. and UNELL, J., *Voluntary and Statutory
    Collaboration: Rhetoric or Reality*. Bedford Square Press:
    London, 1981.
13. Ibid., p. 21.
14. Ibid., p. 151.
15. Ibid.
16. WESTLAND, P., 'The year of the voluntary organisation', *Com-
    munity Care*, 19 Nov. 1981, pp. 14–15.
17. *Social Work Today*, 3 Feb. 1981, p. 1.
18. Ibid.
19. BARCLAY COMMITTEE, *Social Workers: Their Role and Tasks*.
    Bedford Square Press: London, 1982.
20. Ibid., p. 84.
21. Ibid., p. 85.
22. Ibid.

23. Ibid.
24. Ibid., p. 90.
25. WILLIAMS, G., *Inner City Policy: A Partnership with the Voluntary Sector?* NCVO Occasional Paper. Bedford Square Press: London, 1983, p. 9.

Part Four

NEW THINKING ON THE VOLUNTARY SECTOR

Chapter Seven

GOVERNMENT THINKING ON THE VOLUNTARY SECTOR

The preceding chapters offer abundant evidence of the actions of governments in promoting the voluntary sector and in harnessing voluntary social action to public social service programmes. This renewal of official interest in voluntarism and the desire to shift the balance of responsibilities in the welfare state has been demonstrated by both Labour and Conservative administrations – although in different degrees, as this chapter will show, as it traces the convergence of Labour and Conservative thought and the enthusiasms and ambivalences of post-1979 government policies.

Before considering the positions of the main political parties in relation to voluntary social action, let us take a look at what amounts to a more or less common departure point for all recent administrations. Firstly, the context of social policies has changed – in the setting of political limits to the development and financing of state-based social services by the slow-down or cessation of economic growth. Secondly, there has been a growing disenchantment, fostered by social policy writers among others, with the achievements and performance of the welfare state.

The post-war Butskellite consensus on the expansion of the welfare state was predicated on the continuation of economic growth. Public expenditure, and within it social spending, had been expanding at a faster rate than the Gross National Product for some years before the effects of recession began to bite from 1974 onwards. Walker[1] cites a number of factors which have had a cumulative impact on public support for higher public expenditure – the long-term underlying decline of Britain's manufacturing output, combined with the inflationary spiral caused by the energy crisis, the shifting downwards of the burden of taxation, with a consequent rise in public resistance to it, and the escalation of the public sector borrowing requirement. All these factors precipitated financial constraint just at a time when need and demand for the social services was both changing and increasing. Walker sees this erosion of public confidence as the visible expression of tensions which had always been implicit and disguised in the context of economic growth, expressing an underlying 'bias against the public sector and the predominance of narrow economic values over social values'.[2] In other words, the welfare state had been 'the residual beneficiary of the Growth State'[3] where the political will for redistributive social expenditure and the taxation required to finance it, depended upon the felt increase in personal consumption made possible by economic growth. The economic crisis that has put paid to growth has transformed the ideological climate and may lead to the possible restructuring of the welfare state 'by adapting policies to secure more efficient reproduction of the labour force, by shifting emphasis to the social control of destabilising groups in society, by raising productivity within the social services and possibly by reprivatising parts of the welfare state'.[4]

The retrenchments in social expenditure which have been the product of the interaction of economic and political change could not help but precipitate a redefinition of the taken-for-granted role of the state in providing social services. This 'demythologising' of what Margaret Thatcher has called 'the nanny state' has been further compounded by criticisms which have gained force in recent years among the supporters of a positive welfare state who have pointed to its failure to promote egalitarianism. Numerous social policy writers[5] testify to the welfare state's compromises with individualist and market ethics and its failure radically to alter the life-chances of deprived groups in society. From the Right, underpinning the economic arguments, has come the accusation that the welfare state is over-collectivised and has diminished the vital freedoms and choices of individuals – an ideological viewpoint shared by the welfare pluralists who are the subject of Chapter 8. From this battery of criticism has arisen the trend, with all its varying ideological shades, towards a 'reappraisal of the role of the state in social welfare'[6] and the consequent redefinition of the roles of other, non-statutory alternatives.

It was noted above that recent years have seen an element of convergence between Labour and Conservative parties in their support for the voluntary sector as a co-provider of social services. This is not as remarkable a phenomenon as it might at first appear. The parties' ideological positions with regard to social policies *are* different – Labour administrations, as we saw in Chapter 3, have always leaned towards a monopoly role for the state in both financing and delivering social services, while Conservative governments have leaned the opposite way. On specific issues, these differences have represented more than party rhetoric and have emerged in doctrinal clashes over such matters as comprehensive schooling, old age pensions or pay-beds in the health service. Yet, for the most part, in practice, such sharp ideological divisions have been fairly imperceptible and there has been a great deal of common ground. Neither party, when in power, has set out to dismantle entirely the programmes and practices bearing the stamp of its predecessor. The history of the welfare state has, at least until 1979, shown that Labour governments have not been socialist and Conservative governments have not been totally market and private sector oriented. Each, with exceptions like those mentioned, have opted for the middle way in practice. Labour has not fundamentally altered patterns of inequality and deprivation, nor have Conservatives yet actively destroyed the collectivised services developed since the war.

Setting these considerations in the context of government policies towards the voluntary sector, we may note that ministers in both Labour and Conservative administrations over the past decade have exhibited a degree of convergence in their support for the voluntary sector. Both parties have, since the late 1970s, endeavoured to cut expenditure on the social services, and it is arguable that the post-1979 Thatcher government only fulfilled, in some of its policies, the intentions already mapped out by its Labour predecessor. As a corollary to social expenditure cuts made or attempted, and as a gesture to mollify adverse public opinion, both parties sought to make a virtue out of necessity in presenting a glowing case for the superior advantages of voluntary action of all kinds. The growing political interest in the potential of voluntary social services may be directly linked to the desire to make economies in the public sector. Any searching examination of successive policy statements in recent years finds abundant evidence for this link, but it does not explain the whole story. In the rediscovery by politicians of the virtues of the voluntary sector, one may also detect, besides a preoccupation with the expenditure consequences of recession, the adoption and strengthening of distinct ideological positions. Labour ministers, particularly those with responsibilities for social services, shifted towards accepting that the voluntary sector could and should play a valuable complementary role alongside the main-line statutory services, and here they became virtually indistinguishable from the left of the Conservative Party. It is probably fair to say that economies in social expenditure remained the uppermost consideration and that this ideological shift for Labour contained a large dose of pragmatism. Nevertheless, the party had moved in the direction of 'welfare pluralism' both practically and rhetorically by the time the Thatcher government came to power to pursue a rather more drastic reappraisal of the role of the state.

LABOUR POLICIES FOR THE VOLUNTARY SECTOR

We saw earlier that Richard Crossman, after his experience as Secretary of State for Social Services, was to recant from his earlier hostility to voluntary social services. His change of heart may be taken to some extent as the articulation of a wider evolution of opinion within the Labour Party, especially as nationalisation receded as a party objective and as the populist Left became more involved in pressures for participation and power sharing in the late 1960s. The Wilson and Callaghan governments were to develop an enthusiasm for the voluntary sector which, although lacking the doctrinal weight and more central position of voluntarist policies in the Conservative Party, did mean that voluntary organisations continued to receive government funds under Labour. The traditional Labour antipathy to voluntary organisations continued to be much more evident in Labour administrations at the local level. It was a Labour government which had set up the Urban Programme and the Community Development Projects in which voluntary organisations and activities had played a significant part. In 1975, Lord Harris, newly responsible for the VSU, declared government policy towards the voluntary sector to be one of supporting 'participation for volunteers . . . the single most important resource available to the voluntary services – people'.[7] By this time pressures on public expenditure had begun to bite, and Harris urged 'local authorities, central government and other sources of public funds to consider very carefully indeed before deciding to cut the grants they make to voluntary bodies. If they look at the return they can expect from them and compare it with the return from a similar expenditure on their own services, they may find a case for supporting the voluntary body.'[8]

In a House of Commons debate on the financial problems of voluntary organisations faced with inflation, in July 1975, the then Secretary of State for Social Services, David Owen, stated:

> The partnership between voluntary organisations and statutory bodies has been one of the most encouraging developments of recent years. Previously there were suspicions that money given to voluntary efforts could always be better spent by being put into statutory efforts. There has now been a marked change in opinion and an increased willingness to work with voluntary people, particularly those who will accept obligations.[9]

Later in the same debate, the Labour Party's conversion was exemplified in the declaration by a back-bencher of a radical change in his views of ten years before 'that the role of voluntary organisations was somewhat superfluous in a properly organised society' and that 'the government and local authorities should be taking on the great majority of the responsibilities fulfilled by voluntary organisations.'[10] It is perhaps no coincidence that both these speakers were later to switch more completely to a vision of a decentralised society based on voluntary and small group participation, and transfer their allegiances to the Social Democratic Party.

The changing balance of opinion within the Labour Party was very closely associated, not with a vision of a decentralised, participative society, but with questions of expenditure rationing. David Ennals, in launching the Good Neighbour Scheme in 1976, described the use of voluntary effort as 'pound for pound a better buy'. James Callaghan, drawing on Wolfenden's research findings in 1978, declared 'There will always be competition for government funds. But there is an almost inexhaustible supply of good neighbourliness, of good-hearted people waiting to help . . . a recent estimate of the scale of voluntary help is that about five million people per annum undertake some form of volunteer work and probably do as much in terms of manpower as all the paid staff in Local Authority social services departments put together.'[11] This questionable use of the Wolfenden evidence is of course subject to the same reservations that are applied to Patrick Jenkin's use of the same material some time later (see Ch. 4).

The changing nature of Labour's attitudes to voluntarism in the provision of social services can be detected in a succession of policy statements of the mid to late 1970s. The passages selected above also reveal basic conceptual and terminological confusions which are very common and which serve to blur the issues under discussion and, at times, risk the charge of wilful mystification. Politicians of all colours tend to use terms such as 'volunteer', 'good-hearted people', 'good neighbours', 'voluntary effort' and 'voluntary organisations' virtually interchangeably as if they all mean the same thing. Informal care is often indistinguishable from formally organised provisions, the altruistic amateur donor of services blurs with the paid voluntary agency professional. Put in the context of social expenditure and the desire for economies and substitutions, this apparently unlimited reservoir of labour power is taken to be relatively costless or assumed to be more cost-effective than statutory services without any more penetrating questions ever being asked. It is also assumed that volunteers and social service department employees are engaged in the same kind of activities.

Labour's discovery of altruism as a praiseworthy source of voluntary action in providing social services represents a real turnabout in Labour's ideas. The party's traditional hostility to voluntarism has been described by Worpole[12] as leading to 'popular assumptions of the irreconcilability of socialism with individual initiatives and disinterested generosity'. This hostility has led in the past to accusations of social services 'on the cheap'. Worpole observes: 'The voluntary sector has been accused of being amateur, inefficient, patronising and a way of continuing antagonistic class relationships in slightly more disguised forms. The trade union argument strongly adds to these objections the way in which all forms of voluntary labour prevent the creation or continuation of paid jobs.' He suggests that changes in the composition of the voluntary sector have rendered these arguments out of date, and that voluntary activity could now perhaps be seen as the pursuit of the objectives of socialism by other means by working-class activists who have, like himself, drifted away from the Labour Party. The prevalent image of flag-days and patronage and charity has now, he feels, been replaced by a renewed spirit of direct social action. 'In the proliferation of self-organised community nurseries, disabled mutual aid groups, allotment societies, black supplementary schools, women's aid centres, gay counselling services, tenants' cooperatives, public transport campaigns, community bookshops, cyclists' action groups, lies a very old political tradition.'

Worpole is of course right, although only partly. He is right in suggesting that the self-help and mutual aid and campaigning forms of social action which have sprouted since the late 1960s stand in sharp contrast both to the organised and bureaucratic paternalism of social services and unions defended by Labour, and to the outworn stereotype of a Victorian-type philanthropy. Those populist, grass-roots, alternative forms of social action are manifestly different from the traditional social services, statutory or voluntary, and should not be confused with them. He is wrong, though, to conclude that they have transformed the image of voluntarism or that they have replaced the traditional voluntary organisations on a large scale. One of the lessons of the account in Chapter 5 of the bias of Charity Law is that it is precisely the working-class, grass-roots forms of social action which have to struggle for survival, insecure of public support and subsidy in the form of charitable status which is readily accorded to more established, more middle-class and more acceptable voluntary organisations. He makes a well-founded critique of Labour Party thought, however. While it must be acknowledged that Labour politicians have moved away from an exclusive allegiance to the public sector services, does their new 'welfare pluralist' vocabulary of support for voluntary effort, for self-help and mutual aid, align them with the populism of the grass-roots Left? Are Labour politicians referring to anything more adventurous or challenging than self-help playgroups and crèches, or good neighbour alert schemes for the elderly when they extol the virtues of non-statutory alternatives to dependence upon the hard-pressed public services? Are they pluralists in the sense that they welcome diversity and pluriformity but not to the extent that they are ready to facilitate real participation and devolve power? Whatever the conceptual confusion exhibited at national level, it is at the level of local authority resource allocation that a divide between the populism of the New Left and the mistrusts of the middle of the road and traditional Labour Party is most evident. For all the exceptional enthusiasm for grass-roots participation and social action shown by a Livingstone-led Greater London Council and a few other London boroughs in their wide application of their grant-making powers, there are many Labour local councils where antagonism to all but the safest, most service-oriented types of voluntary action has remained high.

The conceptual confusion demonstrated by politicians begins to matter in a fundamental way only when the rhetoric becomes reality. Whether they are talking about volunteers or the professional activities of voluntary organisations or the haphazard altruism of kin and neighbours, or whether they see these various forms of pluralism in terms of power sharing, does not matter until something actually happens to change the existing system. Were there to be a radical dismantling of the statutory services, these unclarities would be crucial, but the Labour Party does not subscribe to any *substantial* alteration in the balance of responsibilities carried by the statutory and voluntary sectors in the welfare state. It has moved along the continuum of pluralist positions, away from an exclusive reliance on the state, but it has not moved as far as the pluralist thinkers that we are going to examine.

Merlyn Rees, the then Home Secretary, made a clear statement of the Labour Party's perception of the legitimacy of voluntary action, as well as an appeal to its special attributes, when he declared: 'The special role of the voluntary organisations in a democratic society is to complement the statutory services and to adapt and apply them to individual cases; to innovate and experiment; and, in all that is done, to provide an opportunity for self-development and an outlet for that spirit of altruism which is essential to the well being and happiness of society.'[13] He reiterated Labour's commitment to voluntary organisations as 'essential partners of the statutory services' in the government's response to the Wolfenden Report in 1978, making the point that 'Whatever the scale of statutory provision, we cannot do without the extra contribution from the voluntary sector.'[14] There is no shift of allegiance here from Labour's customary support of the central importance of the public sector services, for all that the party had now adopted a more pluralist position.

CONSERVATIVE POLICIES FOR THE VOLUNTARY SECTOR

The 'conversion' of the Labour Party to voluntarism was hailed as a breakthrough for Conservative policies by Patrick Jenkin in his speech to the Party Conference in 1980. He observed:

> for the vast majority of the people of this island, the role of the volunteer in society is honourable and infinitely worth while. Today this vast majority includes most sensible members of the Labour Party. It was not always so. It is not so long since Labour used to talk disparagingly about charity. They saw volunteers as a regrettable necessity, to be tolerated only until the day dawned when hte State could take over. The fact that these alien voices are now stilled means that we have won a crucial political argument.[15]

After 1976, in a climate of retrenchment on social expenditure, speeches by politicians from either party were virtually indistinguishable in their appeal to the qualities of the voluntary sector. Mr Jenkin, opposition spokesperson for the social services, took up as a theme-song the assertion that 'the Welfare State can never be a universal provider of answers to all social problems, nor should it try to be. Instead we must return more responsibility for caring to the people, encouraging local neighbourhoods to help to care for the deprived in their midst.'[16] Conservative Party rhetoric shared the useful imprecisions and ambiguities already noted in Labour politicians' references to the voluntary sector. In Mr Jenkin's early speeches, good neighbours, volunteers and voluntary organisations appear to be the same thing. A policy for the voluntary sector must mean 'bringing the voluntary bodies into a close and continuing partnership with the statutory services so that planning, financing and operations can be undertaken jointly to the great advantage of every one concerned'.[17] Voluntary organisations are an extra, 'not a substitute for state provision'. They tend to consist of collections of volunteers which, however, 'cannot be run on thin air and goodwill alone'. Mr Jenkin therefore urges local councils hard-pressed under Labour policies not to make false economies but to consider the greater cost-effectiveness of voluntary bodies which 'can only achieve their best results if they can look to steady and assured sources of finance'. The theme of partnership between voluntary organisations and local authorities was equally enthusiastically taken up by the Community Affairs Department of the Conservative Central Office in its publication *We are Richer than we Think*[18] which documented useful examples of imaginative partnership around the country and advocated their wider replication, particularly with the aid of local authority financial assistance among other sources of revenue.

Support for charity and philanthropy as a principle of social action has a long history in the Conservative Party. The formation and running of voluntary organisations have been a characteristic response to social need and a badge of social respectability, particularly for underemployed Conservative women. Concern for one's social inferiors, especially the deserving poor, has also a solid pedigree in Tory traditions of paternalistic squirearchies and wealthy businessmen turned philanthropists. The voluntary sector, for this strand of Conservative Party opinion, consists of voluntary organisations – typically the local branch of the WRVS or Red Cross or Help the Aged, its chairman (*sic*) characteristically the wife of someone rather important, influential and titled, and its hierarchical composition a perfect replica of the social order. To this school of thought in the Conservative Party, a reinvigorated policy of voluntary involvement as a means of coping with economic pressures was a welcome injection of new life into an old tradition, one which could be viewed as a humane response to the social needs and problems made worse by the recession, an equivalent in the party armoury of another dominant strategy, privatisation. It was the tradition of *noblesse oblige*, a form of paternalism which found resonances among party spokespersons for the social services both before and after the 1979 election.

That this Tory tradition remains separate and distinct from the hardening of attitudes and the rightwards swing of the dominant wing of the party after the election becomes very clear when this faction's social policies are traced through ministerial statements and speeches from about the end of 1979 onwards. What becomes evident in retrospect is a divergence of thought and sentiment between the adherents of old-school voluntarism in its organised form, and the supporters of non-organised, spontaneous and, by definition, publicly costless kinds of informal care. Not that this division of opinion is always explicit, for the policies were neither coherent nor consistent. The point is made, however, in a number of comment-aries[19] that after a certain period of consolidation, the radical Right began to focus its support for voluntary social action on to informal care, and to move away from support of voluntary *organisations*, which it began to class together with the collective social action represented by the statutory services. Roger Lawrence[20] points out that although the Conservative Party's generalised support for voluntary action may be seen 'superficially at least, as being an area of consensus between the two factions', it is not at all certain that people who thought they were in agreement with this policy were aware of the issues involved. The common vocabulary, with its imprecisions and mystifications, of the two wings of the party, managed to placate the *noblesse oblige* tradition with a positive accent on more voluntary social services, while appeasing the Right with its stress on the reduction of public expenditure. It disguises widely variant underlying meanings, the one recognising the obligation to help the less fortunate through the medium of voluntary organisations, and the other being 'concerned less with voluntary organisations than with reducing the role of the state'.[21]

The new government came to power in 1979 committed to curbing inflation and regenerating the economy through strategies based on the monetarist philosophy of Friedman. A central tenet in this philosophy is the belief that wealth production is stifled by the parasitism of public expenditure on the economy and through the depression of incentives by high levels of taxation in an over-collectivised state. 'What cannot be doubted is the central importance to the whole of the government's economic strategy and its political credibility, of reducing public expenditure. It is that which has changed the political equation.'[22] Integral to the strategy of reducing public expenditure and the taxes which feed it is to cut expenditure on the social services.

Equally important and integral to its economic policies was the radical Right's ideology concerning the role of the state. The doctrine of the minimal state, one restricted to such functions as promoting the conditions for a market economy to prosper, as well as to maintaining law and order and defence, but returning many other responsibilities to individuals and lower-order social institutions, is also central to the philosophies of many thinkers on the right of the Conservative Party. For the welfare state, the latter objective implies policies for reprivat-isation and restructuring according to Gough, who comments: 'It is difficult to avoid the conclusion that the welfare state is attacked by the new conservatism at least as much for ideological as for economic reasons.'[23]

Contained within this ideology is an appeal to values deeply embedded in nineteenth-century traditions of liberal political economy with their heavy emphasis on individual achievement and effort as a measure of social deservingness. Moralistic Tory notions of the family as a primary source of authority and assistance combine with an accent on other forms of decentralised social responsibility, radically to shift the locus of collective obligation away from the state and from central government. Timothy Raison took up a number of these themes in a speech to the Voluntary Movement Group in 1980:

> While the public sector will of necessity continue to play the major role in many areas of service provision – for instance, education and the health service, it must be recognised that there are limits to what the state can and *should* do in meeting the needs of the community. While many of the adjustments in statutory services now being undertaken at national and local level reflect the demands of the present economic situation, what I have said about the limits on the role of the state is not solely born of necessity – it is also fundamental to our philosophy. Just as much as self-reliance and self-confidence are the keys to personal success, so helf-help and mutual assistance are the foundations of family, neighbourhood and community life.[24]

The practical implications of these beliefs were contained in the Conservative Party Manifesto: 'In the community, we must do more to help people to help themselves, and families to look after their own. We must also encourage the voluntary movement and self-help groups working in partnership with the statutory services.'[25] Such a policy fitted well with criticisms of the welfare state and the alienation and dependency fostered by it. It also served to focus attention on the government's enthusiastic subscription to the ethos of community care, giving this form of care a new moral and ideological justification for the 1980s.

The sphere of community care, straddling as it does the responsibilities of the health service and the personal social services, and concerned especially with those client groups where the burden of dependency and the demand for what Parker has termed 'tending'[26] is growing most rapidly and expensively, lends itself to such an emphasis more than other areas. The nature of its clientele, the relative simplicity of the tending services required and the fact that by far the largest contribution to community care is made informally, outside the statutory services, makes market options less feasible and less necessary, than in, say, the fields of health, housing or education. Voluntary social action offers the possibility of privatising this part of the welfare state in a non-market form with the added virtue of promoting an array of traditional Conservative values. It was primarily in the context of community care policies, probably because they have always been so ill-defined and vague,[27] that voluntary social action began to change in the minds of politicians from a concept which emphasised organised and formal substitute care to the more diffuse concept of 'informal care' by kinship and neighbourhood support systems. It has also been extended to take in, it seems, many more of the functions customarily performed by local authority personal social services departments. The 'true welfare state' was now to be recognised among all the unsung and invisible carers, principally within the family, who have always provided the bulk of support for needy and dependent persons. This refinement of focus down to the primary supports of family and locality had always been implicit in the political rhetoric of Convervatives in opposition, more especially in their ready confusion of entirely different terms of concepts and their side-stepping of all that this implied. In government, the party line became much more firmly and explicitly tied to a pre-eminent position for informal care, with a consequent relegation not only for the statutory sector but also for the organised voluntary sector. 'We should recognise that the informal sector lies at the centre with the statutory services and the organised voluntary sector providing back-up, expertise and support.'[28]

Although it was constantly denied that government had any intention of 'dismantling the welfare state' or replacing the statutory services, ministerial speeches from 1980 onwards, continued to reinforce this new perspective on first-line care with Mr Jenkin, Secretary of State for Social Services, perhaps of all his colleagues, placing the heaviest emphasis on informal care: 'the first and most natural source of social care is the family, friends, neighbours and communities taking action to help those most vulnerable'.[29] A natural corollary to this assertion is the role Mr Jenkin subsequently assigns to the public sector – 'In the future the statutory services should not be seen as the main provider of care but rather as a source of encouragement and stimulus to the community's own resources.' This sentiment was reiterated by the Prime Minister in a speech to the WRVS much remarked at the time for its heralding of a clear reversal of the state's social service responsibilities, when she declared: 'I believe that the volunteer movement is at the heart of all our social welfare provision. That the statutory services are the supportive ones under-

pinning where necessary, filling the gaps and helping the helpers.'[30]
The Prime Minister went on to spell out a key role for statutory
services and their professionals as a catalyst where voluntary effort is
lacking, organising the resources of volunteers, self-helpers, etc. to go
where help is needed. She went on to deliver a classic statement of
Conservative ideology in saying: 'we politicians and administrators
must not forget that the state has a limited role' and 'The willingness
of men and women to give service is one of freedom's greatest safe-
guards. It ensures that caring remains free from political control.'

Patrick Jenkin gave a more considered account of what has been
described as 'the new monetarist social policy' in a subsequent
attempt to counter criticisms of government as 'trying to get welfare
on the cheap'.[31] In this he lays down three principles for a strategy for
the personal social services. First, that it is the function of both
statutory and voluntary types of organised social service to assist
people to use informal support networks when they are in need.
Second, in the case of the breakdown or absence of these networks, 'it
should be the role of social services to help to restore or replace them
where necessary'. Third, their task should be one of easing pressures
on those who do the caring, 'supporting the supporters'. Beyond the
first line of family and friends, lie the helping activities of self-help
groups and volunteers. The next line of defence is that of the voluntary agencies. The local authority social services department should,
according to Mr Jenkin, 'seek to meet directly only those needs which
others cannot or will not meet'. It should function 'as a safety net, the
final protection for people for whom there is no other, not as a first
port of call'. This safety net function was to operate over and above the
statutory duties of social service departments.

In the developing momentum of these two major themes – the
designation of a pivotal role in the welfare state for the informal sector
and the relegation of the statutory services to the residual role of
gap-filling, of enabling and of supplementing informal and voluntary
sector services, we find a clear divergence from the line adopted by the
previous Labour government. We also find, as indicated above, an
emerging differentiation between different viewpoints in the Conservative Party, strikingly exemplified by Mr Jenkin in his earlier and
later incarnations. Although a campaign to call for the revival of 'the
caring resources of the community' became a concerted ministerial
strategy in early 1980, it is the utterances of the Prime Minister and of
Mr Jenkin which most clearly articulated a return to the extreme
residual model for the statutory services. This is not to suggest that
there was not a powerfully doctrinaire body of support for such a

model in the inner Cabinet. This has been demonstrated subsequently with the *Guardian* newspaper's revelations of the Family Policy Group's advocacy of policies to return more responsibility for caring for the elderly and dependent to the family, and, more especially, to women, who should be encouraged to return to the home from the labour market.[32] That these extreme positions are not universally shared is apparent from the rather more muted and cautious approaches to voluntary sector involvement among other ministers who have carried social service responsibilities at one time or another, and who have also consistently stressed the importance of the organised voluntary sector in addition to, rather than as a substitute for, public sector social services.

So far, we have identified two broad schools of thought discernible in the policy statements of Conservative politicians before and after they came to power in 1979. In the general rhetoric considered, two areas call for a closer focus. First, the qualities and competences attributed to the various forms of voluntary social action advocated. Second, finance policies towards the voluntary sector and the implications of financial relationships with the public sector. The latter issue brings us back to the financial and other policies in relation to the voluntary sector which have been discussed in earlier chapters, and which provide a measure of comparison between what politicians promise and what they actually do.

Reference to the unique and special attributes of the voluntary sector is made most typically by politicans when they wish to anticipate accusations of looking for caring 'on the cheap', and to demonstrate that theirs are loftier considerations than mere questions of economies and cuts in public expenditure. The composite picture of the volunteer contained in the typical speech-maker's kit is that of one of millions, busily involved in interpersonal, helping and reciprocal contacts with the needy, showing caring in an informal way, in practical, down to earth terms, more firmly rooted in everyday life, where his/her 'self-disciplined and sustained commitment expresses values and feelings different from, and, in some respects, better than, the professional's'. The volunteer is compassionate and understanding, often an innovative visionary, and is 'the crucial manifestation of a pluralistic and caring society', giving service not for reward but from a spirit of altruism, although it must also be recognised that volunteers have legitimate needs to fulfil by means of their helping activities. A view that may be held by professionals that the volunteer 'may seem unreliable, paternalistic, inadequately prepared for the job and lacking the understanding of the complexity of the client's need' is based on too little direct experience of working with the volunteer and on an outmoded stereotype. The politician's stereotype of the volunteer is certainly an over-idealisation, particularly in the light of the empirical data in Chapter 4 which show the volunteer as more likely to be engaged in the indirect, though valuable, functions of fund raising or committee-running then in direct help activities, and not necessarily typically to be found where the need is greatest. This is not to decry the undoubted value of the selfless activities of all kinds of voluntary workers in the welfare state. It is to point up the politician's perception of the volunteer as the ready substitute for the professional or trained worker as an important political fact. This perception forms part of policy-making by generalised exhortation rather than by well-considered and systematic examination of the facts, although this lack of coherence is at times acknowledged, as in Timothy Raison's observation: 'more difficult is the question how these autonomous elements can be channelled into an orderly programme for meeting needs'.[33]

The voluntary organisation is seen to add diversity and choice to society. It can act as an independent competitor, its independence giving it a moral superiority and a neutrality not possessed by the public sector, which is inherently political. It is seen as innovative, pioneering and experimental, ready to take risks and adopt new ideas and practices because its members do not generally have the material investments of employees nor the constraints of trade union rules, because the organisation is non-bureaucratised and flexible, and because its status frees it from the constraints of accountability in the public sector. It is thought to be more cost-effective than the statutory services, and it enhances popular participation in a way that the statutory services do not. The voluntary agency is assumed to be beneficent, enlightened and public spirited. Again, the image of the voluntary agency, idealised as it may be, is a significant factor in the political rhetoric of ministers who wish to transfer the burden of social care and to prepare a climate of opinion in support of this. The stereotype of the voluntary organisation is sympathetic, uncritical and unquestioning, being based on generalisations which are the antithesis of equally generalised, often superficial and unproven critiques of the statutory services. As part of an operational blueprint for institutional change in the welfare state, it is less than adequate, but this does not matter greatly. The details are less important than the overall exhortatory value of the message, which is itself also intimately connected with the equally ideological question of the financing of the expansion of voluntary social services, a subject to which we now turn.

GOVERNMENT SPENDING POLICIES AND THE VOLUNTARY SECTOR

The connection between the search for economies in social spending and the surge of governmental interest in an expanded role for non-statutory social services has already been commented upon in relation to both Labour and Conservative administrations. The Thatcher government's ideological objections to public expenditure were, however, particularly prominent in its references to the potentialities of the voluntary sector, even though its spokespersons consistently denied that it was government's intention to use the voluntary sector as a means of cutting back on social expenditure. One of Mr Jenkin's early addresses to the group of voluntary organisation directors somewhat pretentiously known as 'the Moving Spirits', was to include the statement: 'As the Government sets about the tasks for which it was elected – cutting income tax, cutting public spending and curbing the burgeoning bureaucracies of the public sector, we shall be looking to the voluntary movement to take up more of the running'.[34] In his evidence to the Commons Social Services Committee quoted earlier (Ch. 4) where he justified his intended cuts in local authority expenditure on social services, Mr Jenkin went on to clarify his viewpoint on voluntary sector substitution of care with the words: 'When one is comparing where one can make savings, one protects the Health Service because there is no alternative, whereas in personal social services there is a substantial possibility, and indeed, a probability, of continuing growth in the amount of voluntary care, of neighbourhood care, of self-help.'[35] This stands in clear contrast to the claim a year or so later by a junior DHSS minister, that government's policies on the voluntary sector had been misunderstood, that 'their objective is *not* to save public expenditure nor is there any question of Government seeking a takeover by volunteers of work being done by paid employees'.[36]

The post-1979 government did not so much depart from its opposition stance of urging local authorities to continue their financial support of voluntary organisations as expand upon it. Despite central government attempts to prune local authority spending on the personal social services in total from 1979 onwards, it continued to exhort them to make grants to voluntary services. Minimal as they were, these grants did indeed increase. We have also seen that central government financial support was sustained. Mr Jenkin declared: 'I entirely endorse the general thrust of the Wolfenden Report that voluntary bodies can rightly look to the public sector for a substantial slice of their funding, especially that part necessary to meet their normal day-to-day running costs.'[37] The impact of this endorsement depends on what is meant by 'substantial', for the minister said elsewhere that 'the voluntary sector must look largely to the generosity and charity of individuals for financial support'.[38]

In its public statements and in practice the government maintained its financial commitment to the voluntary sector, but, as we have seen, its total grant allocations came nowhere near realistic levels of support for the enhanced voluntary service input it envisaged. Consequently, a dominant and concurrent theme in its policy statements centred around the potential of private sources of funding. The minister had criticised his predecessors and the Wolfenden Committee for assuming too easily that 'the limits of private giving have been reached and that it is only by increasing Government financial support that the voluntary movement can continue to expand its work . . . As income taxes are reduced, I am sure it must be possible to increase the volume of giving from private sources.'[39] Timothy Raison echoed this in saying: 'I believe that we should hope that the voluntary income should continue to grow. I should be most reluctant to believe that the trend detected by the Wolfenden Committee towards a lower rate of giving was irreversible.'[40]

As we noted in Chapter 4, the Thatcher administration did make some effort to encourage private giving through some fairly minor adjustments in fiscal relief, but it stopped short of the more ambitious tax reliefs desired by voluntary organisations. Additionally, the hoped for reductions in personal taxation did not materialise to be a stimulus to more generous donations to charity. Government optimism about the capacity of the voluntary sector to finance itself, while unrelated to the economic realities as spelled out by Wolfenden and the CAF, served the more limited purpose of reinforcing its public commitment to the disengagement of the state and encouraging the pursuit of self-reliance. It also gave the appearance of being concerned about a viable alternative to public finance. A theme which fitted in with this but also had a validity in its own right was the constantly reiterated exhortation to voluntary organisations to guard against the loss of their freedom of action through too close a relationship with government – 'the cornerstone of the voluntary movement is a large degree of financial independence of the state'.[41] The arguments that fund-raising activities represent a time-consuming diversion from the real work of voluntary organisations could be countered by an appeal to autonomy and independence as essential defining characteristics of the voluntary sector, an argument which has some force. Mr Raison illustrates this point of view when he comments:

> I cannot agree with the view that voluntary organisations should simply

be able to look to the State to give it (*sic*) the means to get on with the job. Such an arrangement would result in a serious dilution of the whole ethos of the voluntary movement. While assistance from national and local government is important, voluntary money and voluntary effort can be the only proper foundations for a vigorous and independent voluntary movement.[42]

His concern to see an increase in charitable giving was not motivated by 'a desire to get public expenditure down' but by a real anxiety to preserve the voluntary sector's essential functions of freedom to act, experiment and innovate and also to campaign. This was threatened by a 'growing corporatism' or absorption by the state, and the voluntary ethos was, he feared, diminishing as the availability of government finance encouraged the professionalisation and unionisation of an increasing number of voluntary organisations.[43]

Putting together what we now know of governmental intentions for the non-statutory sector from ministerial speeches and from its policies in practice, we come up with a number of inconsistencies. Its emphasis on the positive attractions of self-reliance and self-finance was entirely consistent with its ideological preference for individualism. What was perhaps not so consistent with this position was its increased support for voluntary agencies from public funds. Yet a government bent on encouraging the expansion of voluntary social action could not be seen at the same time to be cutting the level of its financial support. Paradoxically, too, the major drift of government funding has been in the direction of the formal voluntary sector. As Lawrence comments, 'It is much easier to fund an existing voluntary organisation than to identify, organise and then fund an informal network. This should not disguise the fact that the dominant faction of the Conservative Party is not necessarily committed to the voluntary sector as it currently exists.'[44]

For the period we have been examining, it is evident that some confusion reigned in government thinking on the various constituents of the non-statutory sector, with emphasis being placed at times on informal care, at others on volunteers or voluntary organisations. Although ideologically most predisposed towards the informal sector, the Conservative government found difficulty in encouraging it in other than the verbal terms we have examined. Central government's main instrument for encouraging greater reliance on informal care is a negative one. It can force a fall-back on to it by default, through the attrition of the public services by means of expenditure cuts. The results of such a strategy are of course unknowable, in that the meeting of social need through informal care is invisible. The House of Commons Social Services Committee picked up this point when reviewing governmental emphasis on encouraging more voluntary effort. 'We hope that the Government's strategy will succeed, but we cannot be sure that the vacuum left by expenditure cuts will necessarily and automatically be filled by volunteers and voluntary organisations. In particular, there may be considerable variations, as between different parts of the country, in the ability of volunteers to fill the gaps.'[45] The committee went on to recommend that this process be closely monitored by the DHSS, but failed to suggest how this should be done.

It is not difficult to detect in both government rhetoric and performance the absence of a comprehensive vision and the lack of a coherent strategy. This is unsurprising, for, in respect of the personal social services, it is not clear that any government has ever had either. As we have seen, social policies have always been one-sided in their concentration on the statutory services and on public expenditure to the exclusion of other forms of care. The Younghusband Report and the Seebohm Report on social work and the personal social services both shared this myopia, with a few token references to the potential of voluntary action. Labour governments have tended until very recently to focus mainly on the identifiable, statutory tip of the iceberg, even though they have shared with their political opponents a huge mass of assumptions about the functions of the family and the role of women as the 'natural' source of informal tending, which have formed an implicit and exploitative part of their social policies. The major contribution of the Wolfenden Report, and of the recent work of writers like Adrian Webb, has been to make explicit the existence of the different systems of care (the informal, the private, the voluntary and the statutory) and to underscore the necessity of viewing them as linked parts of a whole. What has been wrong with policies for the personal social services in particular has been the lack of this integration, and the concentration on bigger, more professionalised and more powerful statutory organisations which have not only been starved of the resources to fulfil the duties specified for them, but have also been in many ways the wrong instruments for some of those duties. The major providers in the welfare state have always been, as Patrick Jenkin rightly says, the informal carers. There is a growing body of literature to testify to the way in which they have been exploited and neglected because of the pre-eminence and exclusivity of the professionalised services and, more fundamentally, because of the ideology of the family which has privatised and isolated this struggling social unit, often to the point of crisis. As a number of social policy writers[46] point out, the informal deliverers of 'community care' have saved the state a great deal of money, but the costs to *them* of this primary care are never included in the economic equations. 'Supporting the supporters' has never been an instinctive goal of the statutory social services. More often than not, they have tended to ration their resources and support by 'liable relative',[47] their intervention delayed until the inevitable but initially preventable crisis has made more organised and expensive forms of care mandatory.

CONCLUSION

In this chapter we have reviewed the perspectives and policies of both main political parties with regard to the voluntary sector, focusing, inevitably, on the period when interest in the voluntary sector was at its highest, in the early years of right-wing Conservative administration. What has emerged from this review is a clear picture of the 'supportive philosophical environment'[48] created by the New Right in particular for policies of privatisation and substitution. Such policies, it is evident, do not amount to a 'positive social policy' on the part of government, operating as they do from motives which are relatively unconnected with social need and intimately linked to ideological and economic considerations. This changed climate of thought is demonstrated mostly through the rhetoric of politicians, for their actions so far, as we have seen in earlier chapters, have not proved as radical and far-reaching as their ideas. Their compelling force lies, however, in their function as a source of a steady, drip-by-drip attrition of public support for the statutory services, perhaps preparing opinion for a more severe pruning of the welfare state in due time. A further source of new thinking on the voluntary sector and its relationship with the public services, one closely linked to the ideas discussed in this chapter, is the work of the welfare pluralists to whom we now turn.

NOTES AND REFERENCES

1. WALKER, A. (ed.), *Public Expenditure and Social Policy*. Heinemann: London, 1982.
2. Ibid., p. 11.
3. KLEIN, R. (ed.), *Inflation and Priorities*. Centre for Studies in Social Policy: London, 1974, p. 1.
4. GOUGH, I., *The Political Economy of the Welfare State*. Macmillan: London, 1979, p. 141.
5. LE GRAND, J., *The Strategy of Equality*. Allen & Unwin: London, 1982; WILDING, P. and GEORGE, V., *Ideology and Social Welfare*.

Routledge & Kegan Paul: London, 1976; WILDING, P. and GEORGE, V., *The Impact of Social Policy*. Routledge & Kegan Paul: London, 1984.

6. HADLEY, R. and HATCH, S., *Social Welfare and the Failure of the State: Centralised Social Services and Participatory Alternatives*. Allen & Unwin, London, 1982, p. 2.

7. HARRIS, LORD, House of Commons, 25 June 1975, Hansard, col. 1412.

8. HARRIS, LORD, quoted in ROWE A., 'The Voluntary Services Unit', in K. Jones, (ed.), *The Year Book of Social Policy in Britain 1974*. Routledge & Kegan Paul: London, 1975, p. 191.

9. OWEN, D., House of Commons, 8 July 1975, Hansard, col. 360.

10. Ibid., col. 377.

11. CALLAGHAN, J., Speech to Age Concern, 23 Jan. 1978.

12. WORPOLE, K., 'Volunteers for Socialism', *New Society*, 29 Jan. 1981, pp. 199–200.

13. REES, M., Speech to York Community Council, 27 Sept. 1977.

14. THE HOME OFFICE VOLUNTARY SERVICES UNIT, *The Government and the Voluntary Sector, a Consultative Document*. Home Office, 1978.

15. JENKIN, P., Speech to the Conservative Party Conference (debate on Health and Social Services), 1980.

16. JENKIN, P., Speech to Conservative Association, Watford, 1977.

17. JENKIN, P., Speech to Social Services Representatives, Oxford, 1978.

18. CONSERVATIVE CENTRAL OFFICE, Community Affairs Department, *We are Richer than we Think*. 1979.

19. For example WEBB, A. and WISTOW, G., *Wither the Welfare State?* RIPA, London, 1882; LAWRENCE, R., Voluntary action: a stalking horse for the Right?'. *Critical Social Policy*, Vol. 2, 3, Spring 1985, pp. 14–30.

20. LAWRENCE, op. cit.

21. Ibid., 19.

22. GLENNERSTER, H., Public spending and the social services: the end of an era?', in M. Brown, and S. Baldwin, (eds.) *The Year Book of Social Policy in Britain, 1979*, Routledge & Kegan Paul: London, 1980, pp. 15–30.

23. GOUGH, I., 'Thatcherism and the Welfare State', *Marxism Today*, July 1980, pp. 7–12.

24. RAISON, T., *Speech to Voluntary Movement Group*, Jan. 1980.

25. Quoted in RAISON, Speech to Voluntary Movement Group.

26. PARKER, R. A., 'Tending and social policy', in E. M., Goldberg,

and S. Hatch, (eds.) *A New Look at the Personal Social Services*. Policy Studies Institute: London, 1981, pp. 17–32.

27. WALKER, A., *Community Care: The Family, the State and Social Policy*. Blackwell & Robertson: Oxford, 1982.

28. JENKIN, P., Speech to the Association of Directors of Social Services (quoted in WEBB and WISTOW, op. cit., p. 73).

29. JENKIN, P., Speech to Central Council for Jewish Social Service, Oct. 1980.

30. THATCHER, M., Speech to Women's Royal Voluntary Service National Conference, Jan. 1981.

31. *Guardian*, 21 Jan. 1981.

32. *Guardian*, 9 Mar. 1983.

33. RAISON, T., *The Voluntary Sector: Some Questions*. ARVAC Occasional Paper, 1980, p. 3.

34. JENKIN, P., Speech at a dinner of the 'Moving Spirits', June 1979.

35. HOUSE OF COMMONS, Social Services Committee, *Report on the Social Services 1979/80* HMSO: London, Q. 247.

36. YOUNG, G., Speech to the National Conference of Volunteer Bureaux, Apr. 1981.

37. JENKIN, P., Speech to AGM of Volunteer Centre, Dec. 1979.

38. JENKIN, P., Speech to Central Council for Jewish Social Service, Oct. 1980.

39. JENKIN, Speech at dinner of 'Moving Spirits'.

40. RAISON, *The Voluntary Sector*.

41. RAISON, Speech to Voluntary Movement Group.

42. RAISON, T., Speech to AGM of Northampton Council of Voluntary Service, July 1981.

43. RAISON, *The Voluntary Sector*.

44. LAWRENCE, op. cit., p. 19.

45. HOUSE OF COMMONS, op. cit., Section 33.

46. For example, NISSELL, M., *Family Care of the Handicapped Elderly: Who Pays?* Policy Studies Institute: London, 1982.

47. PARKER, op. cit., p. 23.

48. WEBB and WISTOW, op. cit., p. 74.

Chapter Eight

WELFARE PLURALISM

To try and trace out the ideas behind the concept of welfare pluralism and to classify distinct, prescriptive models which neatly encapsulate the arguments, is to impose an artificial structure on what are in reality less well-formed or articulated ideas. It has been suggested[1] that the lack of conceptual clarity that swiftly becomes evident in writings on the subject may have a change function all of its own in contributing to 'the modification of assumptive worlds' where 'Uncertainty and confusion may be the prime stimulus for breaking the mould of established behaviour.'[2] Be that as it may, it is certainly difficult to distil out from a relatively consensual body of opinion clear viewpoints which represent more than different degrees of emphasis on the desirability of a healthy voluntary sector in today's welfare state. In the personal social services sphere there already exists a 'mixed economy of welfare' as we have seen. How far beyond this does the notion of welfare pluralism take us? What kind of 'mix' of the various systems of social care is being advanced as ideal and how much of a retreat is being advocated for the state? We need to look at some of the arguments themselves to see if there are any answers to these questions.

The essence of a pluralist approach to the provision of social services would appear to be, at its simplest, the advocacy of pluriformity and diversity as a principle of organisation. This is opposed to the concentration, in a monolithic organ of the state, of responsibilities and functions which are its exclusive preserve. Welfare pluralism stands midway between a collectivist or institutional mode of welfare provision and an individualist or residual one. Its proponents oppose a statutory monopoly of service provision and likewise reject the minimalist call for disengagement by the state. Instead, they see the state as the enabler and regulator of voluntary groups and organisations which provide the mainspring of social action. The state is a necessary and important participant in a mixed system where the virtues and defects of the different actors can be set off against each other to produce a whole that is better than any one of its constituent parts. It does, however, cede its service delivery role to voluntary agencies and confine itself to financing and ensuring the equitable distribution of the mass of self-governing, decentralised services that results from spontaneous voluntary enterprise.

Alongside this notion of pluriformity, lies for some a more ideologically based objective – that of procuring the wider dispersal of power. Not all supporters of diversified forms of social service and social action take their analysis explicitly to this point. Those who do are borrowing from the political philosophy of pluralism, a model for the distribution of power which has been developed by political scientists in the United States and which has been subject to challenge from a number of alternative perspectives. Both interpretations of pluralism as applied to the provision of social services are to be found among the writers examined in the following pages.

THE WOLFENDEN REPORT AND PLURALISM

We have observed already in our account of the Wolfenden Report, that one of its concerns in recommending an expansion of the role of the voluntary sector and a long-term strategy for its interrelationship with the statutory and informal systems of care, was to maintain 'a pluralistic pattern of institutions'. In part, this meant the practical provision of a wide range of alternative modes of service which would enhance variety, choice and competition for consumers. A dominant role for the state was part of the plurality envisaged – 'We believe it to be generally accepted that statutory bodies have the ultimate responsibility for planning and provision of social services and for looking at the needs of the areas they serve as a whole: and that voluntary action is one means of helping to meet such needs.'[3] The state's essential superiority in certain aspects is frankly acknowledged – its capacity for ensuring universal coverage, for redistribution to minority groups, for achieving equity and maintaining standards, for integrating planning and for preserving democratic control, are all positive features. On the negative side, however, statutory services are seen to be expensive, too large in scale, and therefore likely to be rigid, bureaucratic and change-resistant. Voluntary services can counteract some of these disadvantages because they are often small, they have a tradition of spontaneity and innovation which enables them to search out and react to new problems speedily and flexibly, and they can call on fresh, extra-statutory resources in voluntary work and voluntary loyalties. Although they should be essentially autonomous and independent they are also in need of a symbiotic relationship with the state. The state, as we saw in Chapter 3, must, according to Wolfenden, provide the finances necessary for the voluntary sector to expand. It should also seek to counteract what Wolfenden described as the main limitation of the voluntary sector – its unevenness. 'Its very diversity and specificity, and the small size of the financial resources at its command, mean that the voluntary sector is less able than the statutory to remedy mismatches between needs and resources that become evident when an over-view of social provision is taken.'[4]

So far we have looked at the practical, functional gains of an expanded role for the voluntary sector in relation to the statutory sector, a relationship described by Wolfenden as ' "pluralism", the principle that the State and the voluntary sector should be partners'.[5] This is the first strand of the pluralist model which has been articulated increasingly in recent years, a simple framework for stressing plurality and diversity. There is in Wolfenden, however, a second strand of thought beyond the practical advantages of an expansion of voluntary social services. This is the concept of a pluralist system as one 'in which power is spread over several political, social and economic institutions and not concentrated in a few monolithic structures'.[6] There is a clear conceptual distinction between the two strands, but the emphasis of the second, on the diffusion of power, is dependent upon the pluriformity contained in the first meaning, in a sense that does not apply the other way round. Hence many writers refer to pluralism as a shorthand term for all those diverse features we have discussed, but are not necessarily referring to the transfer of power. The Wolfenden Report itself often uses the term solely in this first sense.

Wolfenden makes two additional criticisms of the statutory system of social services over and above its functional characteristics. Because these services tend to be large in scale, complex and bureaucratic, they also tend to be remote and alienating and insulated from popular control either in the form of consumer participation and influence, or in terms of a more general, public involvement in their affairs. Control and answerability in the various statutory agencies are deemed to be vested, as far as clients and public are concerned, in their representatives in the electoral system. In theory, this system is supposed to be democratic, but, in practice, it remains relatively impenetrable to the grievances and preferences of those who are represented. The second defect of the statutory services consists of the deterrent effect of their professionalism and paternalism on direct public involvement in the actual delivery of services.[7] Viewed from this perspective, the voluntary sector not only has the practical function of extending, improving and substituting for statutory services, but the political function of dispersing power more widely because it can be 'a means of enabling widespread, direct public participation'.[8] By joining voluntary organisations, disenfranchised consumers or members of the public can effect change in society. This they will achieve not only through their own direct activities, but also 'less directly, through the signals sent by these activities to the statutory system on the nature of shifts in public interests'.[9] Wolfenden sees as a by-product of this participation, a reduction in people's sense of alienation and an education for their other social roles.

So far this account has distilled out from the Wolfenden Report the basic elements of its theoretical framework of pluralism. We have already noted that, for all its positive contribution to debate in supplying valuable data about the voluntary sector and in clarifying and stressing the significance of the various systems of social care, the report fails to come to grips with the operational 'long-term strategy' it urges on the statutory authorities for the integration of those systems of care. The report was criticised for lacking a clear philosophy[10] for the balancing of roles between the different systems. Its philosophy is pluralist, but it is undeniable that it is neither deeply thought out nor critically evaluated in its application in the report. Wolfenden borrowed from the ideas of pluralism in viewing the state as one participant among others in the social welfare system, but, in allocating to it the major role and in some senses making it a reference point for defining the contribution of the contribution of the voluntary sector, it failed to sort out clearly its ideological position with regard to the proper role of the state, or to specify precisely where its functions should begin and end. With regard to the other political strand of a pluralist philosophy alluded to earlier, the objective of a wider diffusion of power, there is no doubt that the report makes a smooth and uncritical equation of voluntary action with participation and of participation with the spreading of power, as if these were synonymous concepts. Some of these issues will become clearer in the more developed analyses of the writers now to be considered.

PLURALISM AND DECENTRALISATION

Continuing the pattern of critique of statutory performance, promotion of the compensatory virtues of the voluntary sector and stress on the political value of 'participative pluralism', the work of two writers closely associated with the Wolfenden Report, Stephen Hatch and Roger Hadley, develops the arguments further. Hatch's study *Outside the State*[11], an account of an empirical study he conducted for Wolfenden, of voluntary organisations in three English towns, ends with a thoughtful reflection on what he considers to be the changed terms for debate. No longer should this focus on the old extension ladder/parallel bars argument 'about whether the state should play a central role. The essential questions now are about the nature of the relationship between statutory, voluntary and informal sectors.'[12] Hatch poses those questions by asking 'whether voluntary action is merely marginal to the statutory services, or whether it plays an integral part in service provision'.[13]

Voluntary action may extend the provisions of the statutory services by offering more services, or higher-quality or different ones. In some cases, as in the area of information and advice work, for instance, it may be the main provider. Either way, it can offer flexibility, innovatoriness and personal commitment to counteract the domination of statutory services by bureaucrats and professionals. It is in need of the state, however, because it lacks a universal authority, it is distributed unevenly and does not possess sufficient resources. The two models that Hatch puts forward, the marginal and the integral, embody reverse images of the roles of the state and the voluntary sector. The marginal model, one enjoying much support still, sees the voluntary sector at the fringes of state-organised welfare, pioneering services and activities which are then rightly taken over by the state which has the professional and financial resources for developing them. This model, Hatch feels, has essential weaknesses, being faced with limitless demand on finite resources and being subject to professional and political constraints. The integral model, on the other hand, gives voluntary action a more central role and sets limits to the involvement of the state which is to provide the framework within which other forms of provision can flourish – 'the second model pins its faith to the integration of different sources of care, and calls for a shift in the balance of statutory services from direct provision towards enabling and supporting'.[14] This is the model which Hatch advocates as a basis for future development, one which he sees as resting on 'a philosophy of participatory pluralism, incompatible with a narrow and exclusive adherence to the traditional forms of representative democracy'.[15] Voluntary organisations, functioning as critics and pressurisers, sharing in decision-making or service delivery, must be seen as 'ways of enhancing rather than eroding democracy'. The state retains a strong, positive role in counteracting the deficiencies of the voluntary sector, and it is this function that distinguishes Hatch's integral model from the minimalist, residual role for the state advocated by the right wing of the Conservative Party.

Outside the State did not set out to explore these issues at any greater depth. In a later work, with Roger Hadley, Hatch develops themes which echo the earlier writings of such American pluralists as Berger and Neuhaus,[16] who write of 'Empowerment through pluralism' in a critique of social planning, bureaucratisation and professional power, or Peter Drucker[17] who, from disenchantment with government, looked towards 'a society of institutional diversity and diffusion of power'. Hadley and Hatch take up a similar perspective with a critique of centralised social services and an argument for developing an alternative to them in a 'pluralist, decentralised and participative pattern of services'. In *Social Welfare and the Failure of the State*[18] Hadley and Hatch consider the achievements of the welfare state which, they feel, have failed to match its early promise to promote equality, liberty and fraternity, despite substantial expenditures. Intervening more and more extensively into the lives of citizens, it has become less and less capable of meeting the expectations it generates, and more and more remote from the preferences and influence of the consumers it serves. This is because, biased towards bureaucracy and expertise, the statutory services have concentrated power in the hands of civil servants and professionals, two groups of personnel increasingly subject to criticism on grounds of inefficiency, ineffectiveness and resistance to change. Successive structural reorganisations such as those in the NHS, in local government and in the local authority social services, have been founded on the wrong values and have therefore failed in many of their objectives. All have been geared to a view of society where standardisation is preferred to diversity, an attachment to uniformity which then requires central control. Their overriding concern has been with promoting efficiency rather than democracy, and to this end the various services have been organised on the basis of economies of scale, in units so large that ordinary consumers have been lost in them, powerless to make any impact on their management. Remote and impersonal modes of operation, which are the antithesis of local-level, small-scale participative democracy, have been rationalised by being set in the context of the system of representative democracy through which, in theory, the services are publicly accountable. These assumptions have, according to Hadley and Hatch, the character of a mythology – 'one which serves to insulate managers and professionals from the demands and criticisms of consumers and lower-ranking employees by arguing that the representation of interests is something that should be carried on through separate political institutions'.[19]

Hadley and Hatch point out that the statutory services are not the only providers of care, although they 'often act in isolation from other sources of care and behave as if they were at the centre of the caring universe'.[20] Three alternative and substantial contributors to care are the other systems named by Wolfenden – the informal, voluntary and commercial sectors. Each of these has its own positive characteristics and particular limitations which could respectively be capitalised upon and countered by the operation of the statutory services. The informal sector is acknowledged as playing a central role in the provision of care and services, yet being crucially dependent on statutory policies and support which are often inadequate . . . 'both nationally and locally the policies of the statutory social services towards the informal sector appear to be haphazard, piecemeal and half-hearted'.[21] The voluntary sector's substantial contribution to the personal social services is cited, but the authors find that, for all its positive attributes, it is 'essentially marginal to the statutory sector, in terms both of its financial resources and of the way it is treated by the statutory services'.[22] The virtues of the voluntary sector – its flexibility, responsiveness, opportunities for involvement, etc. are set against the limitations of its unevenness and unreliability, lack of correspondence to need, its specificity and its lack of coherence. 'The essential problem is that voluntary organisations are difficult vehicles through which to aim at a broad policy objective and provide universally available services of specified standards.'[23] This poses the question, for Hadley and Hatch, as to how a statutorily provided framework may enable the voluntary sector to compensate for such defects. Similarly, they find both positive and negative attributes in the provision of social services by the commercial sector, noting that this sector also 'can contribute usefully to a plural system of services'.

The three alternative systems of care all have the virtue of being in existence, despite being ignored or neglected by the state. None of them, the authors feel, could or should stand alone as sole providers of care and services, yet all could make a positive input within a pluralist strategy which maximised their strengths and compensated for their limitations. The study goes on, in fact, to focus more or less exclusively upon the role of voluntary organisations, advocating an expanded role for them, alongside the democratisation of the statutory services. To the state it assigns the central function of devising a pluralist strategy and for providing a framework within which the alternative systems could operate. 'Such a framework would have to provide for the equitable redistribution of resources; it would have to ensure adequate standards of provision; and where the provision of services was devolved to organisations not directly accountable to it, government would still have the duty to police whatever alternative form of accountability was decided upon.'[24] The state, therefore, far from retreating to the minimal role advocated by the Right, would retain an essential distributive and monitoring function. Quite how it would achieve this alongside a substantial decentralisation and privatisation of power, functions and resources, remains far from clear.

Having moved on from a critique of the failure of the welfare state, to the advocacy of a more pluralist pattern of service provision underpinned by the state, Hadley and Hatch then place their twin themes of decentralisation and pluralism within the context of a system of participatory democracy. Throughout the book so far, cogent and telling criticisms have been made of the defects of the representative democratic system which has, quite clearly, not enhanced the wider involvement of citizens in the institutions of the state. Participatory democracy exists where ordinary citizens can 'define issues, decide and act for themselves and in so doing to achieve a measure of self-realisation and fulfilment'.[25]

One of the ways of promoting such involvement, besides the decentralisation of statutory services, is pluralism – understood here as 'the ideas that social services can come from a variety of sources, not just from staff directly employed by government, and that for numerous reasons it is desirable to maximise the involvement in care and service provision of people outside the statutory agencies'.[26] The authors go on to catalogue a series of examples of 'theory into practice' where through such voluntary initiatives as neighbourhood councils and centres, self-help groups, housing associations, etc. the voluntary sector contributes to plural provision. An essential factor here is the right to take initiatives – for instance, to set up an alternative school, or health facilities – which would be backed by public money. Although conceding that voluntary organisations do not necessarily encourage consumer and community involvement, the authors emphasise their potential for increasing participation. Their initiatives 'would alter the prevailing norms and the balance of power and expectations, and consequently the way in which larger parts of a system worked'.[27] Besides the competitive effect of alternative institutions, this strategy should also lead to greater involvement of both consumers and alternative providers in statutory decision-making. The authors specifically recommend, in their outline of a new structure, that alongside a greater national and local government role in monitoring and inspecting those voluntary organisations with whom they have contractual relations, would develop forms for this kind of participation in the representative system so that 'legitimacy would cease to reside exclusively with representatives selected by existing methods'.[28]

What becomes evident here, although it is not made explicit, is that the authors are operating on the basis of two different concepts of pluralism. The first, clearly defined, conveys the idea of variety and choice of social service provision as opposed to a statutory monopoly. The second concept, more generally assumed rather than articulated, links the alternative provision of services with the advancement of participative democracy and the 'dilution' or 'enrichment' of the representative system. In a later work,[29] Hatch makes a clear distinction between 'welfare pluralism' (the participation in service provision of numerous systems of care) and 'political pluralism' (a system in which 'many different interests have a voice in the political process'). He thus differentiates between participation in service provision and participation in decision-making, and does not assume a necessary connection between the two. In *Social Welfare and the Failure of the State* the two concepts are not clearly distinguishable and at times are totally blurred in a haze of wishful thinking. It is true that one part of the authors' recommendations (already referred to above clearly advocates the sharing of decision-making, through the co-option of the voluntary organisation providers into the statutory political process. How much influence on this process they would achieve is not explored, nor is the basis of their legitimacy investigated, given that their status would, of necessity, have to be representative, albeit not electorally so, because direct participation of every voluntary provider of services would be impossible. Still, here is clearly a form of political pluralism corresponding to Hatch's definition.

The major emphasis in the book's discussion of pluralism, however, is on the provision of plural services. Besides its contribution to variety, choice, involvement, etc. the act of providing alternative services is seen as effecting a shift in the balance of power in a particular area of service provision. Hence, for example, the creation of alternative schools, or even the possibility that they could be formed 'would significantly alter the balance of power within the traditional school system'.[30] Presumably the shift in power would occur through the exercise of consumer preference and self-determination on the one hand, and on the other, through the competitive effect on providers, of the exercise by consumers of a negative sanction when dissatisfied with the product. This is an attractive idea, and it is clear that it would work well for some people. It is difficult to see how it would supply universal solutions to the ills of the statutory social services. The idea has resonances of the educational voucher scheme, with all the attendant risks of that scheme which are that the sections of the population which would exploit it to greatest advantage would be, as always, the middle classes. As with other areas of social policy where public subsidy is made available to maximise choice and autonomy, such as mortgages, occupational pensions and private health care, it is inevitably the middle class which gains and the working class which, while helping to pay for those subsidies, do not reap proportional benefits and thus are left, in the end, with inferior-quality options in a ghettoised public sector. In the personal social service sphere, which is mainly directed at the poor, this already happens. Those with independent buying power buy in their own services and do not use local authority social service departments. It was suggested in Chapter 4 that government subsidies are already operated preferentially on behalf of the middle class to some extent, enabling them to bypass, by means of their own voluntary organisations and charities, the public sector. There can be little confidence that this system, if escalated in the way that Hadley and Hatch suggest, would add anything to the political leverage and participation of those groups who are deprived and disenfranchised in the present system. Here, however, is the nub of the problem of pluralism as a political doctrine, and further evaluation must await some discussion of the major proponents of a welfare pluralist system, Francis Gladstone[31] and others [32] from the NCVO.

GRADUALIST WELFARE PLURALISM

One of the strongest appeals in recent years for a 'de-monopolising strategy' which would replace the statutory social services by voluntary action is Francis Gladstone's *Voluntary Action in a Changing World*.

Gladstone, as senior policy analyst for the NCVO, the voluntary sector's major, generalist umbrella body at national level, supplied in this study a fresh blueprint for the voluntary sector to expand its role in the welfare state and to redefine its relations with government and with the statutory services. Essentially, Gladstone's book shares the preoccupation of Hadley and Hatch's work with the extension of voluntary action, and with decentralisation, destandardisation and deprofessionalisation. It gives less attention to the statutory services themselves, however, and *Voluntary Action in a Changing World* is both more diffuse in its assessments of modern society and more closely focused on the replacement of statutory by voluntary action. The latter is what Gladstone means by 'gradualist welfare pluralism'.

Gladstone bases his case for changing the structure of the welfare state on a critique that is similar in tone to that of Hadley and Hatch. He notes criticisms from bodies like the Institute of Economic Affairs, on the Right, of the steady erosion in the welfare state of individual freedom and choice, and, from the Left, a progressive disillusionment with the failure of egalitarianism. Further indictments concern 'the remoteness and inefficiency of large-scale bureaucracy', and the ineffectiveness, demonstrated by researchers, of many of the social programmes of the welfare state. All these problems, according to Gladstone, 'must raise serious doubts about the "Grand Design" approach to social welfare. Might it be, in fact, that local mass production from a centrally determined blue-print is not the ideal recipe for effective social welfare provision?'[33]

In the face of an uncertain future, where the social and political limits to growth have been reached, where new meanings have to be given to work and leisure, where far-reaching social changes have their effect and where demographic pressures will have 'profound repercussions', there is a need to rethink the structure and logic of the social welfare system. This cannot be achieved through a continuation of the dirigism and social engineering which have characterised our efforts so far. Gladstone examines and dismisses a number of options – existing statutory programmes are unsatisfactory and function within a fast changing society, so the maintenance of the status quo is not an option; he dismisses the individualist, market option as being divisive and unjust, and sees a case for greater collectivism as appropriate only for income maintenance, not for welfare services. What then, is Gladstone's own remedy for the ills of the welfare state and the means by which we may achieve his 'preference guided society' based on decentralised decision-making and social interaction?

Tracing a path between the individualist and the collectivist options, Gladstone opts for ' "a radical welfare pluralism" model in which statutory service delivery would be replaced by voluntary action'.[34] Far from minimising the role of the state, he carefully separates out its key functions of enacting legislation and allocating resources from the less fundamental role of service delivery, which can be left to voluntary action. The evolution of this hand-over by the state to the voluntary sector is termed 'gradualist welfare pluralism', which will bring in its wake more local involvement in decision-making, more support for innovative and experimental programmes and more emphasis on informal caring and self-help together with a shift to prevention and the horizontal integration of services.[35] 'In such a scenario', Gladstone comments, 'the role of the government gradually becomes the upholding of equity in resource allocation, the enforcement of minimum standards, the fostering of more pluralistic legislation and the use of fiscal and regulatory law both for income maintenance and to reinforce a preventive approach.'[36] Thus, voluntary action contributes positively to the welfare system in bringing to it its 'tradition of innovation and experiment and greater flexibility'[37] and the state redresses the negative characteristics of voluntary action such as its uneven distribution and access and imperfect accountability. This gradual increase of voluntary action should not, Gladstone feels, require a huge increase in government expenditure – 'even if the level of support were trebled the voluntary sector would receive less than 2 per cent of total public spending'.[38]

Gladstone's approach to welfare pluralism is eclectic and visionary. A more concise account of this viewpoint, and one which clarifies some of his main proposals, is given by Nicholas Hinton and Margaret Hyde, both from the NCVO. They suggest that 'the framework of voluntary action offers a potential for innovation, sensitivity to change, responsiveness to local and individual variations, and for user and community influence over decisions affecting their lives; a potential which the statutory sector by itself does not share'.[39] There are certain essential elements to this pluralist approach, which they list. First, they state that it is the task of government to fund welfare services – here is a very clear declaration to those on the right of the Conservative Party who would privatise not only the delivery of social services but also their finance. 'Funding for the bulk of our welfare services', say Hinton and Hyde, 'must remain a major responsibility of the state.' Alongside the financial role, all levels of government must work to promote equity and justice by distributing resources fairly. Third, all social services should have the possibility of citizen participation built into them. Lastly, and it is here that gradualist welfare pluralism is called for, 'a gradually increasing number of groups should have access to central and local government funds for the purpose of providing welfare services'.[40] The authors do not envisage that this gradual enlargement of voluntary and community action supported by public funds will greatly diminish the part played by the employees of the statutory social services, 'although it would certainly change'. They foresee the diversion of more public expenditure and the transfer of some public sector employees to the voluntary sector, as well as changing requirements for the training of professionals. In the short term, at least, they do not see the evolution of 'a pluralistically provided welfare state' as a cheaper alternative, although they do see some potential for the freeing of resources in the long term by the adoption of more effective and less costly forms of social intervention on a voluntary and community basis.

An evaluation of the case for gradualist welfare pluralism put forward by the NCVO can approach their argument at two levels: it can examine their specific proposals and the implications, feasibility, etc. of these. It can also single out for special attention the political ideology that is implicit within the authors' use of the concept of pluralism. The intention here is to do both. On the first count, the main lines of the argument are that, given the deficiencies of the statutory social services and the compensatory values of the voluntary sector, voluntary social action should gradually, and to an unspecified degree, replace parts of the statutory social service delivery system with the aid of public funds. Let us look at these elements more closely. The alleged 'failure' of the welfare state is the key launching pad for building the case for welfare pluralism, yet as an allegation it remains relatively untested in these works. Complaints from the Right that the welfare state has eroded personal freedoms are not measured against a wider philosophy of social justice and a broader concept of freedom. The verdict from the Left on the failure of egalitarianism is not balanced by a positive appraisal of what the welfare state *has* achieved. 'It is . . . easy to look back and criticise the weak points of welfare state policy-making and forget how much better it all was than what has gone before.'[41] Specific social programmes, such as the NHS or the personal social services are given the grossly over-generalised label of 'ineffective' or 'dysfunctional'. Gladstone's critique of the former accurately locates NHS deficiencies in the individualised and curative nature of the medical model, yet here, he is attacking a particular philosophy of health care rather than its administration by the state. There is little encouraging evidence from the more pluriform health care systems of Western Europe that a voluntary approach does much to correct this bias – in fact, the opposite is the case.[42] Similarly, the personal social services are criticised for their methods and philosophy, yet we have no indication of how their replacement by voluntary services would transform this orientation.

If we take up some of the other issues cited as a case for change – dominance by professionals or administration by bureaucrats – we are compelled to ask similar questions. While accepting that these and other features of the statutory services can be and are at times harmful or oppressive, or remote and alienating, do they not also have their positive aspects and make a necessary contribution towards meeting a vast and complex range of needs in our society? For all the attractiveness of a 'preference guided society' where decentralised voluntary and community initiatives hold sway, will such a society not also need a measure of rational organisation and planning, the experience of professionals, etc.? To alter the balance of power where professionals and planners dominate, is it necessary to eliminate them? It is not in fact more desirable that they be required to put their skills at the service of society under a more genuine and effective popular control?

Moving from the generalised defects of the welfare state, we find when we turn to the characteristics claimed for voluntary action, that, although its major shortcomings receive frank acknowledgement, some of its more positive attributes are rather unquestioningly portrayed. Voluntary action's capacity for innovation and experiment, its greater flexibility and ability to adapt, the greater scope it offers for participation – all these claims *may* be true but are not necessarily true of today's voluntary groups and agencies. They are certainly widely assumed to be more or less universal features, and Chapter 9 will examine some of these assumptions. The key question here relates to an issue that must come to the fore shortly. Accepting these attributes as given facts for now, for the sake of argument, how far do they rely on the *ancillary* nature of the voluntary contribution and would they survive the wholesale expansion of the voluntary sector advocated by Gladstone?

The third element in our summary of the NCVO position was that voluntary action should replace statutory services. This is clearly stated in Gladstone's book and in Hinton and Hyde's paper. They advocate the progressive switch of public funds to community and voluntary groups, at first possibly maintaining the public sector institutions to be replaced until the transition is complete, but eventually achieving a 'devolved, differentiated and participative system of service delivery' instead of the statutory services. This process would necessarily be a slow one to allow for institutional adjustment and to take account of the essential nature of voluntary action.

The essence of 'welfare pluralism' is that it cannot be planned from above, only regulated and encouraged; hence it is not a real option for the present as much as a framework or an orientation for a gradualist approach. Unlike statutory services, voluntary action cannot be created overnight by legislative fiat so that any move towards greater welfare pluralism would need to be conceived as a long-term strategy.[43]

It is difficult to discern, from a careful reading of either source, which social service programmes which are presently run by statutory authorities would be 'voluntarised'. Gladstone talks in terms of a 'family choice model' for education (which might or might not involve the evolution of more voluntary schools) and extends his thinking to the NHS, surmising that substantial parts of it could be removed from the statutory monopoly. Hinton and Hyde rule out any substantial replacement of the statutory role in these areas, settling for greater consumer influence and participation. The main emphasis appears to lie on transfer of the personal social services, community care and community work – where, as we know, the voluntary role is stronger. How far this transfer would extend is not specified and certain key problems of such a transfer of responsibilities can be identified which receive little or no attention in the arguments for welfare pluralism. In replacement of many or most of the activities now carried out by local authority social services departments, for instance, with the transfer of funds and possibly staff to a multiplicity of voluntary and community groups and agencies, a number of difficulties come to mind. Reading the NCVO case as it stands, we find that the local authority role would be reduced to providing finance, ensuring access and distribution and maintaining a measure of public accountability for the use of public funds. That the Local Authority Social Services Department (LASSD) performs a range of statutory duties in fulfilment of legislative requirements, that it acts as a primary point of reference for a generic range of human and social problems on the Seebohm 'one-door' philosophy, that it has, potentially at least, an integrative and coordinating role, and that it is supposed to maintain emergency services, are facts that are not adverted to nor given practical consideration in the NCVO case. Gladstone refers to the welfare system in the Netherlands as an example of a welfare pluralist system which might be copied to some degree here. I have written about the shortcomings of the Dutch system elsewhere,[44] and will enlarge on them briefly in Chapter 9. It should suffice to say here that all the objections raised above have relevance in the Dutch welfare system also, plus the additional, important consideration that the Dutch welfare services have been funded at more than adequate levels in comparison with our personal social services, statutory or voluntary.

The lack of precision of the NCVO case for gradualist welfare pluralism gives it the quality of a vision and the effect of a stirring exhortation rather than establishing a firm basis for concrete action and systematic development. It is perhaps unfair to demand precision of an argument which was possibly not intended to do more than sow ideas and rouse imaginations. It is clear that the dream cannot become reality however, without a great deal more hard-headed attention to the practical dimensions of the long-term process it advocates.

To turn briefly to the second area of evaluation mentioned earlier, that of the political ideology inherent in the NCVO's understanding of welfare pluralism, we find a similar set of assumptions, less clearly articulated, to those contained in Hadley and Hatch's use of the term. These concern first an equation between pluriformity and diversity and the political process of participation, and, second, a rather more implicit belief that from this participative process will result the wider diffusion of power. Gladstone's treatment of participation is rather lightweight, in that he neither specifies what he means by the term nor does he examine its feasibility in the context of gradualist welfare pluralism. Of course there may be very positive by-products from the gain by a group or agency of control over the activities and resources connected with a certain function, but how significant a form of participation is this in a wider context? An autonomous residential home, for example, may score very well on the Arnstein 'ladder of citizen participation' quoted by Gladstone, in running its own affairs, disposing of its own budget, etc. In the context of local authority resource control, however, it may exercise little or no influence and will score very low. Gladstone acknowledges that participation is not always a high value even within voluntary organisations in the sense that members or clients gain access to decision-making. The whole tenor of the case for gradualist welfare pluralism rests in part on being antithetical to the dirigism and bureaucracy of centralised control, in restoring to citizens control over their own life-space, yet neither the possibilities genuinely offered by a more pluriform system for this, nor the structural constraints and limitations which would crucially determine its form and scope, are adequately analysed.

A similar criticism may be levelled at the rather more hidden assumption that pluriformity of social service inputs and whatever kind of participation might result, also contributes to the wider diffusion of power. Gladstone acknowledges the association of pluralism with 'a view of the political process in modern Western democracies which emphasises the extent to which power is widely diffused and the role of government to reconcile competing interests . . .'[45] and notes possible alternative explanations. His own use of the term, he feels is in an older, different sense – 'in the present context, therefore, "radical welfare pluralism" implies diversity of welfare provision and service delivery'.[46] So far as this understanding is concerned it is perfectly acceptable, although pluriformity might be a better word. There is more than a hint, however, in his work that suggests the deeper, political understanding of pluralism, although he tends to refer to the work of others in this regard rather than spell out their ideas in terms of his own position. Hence, he quotes from A. H. Halsey, who expressed the desire 'for a pluralistic society, an equal distribution of power and advantage'.[47] Hinton and Hyde end their paper by describing voluntary organisations as 'a means of enfranchising thousands of people in this country for whom other opportunities to meet human needs and influence decision-making are remote and haphazard'.[48] The hidden agenda here is a belief that power is unduly concentrated, but *where* it is perceived to be concentrated, is far from clear. Webb and Wistow point out that if power is believed to be concentrated in the state, then the proposal of a non-statutory alternative 'could conceivably be a solution and reform of state services would not be an alternative'.[49] If, however, it is thought to lie in the hands of bureaucrats, then state reform in this respect would be possible; if in the hands of professionals, then a good many voluntary organisations are also in need of reform.

CONCLUSION

The assumption underlying the welfare pluralists' polarisation of the alienating, bureaucratic, *dirigiste* and non-participative welfare state with the spontaneous emergence of voluntary groups and their active participation in service provision, decision-making, resource distribution and other processes hitherto reserved mainly to the public authorities, is that power is automatically diffused through the activities and interactions of non-governmental groups and institutions. The levels of their analysis are far from clear. As Webb and Wistow indicate, they are at times oriented to a critique of professional or bureaucratic power, and at others address themselves to the workings of the state itself, to the functions of government and the democratic process. Here they face a basic conflict, between the imperatives of the distributive justice ethic enshrined (along with other considerations) in social.policies, which have been taken to require a measure of centralised control and resource allocation as well as certain economies of scale, and the equally important values of local, decentralised, participative democracy. Additionally, they tend to assume that direct popular participation will automatically redress the shortcomings of the representative democratic system, and spread power more widely among individuals, groups and communities.

A central tenet of political pluralism which has been absorbed, more or less confusedly, by the welfare pluralists examined here, is the belief that political resources are dispersed in society through the participation of a multiplicity of groups which bargain with each other in a self-regulating system of checks and balances, where no group or class or institution can then sustain a monopoly on power. This system is thought to tend towards a natural end-state of harmony and cumulative equality, because the power asserted by one coalition of groups or interests, is soon balanced by the countervailing power exercised by others. Such coalitions form and re-form constantly according to the issues at hand. The state, in this process, is both another interest group among many and, by virtue of its legitimacy and power of sanction, is the neutral, benign arbiter in group interaction and conflict. Welfare pluralism or the institutionalised diversity of non-governmental groups in the provision of social services is seen as part of this system of checks and balances and therefore as contributing to the broader spread of power. This is to assume – wrongly, as Lowi observes – 'that social pluralism . . . creates *political* pluralism'.[50] Even where diverse groups and organisations participate in the political process, the pluralist analysis runs the risk of confusing the political *process* itself with political *power*.[51] The origins of American pluralist thought lie in case studies by political scientists of local decision-making processes. Newton specifically tested the pluralist hypothesis in his case study of the participation in local politics in the city of Birmingham of local voluntary organisations. He found among the 4000 voluntary groups he studied a political participation rate of only 30 per cent in a twelve-month period. The empirical evidence shows, he claims,

> contrary to pluralist arguments, that group resources are distributed with cumulative inequalities; that groups generally operate unilaterally within their own sphere of interests, with little or no organized opposition; that coalition-building and the escalation of group politics are the exception rather than the rule; that the great number and diversity of groups (social pluralism) should not be equated with political pluralism, if only because the breadth of group activities may conceal a narrow range of activists, most of whom appear to be middle and upper-class.[52]

Through their critique of the over-centralised state and their advocacy of welfare pluralism, Hadley, Hatch, Gladstone, etc. appear to borrow substantially from the assumptions of political pluralism.

Their model of society has no class analysis whatever. In their view, beyond the state's distributive and regulatory functions, society's welfare is the natural product of the voluntary enterprise manifested by a multiplicity of groups and organisations outside the formal political system. Once the state sheds its overbearing controls, it retires to an enabler role. Individuals are enfranchised not only by gaining choice from a range of services and strategies, but by exercising their political will directly through them. At the micro-level of direct, local service provision and activity, this participation is meant to empower people in their own limited local spheres of interest, so that they can countervail the power of bureaucrats or professionals. At the macro-level, the sum of democracy is enhanced by this wider participation. There is no space here for a structural view of society as the arena of conflicts between the interests of institutionalised and concentrated power and the powerless, between a class which keeps an iron grip on essential economic and political resources and a class which, give or take concessionary welfare services, is confined to a permanently unequal position in society.

NOTES AND REFERENCES

1. WEBB, A. and WISTOW, G., *Whither State Welfare? Policy and Implementation in the Personal Social Services, 1979_1980*. RIPA: London, 1982.
2. Ibid., p. 64.
3. WOLFENDEN COMMITTEE, *The Future of Voluntary Organisations*. Croom Helm: London, 1978, p. 95.
4. Ibid., p. 60.
5. Ibid., p. 61.
6. Ibid., p. 15.
7. Ibid., p. 25.
8. Ibid., p. 29.
9. Ibid.
10. WEBB and WISTOW, op. cit.
11. HATCH, S., *Outside the State: Voluntary Organisations in Three Towns*. Croom Helm: London, 1980.
12. Ibid., p. 124.
13. Ibid.
14. Ibid., p. 149.
15. Ibid., p. 142.
16. BERGER, P. and NEUHAUS, R., *To Empower the People: the Role of Mediating Structures in Public Policy*. American Enterprise Insti-

tution for Public Policy Research: Washington DC, 1977.

17. DRUCKER, P., *The Age of Discontinuity*. Heinemann: London, 1969.
18. HADLEY, R. and HATCH, S., *Social Welfare and the Failure of the State: Centralised Social Services and Participatory Alternatives*. Allen & Unwin: London, 1981.
19. Ibid., p. 86.
20. Ibid., p. 100.
21. Ibid., p. 93.
22. Ibid., p. 96.
23. Ibid., p. 98.
24. Ibid., p. 158.
25. Ibid., p. 105.
26. Ibid., p. 112.
27. Ibid., p. 167.
28. Ibid.
29. HATCH, S. and MOCROFT, I., *Components of Welfare*. Bedford Square Press: London, 1983.
30. HADLEY and HATCH, op. cit., p. 163.
31. GLADSTONE, F., *Voluntary Action in a Changing World*. Bedford Square Press: London, 1979.
32. HINTON, N. and HYDE, M., 'The voluntary sector in a remodelled welfare state', in C. Jones and J. Stevenson (eds), *Yearbook of Social Policy 1980–81*. Routledge & Kegan Paul: London, 1982.
33. GLADSTONE, op. cit., p. 44.
34. Ibid., p. 83.
35. Ibid., p. 101.
36. Ibid.
37. Ibid., p. 63.
38. Ibid., p. 104.
39. HINTON and HYDE, op. cit., p. 12.
40. Ibid., p. 14.
41. ABEL-SMITH, B., 'Assessing the balance sheet', in H. Glennerster (ed.), *The Future of the Welfare State*. Heinemann: London, 1983, p. 13.
42. MAYNARD, A., 'The inefficiency and inequalities of the health systems of Western Europe', in M. Loney, D. Boswell and J. Clarke, (eds). *Social Policy and Social Welfare*. Open University Press: Milton Keynes, 1983.
43. GLADSTONE, op. cit., p. 100.
44. BRENTON, M., 'Getting a grip on the Dutch voluntary sector', *Voluntary Action*, NCVO, Spring 1980; BRENTON, M., 'Changing

relationships in Dutch social services', *Journal of Social Policy*, Vol. 11. Part 1, January 1982.

45. GLADSTONE, op. cit., p. 83.
46. Ibid.
47. Ibid., p. 103.
48. HINTON and HYDE, op. cit.
49. WEBB and WISTOW, op. cit., p. 67.
50. LOWI, T., quoted in NEWTON, K., *Second City Politics–Democratic Processes and Decision-making in Birmingham*. Clarendon Press: Oxford, 1976.
51. HALL, P., LAND, H., PARKER, R. and WEBB, A., *Change, Choice and Conflict in Social Policy*. Heinemann: London, 1975, p. 130.
52. NEWTON, op. cit., p. 62.

Chapter Nine
EVALUATING THE ARGUMENTS

The preceding chapters have focused on contemporary arguments in support of voluntary action, its extension, or its substitution for the statutory social services, which stem not so much from an 'ideology of voluntarism' in its own right, but more from distinct ideological positions regarding the role of the state and a negative reaction to its role and performance as provider of the welfare state. There is to be found in such advocacy, in other words, a preoccupation not just with an alternative service delivery system but with an alternative political model – 'less government' – whatever the party affiliations of its proponents or the disparity of meanings to be found among them. Residual government and a return to private enterprise and competition on the one hand, and the demand that government facilitate a popular participative democracy on the other, are different perspectives which share an orientation to voluntary social action that, although reinforced by more pragmatic arguments concerning the effective use of resources or the delivery of better-quality services, is not always primarily directed to such considerations. In the context of the economic recession, these two perspectives share, in terms of ideology, a great deal of common ground and both feed, in effect if not by intention, the anti-welfare sentiment that is fostered by a sense of scarcity and crisis in recession. But this is for later discussion. This chapter first seeks to assess what we have learned of the voluntary sector and its potential for the future options assigned to it.

In Chapter 1, we identified practical operational questions about the specific attributes and functions of the voluntary sector in providing social services, and its capacity for some degree of direct substitution for the public sector in providing an alternative social service delivery system. References to such attributes and capacities have, as we have seen in Chapters 7 and 8, frequently figured in the speeches of politicians and the writings of welfare pluralists. These are claims which have to be tested as far as possible against what we know about the voluntary sector. We now take up some of the questions and hypotheses mooted in Chapter 1 regarding the kind and quality of social services that a society such as ours ideally requires, asking whether a voluntary sector delivery system would achieve as much or more than the statutory services. To this end, too, we briefly consider the prototype experience of a country which either largely or wholly relies on the non-statutory provision of social services. Such an evaluation will inevitably be couched in hypothetical terms, and, given the realities of the political and economic climate of Britain in the 1980s, is of little use unless also set against considerations of political and economic feasibility. The options opened up for voluntary action in this new era of the welfare state are crucially determined by the fortunes of the public sector and by future trends in welfare expenditure.

SUSTAINING OR DISMANTLING THE PERSONAL SOCIAL SERVICES?

The central proposals contained in the arguments of both Conservative right-wing politicians and of the supporters of welfare pluralism are, so far, only proposals. They are general and unspecific as blueprints for change, prescriptive in vague terms and creative of a moral climate, a way of thinking, more than of a positive strategy for action. As a collection of ideas, they may still have potent effect in the long term on developments in the social services. So far as they may be distilled from their various sources, these proposals would seem to suggest the following: that the statutory role in the provision of social services should diminish; that the role of the organised voluntary sector should increase; that the contribution of the informal sector should be recognised and supported. This much constitutes a common denominator between the two schools of thought – although it should be stressed that in neither are the precise degree and form of change that are advocated clearly specified. *How much* substitution of the public services is thought desirable, and how far the minimal or residual role of the public authorities should extend are key questions that are never fully addressed. A clear difference of opinion on the continuing role of the latter is apparent, as we have acknowledged, and there are also crucial disagreements concerning public finance and also on the extent of reliance on informal modes of care – issues which are of course related. In these differences we find the re-emergence of the two hypothetical situations suggested in Chapter 1. These were, firstly, that the replacement of any statutory by voluntary sector services would be accompanied by a transfer of social expenditure at least to the measure currently received by the statutory social services. This is the welfare pluralists' position, and does not as such betoken a radical switch from formal to informal modes of social provision. The second possibility was that there should be no such transfer of resources, but that the handing over of responsibility for social caring to the organised voluntary sector, to volunteer effort and to informal care would involve not only a change to an alternative delivery system but also a fundamental alteration to the state's role as financer of social services. This is the logic of much policy discussion in the New Right of the Conservative Party, and the reality of cuts and potential cuts in social expenditure.

Staying with our original orientation to social provisions within the sphere of the personal social services, and taking these two models as feasible options for the sake of the present discussion, we must then explore what each implies in terms of the continuation of our current levels of expectation of acceptable standards in the personal social services or the adjustment of both our expectations and those standards. What measures would we use as a guideline for assessment? Standards of service provision in the statutory sector have an abstract and somewhat unreal quality in that the expectations of legislators and ministerial norms have seldom been backed for the personal social services with the requisite resources for the duties laid on local authorities. Furthermore, there is, at the level of public expectation, a dissonance between the demand that the social services department prevent every case of child battering or death through self-neglect, and an equivalent popular resistance to the notion of paying adequately for such an intensive service. Nevertheless, it is clear that the local authority social services department is constituted on the basis of a range of statutory and non-statutory requirements, and, as the history of its development testifies, it is meant to operate by certain principles and to meet certain official norms, at least ideally. To summarise the functions of social services departments briefly, they are expected to be universally available in a geographical sense, to be accessible as of right to certain categories of the population and of social need, and to provide a comprehensive range of supportive and protective material and non-material services in execution of their statutory duties and powers. In certain instances, such as in the provision of home helps for elderly persons, residential care places, etc. they are at least notionally governed by norms and quotas of provision officially laid down by central government. The philosophy of the Seebohm Report, not substantially changed by

Barclay, was that local authorities should operate a one-door policy so that citizens should know where to look for assistance, that they should be organised to a certain degree on generic rather than on narrowly specialist lines. They should be in a position to compete with other local services for resources, and to foster the integration and promote the coordination of diverse forms of care, particularly in relation to the NHS. All these objectives may be regarded as ideal goals for the personal social services, goals in the process of being realised here and there to varying degrees, but in many respects far from being achieved throughout the country.

For our purposes, however, they supply a reasonable template against which to measure alternative provisions and enable us to ask what targets and standards we would regard as equally essential for a system of voluntary sector social services, and without which we would regard the personal social services system as having not been *replaced* by a different but equivalent system, but effectively *dismantled*. Before we ask such questions, however, let us return to the voluntary sector and try to pull together some of the dimensions which have surfaced in relation to it all through this study, and particularly in the arguments of Chapters 7 and 8. Occurring as a consistent refrain in many of these arguments are a number of claims for the voluntary sector. These are that it is innately innovative, that it is more cost-effective than public sector services, and that it is also more participative. The following sections attempt to evaluate these claims and ask whether such attributes, if genuinely possessed by the voluntary sector, could withstand the assumption of a virtually total responsibility.

INNOVATION AND THE VOLUNTARY SECTOR — Some are not all.

An attribute of voluntary organisations that has been acclaimed in commentaries on the voluntary sector from the Webbs to the Younghusband Report, to Wolfenden, Barclay and a whole host of literature in more recent times, is their 'capacity for innovation'. The Wolfenden Committee, for instance, observed: 'The role of voluntary organisations in pioneering many of the services that were subsequently incorporated in the welfare state is well recognised. There is also widespread recognition that pioneering continues to be a valuable role of the voluntary sector.'[1] Francis Gladstone casts doubt on the capacity of statutory welfare provision to experiment in different ways of meeting problems, with 'its tradition of standardised programmes and centralised planning', and considers risk of failure or controversy poorly compatible with statutory forms of accountability. 'By contrast', he writes, 'voluntary action's tradition of innovation and experiment and greater flexibility in general seems encouraging.'[2] The Barclay Committee, commenting on the variety of innovatory activities generated by a voluntary residential establishment, attributed this to its being part of the voluntary sector and therefore 'able to assess needs in new ways and pioneer new methods of care largely because it is not publicly accountable to a local authority and is prepared to concentrate unashamedly on certain people and a certain area, while leaving local authorities to support others'.[3] The Barclay Report gives other examples of the voluntary sector's flexibility compared with the statutory sector – in responding to urban aid initiatives, for example, and in providing 82 per cent of Good Neighbour Schemes. This relatively solid consensus is shared, as we have noted, by politicians of all colours, and forms a major component of support for the voluntary sector and arguments for its transformation into a mainstream provider of the social services. How accurate a judgement is this? Do voluntary organisations provide 'above all, an outlet for change, creative innovation and improvement',[4] particularly when compared with the local authorities?

If we unravel some of the assumptions around this question of innovatoriness, we find some diverse aspects. Dominant among these is what is perceived as the historical pioneering capability of voluntary agencies, termed by Kramer,[5] who has made one of the few investigations into this, as 'the trailblazing role' from 'private invention to public adoption'. In this role, voluntary bodies originate programmes and services, prove their necessity and feasibility, and then hand them over for replication by statutory bodies. This historical 'vanguard' role may be distinguished conceptually from other elements assumed to characterise the voluntary organisation – that it is flexible, adaptable to new needs, creative and uniquely fitted to take risks and experiment. The reverse side of these assumptions is, of course, the assumption that such capabilities are not possessed by the public services, or are possessed to a markedly lower degree. No one would claim that every single voluntary agency is intrinsically pioneering and innovative, but the vast majority are assumed at least to have the edge over the public sector in this regard.

The pioneering or vanguard role is one that voluntary organisations clearly established for themselves by virtue of organising to combat social problems from the nineteenth century onwards, before the public authorities had developed such a role. We saw something of this process in Chapter 2. Thus the two elements identified by

Kramer as 'private invention' and 'public adoption' are a matter of historical fact and are closely linked in a general perception of voluntary agencies as pioneering. The two elements are, however, no longer so closely joined – largely because the statutory services are already so comprehensive, and it frequently suits the authorities to fund voluntary endeavour rather than run their own services. The expectation has arisen, none the less, from the traditional concept of pioneering, that voluntary agencies will either close down or move to new pastures when superseded by statutory services. Many voluntary agencies have long resisted any such imperatives, defending themselves against statutory encroachments and becoming permanent fixtures, with, consequently, little further claim to be pioneers. Kramer's study of twenty national voluntary organisations in the handicap field[6] throws some light on the subject. He finds that the historical process of public transfer and universalisation applied to some voluntary bodies in the last century but not to others, and that the process itself was more or less complete by the 1960s, since when, 'much of what is often termed pioneering or innovation in the voluntary sector has consisted of previously overlooked-unserved or under-served persons'.[7] Of the new services initiated by the agencies in the preceding twenty-five years, most, he found, were 'small-scale, incremental improvements or extensions of conventional services with relatively few original or novel features'.[8] Little risk or controversy was attached to them, and 'In contrast to the conventional wisdom that the results of voluntary agency pioneering are adopted and universalized by government, 70 per cent of these programs were continued by the sponsoring agency, with half of them receiving some form of statutory support . . .'[9] Often, Kramer noted, programmes continued under voluntary auspices until they became routine or standardised, or too large for the sponsoring body to manage, and frequently 'the adoption of a voluntary agency program was much more a process of "bailing out" on the part of a local authority than an orderly transfer of a demonstrated service program'.[10]

Kramer pinpoints some of the conditions which obstruct the transfer of functions: on the statutory side the difficulty is more likely to be shortage of resources rather than the lack of a defined public responsibility. Also the voluntary programme may be too small for public adoption or its values too sectarian, unpopular or controversial. Additionally, it may be organised across local authority boundaries – a lack of congruence which makes transfer problematic. On the voluntary sector side, he notes that there may also be 'intrinsic resistances within voluntary agencies to the transfer of their services to the government'[11] on ideological grounds or in defence of standards and of participation.

The mystique of the vanguard role, or the propensity of voluntary organisations to innovate, lacks supporting evidence, according to Kramer, and the role itself needs to be reconceptualised. His suggested alternative provides for four possible outcomes, once a voluntary agency has demonstrated a programme and drawn attention to it. These are: (1) adoption by other organisations; (2) transfer to a statutory body; (3) continuation by the original sponsor; (4) cessation. Public adoption is thus removed as an inevitable expectation. Furthermore, the programme itself may not be unique – Kramer found little in the way of 'authentic social inventions, true innovations that are original or first of their kind'. Voluntary agencies are at best only *potentially* innovatory, and this at an early stage of their development before they become institutionalised and bureaucratised. This was a feature recognised by Wolfenden – 'It is an interesting question how far voluntary organisations continue to act in a pioneering role once their opening phase is over.'[12]

If pioneering in the traditional sense is not a hallmark of voluntary organisations any more, what of the other characteristics identified above as innovatory? Are voluntary agencies predisposed towards flexibility, experimentation and risk-taking, at least in their early stages? Do they demonstrate these capabilities more readily than statutory bodies? Kramer's study was limited to a narrow range of voluntary organisations where a goodly proportion were likely to be of the long-established kind. There are voluntary agencies, particularly those which have come into existence since the 1960s in the phase of new development documented in Chapter 3, for whom the notion of public adoption has not been seriously on the agenda. Some, like the Citizens' Advice Bureaux or the Samaritans occupy a virtual monopoly role in their respective fields. Kramer proposes the restriction of the attribute innovative to 'an original, first-of-a-kind mode of intervention or service delivery system, that is, one that is substantially different from previous efforts'.[13] It is clear that some initiatives in the voluntary sector do qualify under this rubric. Johnson cites as examples the growth of self-help groups and advice and information services and the spread of refuges for battered women – all of which uncovered needs which were previously unrecognised or neglected. He concludes that 'both their past records and their present performance support the view that voluntary organisations are an important source of experiment and innovation in the social services'.[14]

It is probably more accurate to stress that *some*, and not *all*, voluntary agencies present such possibilities. A more convincing claim is that which attributes innovative capacities to the voluntary *sector*, capacities which are realised largely, but not exclusively, by the creation of new agencies to meet new needs, or to meet old needs in new ways. Kramer writes: 'Because voluntary agencies are more likely to be trail-blazers in their early stages, their high birth rate, more than their proverbial low mortality, helps ensure changes in the social services. Paradoxically, the oft-criticized "proliferation" of voluntary agencies expresses a resurgent vitality and constitutes one of the prerequisites for the performance of the vanguard function.'[15] He would not preclude the more established agencies from this innovative function, finding in their very bureaucratic rationality, their professionalisation and their needs for organisational maintenance some pressures conducive to new developments.

The discussion so far has suggested the need for a modification of the claims noted earlier for their sweeping attribution to voluntary organisations of a range of positive, innovative qualities. It is clear, from the recent history of the voluntary sector, that new needs and methods are indeed thrown up from time to time – mostly by means of 'fission' or the creation of new agencies or groups – and that this phenomenon is not so widespread or frequent as is claimed. Voluntary agencies do often, but not always, enjoy comparative freedom of action and experiment because they are not part of the public accountability system, because they may be small, informally organised or not unionised. On the other hand, there are also considerable numbers of voluntary agencies which can and should be criticised for their inherent conservatism. It is arguable that some voluntary agencies have survived as long as they have precisely because they have resisted change, have never campaigned with sufficient zeal or political acuteness for change and for the *public* resolution of the problems they exist to succour. Others have been criticised for their outdated methods and attitudes – bodies like the Salvation Army, for example, have been accused of pursuing nineteenth-century institutional policies in building large, impersonal and regimented hostels inappropriate to the 1980s.[16]

Some of the large national disability organisations may be justly accused of over-identification with the establishment, of patronising attitudes to their clientele, and the perpetuation of sadly out-of-date and pathetic images of dependent people in need of charity. Smith suggests that it is 'much too simple . . . to argue that voluntary organisations should carry the responsibility for pioneering. Many areas are much too important to be left to the always patchy and usually under-capitalised voluntary movement.'[17] In this view, voluntary agencies offer an unsatisfactory prospect on account of their lack of resources and monitoring capability for testing innovation, their channelling off from public concern social problems which should be of universal importance, and their obsolete methods and practices.

Voluntary organisations in general cannot then be described as uniquely creative, flexible and innovatory. How does the statutory sector fare in comparison? We have already noted Gladstone's pessimism in this regard, but his verdict on the statutory authorities does not seem to be universally shared. The Barclay Committee writes: 'While much innovation comes from the voluntary sector, there is also clear evidence that innovation is increasingly common in local authority social services departments, though interestingly it was rarely cited in their evidence to us.'[18] Johnson[19] cites developments in the statutory sector such as preventive work in child care and intermediate treatment as well as the Community Development Projects and the Comprehensive Community Programmes as evidence of the innovatory capacities of public authorities. Kramer views the broader scope and complexity and the larger resources of governmental organisations as factors favourable to experimentation – 'There is considerable evidence of the ability of local authorities in England to initiate new programmes.'[20] Again, the research findings reviewed in Chapter 4 offer an interesting connection here – the most significant source of stimulus to the growth of new voluntary agencies in the three towns was found to be the official or semi-official activities of statutory agencies' staff.[21]

It would appear that the actual expression of innovatory forces within the statutory sector is sometimes more easily channelled through non-statutory groups and agencies. This is unsurprising, given that they are often mobilised on behalf of small consumer groups in an *ad hoc*, immediate and flexible response to special needs, in a way that the more generic responsibilities of statutory departments, and their public accountability, might impede. The voluntary sector therefore acquires the appearance of innovatoriness, but is to some extent, in reality, acting as the creative arm of the statutory sector – a complementary relationship which seems ideal.

The stereotypes of the voluntary organisation as innovative and the statutory authority as non-innovative are, as we have seen, founded on far from convincing evidence, but they are pervasive none the less. They emerge quite powerfully in the utterances of politicians and the arguments of the welfare pluralists examined in Chapters 7 and 8. One explanation for the support they command has already been suggested

– the historical legacy of the pioneering image of voluntary organisations. A second has been suggested above – statutory bodies often use voluntary agencies as a form of innovation. A third explanation is related to the first – the pioneering image, combined with the tenuous financial position of many voluntary agencies and the need for a special rationale for their coexistence with statutory services, has become a vital element in the pursuit of grants. Although, as we have stated, the voluntary sector has very real claims to some innovative capacities, there is an inevitable tendency to overinflate such claims in grant applications, especially where funding agencies specifically tie grants and subsidies to notions such as 'seeding' or 'start-up' money for 'demonstration projects' or 'experiments'. Such conditions are a means of distinguishing between claims on finance, a way of rationalising the funding body's short-term commitment to a project and its avoidance of the long-term implications, and a way of justifying, particularly for governmental bodies, the diversion of public funds to non-governmental agencies. Thus both sides collude in sustaining a convenient mythology that serves the interests of each.

The stereotypes may go no deeper than the language used to convey them. For instance, drawing on his experience of working in both sectors, Jef Smith describes[22] how identical projects may attract contrary labels, depending on their origin. The voluntary suitor has to stress a project's creative potential as 'innovatory' or 'experimental', and the statutory project has any such potential played down and disguised for a cautious bureaucracy by being projected as 'orthodox' or 'an extension of existing practice'. In the voluntary sector, then, as Kramer observes, 'innovation' often becomes 'a ploy in the game of grantmanship as agencies describe minor modifications and marginal extensions of conventional programs as original breakthroughs in order to compete for funding'.[23] The funding game thus becomes an endless series of quests for finance which is allocated on a short-term basis for projects and programmes the innovatoriness of which is rarely monitored, given the pervasiveness of the myth surrounding voluntary agencies. The capriciousness of short-term finance makes a nonsense of any concept of planning, and often means that promising new ventures are 'demonstrated' but not replicated. Alternatively, the fictional 'transience' or 'short life' of the voluntary agency which forms part of the pioneering image and justifies its funds, becomes, through one grant application after another, a means of extending its life into permanence, however insecure.

COST-EFFECTIVENESS AND THE VOLUNTARY SECTOR

An argument often employed, particularly by politicians, to support proposals for an expansion of the voluntary sector role in providing social services is that this could be accomplished for less money than in the statutory sector. The claim here is not just that voluntary social services are cheaper, but that they are more cost-effective, achieving a greater return on expenditure than their statutory equivalents. This is an argument that obviously holds a compelling attraction, given requirements for cuts in social expenditure and the extent of unmet and new demand. Thus politicians may argue: 'local authorities should make the fullest possible use of voluntary bodies; pound for pound they are a better buy'.[24] Official advice may suggest: '. . . support for voluntary effort and encouragement of self-help schemes may represent better value for money than directly provided services . . .'[25] The cost-effectiveness advantages of voluntary social services are held to represent a rational way forward in today's straitened circumstances where 'Only a change in the average costs per unit of labour can achieve the stretching of the resources necessary. The only way of achieving this end seems to be much better use of voluntary activity and to procure support and care more effectively.'[26]

How well founded are these cost-effectiveness assumptions? It is clear that their wide appeal derives to some extent from the terminological confusions and fudging of issues fostered by 'ideologically biased wishful thinking' to which we referred in Chapter 7, where the distinctions between voluntary organisations and volunteers, and between those voluntary bodies which employ paid staff and those which rely on unpaid labour, are blurred. The Wolfenden Committee commissioned a small amount of research on cost-effectiveness, but concluded 'that on the basis of the very limited evidence available there was only a little support for the claim that voluntary organisations were much cheaper than statutory agencies'.[27] Where the evidence for greater cost-effectiveness was strongest was, predictably, where volunteers were used most extensively. For the rest, Wolfenden stated: 'it is more difficult to tell whether voluntary organisations are more cost effective than local authorities when both are relying on paid staff'.[28]

Where the deployment of volunteers rather than paid staff is concerned, there can be no doubt that money is saved, although even here it should not be assumed that the use of volunteers is always costless, and, furthermore, it is not axiomatic that the use of volunteers is always and everywhere effective or beneficial. As Hatch indicates, it may be difficult to assess the cost-effectiveness of volunteers who are utilised through voluntary organisations, and few serious attempts have been made to calculate the financial benefits of their use where such assessments are in fact easier – in their direct use by social services departments.[29] Hatch comments:

> the costs of using volunteers even in a well conceived way are not insignificant. Second, poorly conceived schemes for using volunteers may represent a wasteful use of SSD resources. Third, if volunteers are to be an important element in the government's strategy for allocating resources to the personal social services, it is time that some serious attention was given to the costs and benefits involved in the different ways of deploying them.[30]

There is some research evidence to support the cost-benefit advantages of the use of voluntary labour. Hatch and Mocroft cite, for instance, some DHSS research into voluntary meals on wheels services which showed significant cost advantages compared with their equivalents in the public sector, saving local authorities between 50 and 90 per cent of costs.[31] The Kent Community Care Project is based clearly on the premiss that 'There is a vast difference in the unit costs to the organisation of volunteers (and quasi volunteers) and labour paid at the full rate.'[32]

This project has demonstrated the considerable value and effectiveness of the volunteer who is supported adequately by social workers encouraged to analyse the costs and benefits of the various strategies open to them such as residential care or maintenance at home. The Kent project makes small payments to its volunteers to cover expenses, establish a kind of contractual relationship and enable people to volunteer who otherwise could not afford to. The essential factor here, according to Davies[33] is to avoid inflating volunteers' expectations – 'If helpers came to expect to be paid the rate for the job, the crucial cost-effectiveness incentive to local authorites to adjust their procedures and recruit volunteers would be undermined.'[34] Davies sees such volunteers as essentially a complement to the work of social workers along the lines suggested by Holme and Maizels,[35] and warns of the dangers of substituting untrained for trained social workers just on the grounds of cost.[36]

With regard to the substitution of statutory services by those of voluntary organisations with paid workers, cost–benefit arguments are very much weaker. Hatch and Mocroft review a number of studies in this area, including their own attempts to assess comparative costs of residential care for children between statutory and voluntary provisions. In the latter study, differences in average running costs between the two sectors were considerable, but these were much reduced when the differential effects of occupancy rates were standardised for, reflecting the differing circumstances or requirements of each type of home. Such differences as remained were largely attributable to differences in staff costs, with voluntary home care staff not being paid for overtime, and including more domestic work than their opposite numbers in the statutory sector. A study of the comparative costs of running hostels for single adults showed great differences, but these results are likely to have been grossly distorted as the relevant populations compared were significantly different. Barr and Carrier's study of the cost of a voluntary women's refuge reached the conclusion that for a local authority to run it would increase costs by half as much again.[37] Klein compared the cost of local authority and voluntary old people's homes and found that 'costs in local authority homes were 78 per cent higher than in the others and rising much faster'.[38] The pitfalls of such a conclusion are illustrated by his subsequent speculation as to the reasons for this – that local authorities may have higher standards, that their residents may be more infirm or that different accountancy practices might be responsible. An alternative explanation, he writes, 'may be that small organisations are more efficient – if only because they are less circumscribed by Trades Union rules . . . if that is so, then perhaps we should be thinking much more about the creation of a social market in the provision of social care'.[39]

The number of research studies into this cost-effectiveness factor is too small, and their findings too inconclusive to sustain the claims and arguments frequently made for the relative cost–benefit advantages of voluntary organisations. There often are clear differences in the rates of pay and conditions of work of paid staff in voluntary bodies when compared with staff in the public sector, which, as Hatch and Mocroft point out, may be seen as evidence of greater commitment on the part of the former or their greater exploitation. Overheads may well be lower in the voluntary sphere, where they do not have to meet the same requirements as in the public sector, cater for the same intensity of demand, etc. Hatch's work also establishes a discernible trend among voluntary agencies with paid staff towards replication of conditions in the statutory sector – 'though voluntary organisations are sometimes cheaper, this is not always so. Indeed, as they become more established and institutionalised, the costs of voluntary organisations tend to catch up with those of the statutory services.'[40] It is clearly essential for researchers to ensure they compare 'like with like', that they allow for change such as the slowly growing unionisation of the voluntary sector, and that they give as close attention to measures of equivalent effectiveness as they do to comparisons of cost.

There is little demonstrable fiscal advantage for government in transferring existing social service functions from the statutory sector to voluntary organisations except where the substitution is of paid workers by volunteers. Volunteers may be used in a number of ways – to replace expensive resources like social workers, to replace untrained ancillary workers or to cover areas of current neglect, thus perhaps preventing needs arising for paid or professional input. Whether the replacement of professional social workers is seen as a liberating or a deskilling exercise, other factors besides those of immediate costs have to be considered. It is more likely that voluntary labour would be used in the other two ways, but there are further important issues here which must be addressed. Accounts of projects such as the Kent Community Care Project testify to the real benefits of flexible and personal forms of care given by volunteers and quasi-volunteers, and seem to demonstrate a significantly cheaper way of expanding care of elderly and frail people at present scandalously neglected by our society. However, when seen in a broader structural perspective, they neglect other extremely important considerations and may risk perpetuating other social ills. Davies, for instance, perceives the local project's potential as largely dependent upon 'the state of the local labour market for women'[41] – in other words, where opportunities for paid employment are few, local projects will reap the benefit of a pool of unemployed female labour. 'Community care' thus becomes a by-product to some extent of female poverty, and an effective force in perpetuating the exploitative stereotype of the 'caring woman'. Equally, Davies's concern with maintaining a sufficient differential between the 'quasi-volunteer's' allowance and the rate of pay for similar work by the local authority employee, while understandable in terms of his particular objectives, has to be seen in the context of helping to undercut what are already very low rates of public sector pay for such work, and to undermine even further women's purchase on jobs in the public sector where expenditure cuts have hit women especially hard. In Kent, for instance, there have been significant cutbacks in the numbers of some home helps employed during the last few years.[42] That the disappearance of women's jobs leads to an increase in family poverty is incontrovertible. In the context of the Kent Community Care Project's focus on elderly persons, women who are dispossessed even of low-paying jobs today are themselves the poor elderly of the future. It is a final irony, then, that they are now encouraged to volunteer the same kind of services for free, or for real 'pin-money'.[43]

A similar critique may be extended to other issues. Why, for example, is it socially desirable that those voluntary agencies which employ low-paid, non-unionised labour should be seen for that reason as a preferable form of social care to that supplied by the public sector? Exploitation and abysmal conditions of service are social ills too. Timothy Raison, while minister responsible for the VSU, posed the question whether low pay could be assumed to guarantee personal commitment in the voluntary sector as is often claimed, or, conversely, whether it in fact results in the appointment of low-calibre personnel. 'I fully accept', he declared, 'that the principle of a proper rate for the job should apply wherever possible. Moreover, where voluntary organisations are large employers, their employees are entitled to the same degree of protection and support offered by union membership as is the case both in the public and the commercial sector.'[44] A further question arising from some of the arguments on cost-effectiveness concerns the desirability of using voluntary bodies for social services where their advantageous costs are based on the operation of lower standards of care or physical amenity for consumers.

That concern for 'lower costs' in terms of a reduced need for social services expenditure has been a major preoccupation of recent governments in promoting the expansion of volunteer effort through all kinds of new programmes, is apparent from a reading of earlier chapters. What is not equally obvious or discernible is a parallel concern with 'effectiveness'. When local authorities are urged to deploy volunteers and use voluntary organisations on the grounds of their 'greater cost-effectiveness', that phrase has the status of an untested myth. Where local authorities find themselves forced into such deployments by expenditure cuts, or rate-capping, there develops in effect a slow process of substitution of paid workers by unpaid or possibly lower-paid labour. That this does not happen on a job-for-job exchange basis does not alter the long-term effect. It also facilitates the avoidance of searching questions about equivalence. The 'central question' here, write Webb and Wistow, is 'in what circumstances can non-statutory provision offer services of the same quality and acceptability as the state at lower cost or, alternatively, in what circumstances can services of a reduced but agreed level of quality be offered at a lower cost?'[45] Belief in the cost-effectiveness of the various forms of voluntary sector input furnishes a rationale for cuts while sustaining the illusion that this central question has indeed been addressed. Carefully supported and monitored schemes like the Kent project have attended to the concept of equivalence or acceptable substitution, but these are very much the exception. Most of the volunteer schemes developed recently in rapid response to the availability of central funding are unlikely to have been based on precise measurements of equivalent or acceptable standards. Nor are they likely to have allowed for the costs of 'the knock-on effects' of the deployment of volunteers who are likely to stimulate or articulate greater levels of demand on the statutory services.

PARTICIPATION AND THE VOLUNTARY SECTOR

The voluntary sector's image as an alternative mode of citizen participation has featured strongly in the work of the welfare pluralists examined in Chapter 8, and has, indeed, contributed to arguments in support of the voluntary principle over a long period of time. Being a volunteer or member of a voluntary organisation is variously held to compensate for the lack of personal autonomy in other areas of life; to provide concrete opportunities for involvement in areas which are of communal or public importance, and to educate the individual for an intelligent role in civic affairs. It can also, some maintain, afford the citizen a measure of influence, even power, over resources and decisions in the political sphere. In so far as such opportunities are offered in and through the voluntary sector, their positive benefits are undeniable and they should be welcomed and encouraged. The limits to which such participation extends in the political sphere, and its equation with access to economic or political power, have been strongly questioned in the critique of the doctrines of welfare pluralism in Chapter 8. Without returning to these arguments, let us now take a step back to ask whether the seemingly universal assumption of participativeness as an attribute of the voluntary sector is accurate.

Participation can be understood in a restricted sense as meaning to take part in voluntary activities, to be a member of a voluntary organisation. Both Chapters 1 and 4 of this book remind us of the caution needed in defining either of these categories and in measuring the extent of such participation statistically, but it would be true to say that a significant (mostly middle-class) minority of the population is engaged in such ways, and that this is evidence of a lively tradition in British society. We know little from such findings, however, of the precise nature and extent of this form of participation and its impact on people's lives, or of the access it affords into any aspect of public affairs. Helping with a raffle or a jumble sale, doing odd jobs or sitting on a committee are forms of participation which have a real value. They can represent an enrichment of an individual's life and an opportunity to develop broader perspectives and a sense of usefulness, and the more scope for such participation, the better. As a means of linking the citizen with the general run of communal or public affairs, in the way that is often claimed, their importance is perhaps exaggerated. We have already noted in earlier chapters some examples of voluntary agencies' participatory status within public bodies such as the local social services committee, the joint consultative committees or the Community Health Council. There are also the various forms of partnership, such as those considered in Chapters 5 and 6, where they are potential participants in public programmes and decision-making, even if their influence is more advertised than real. Informal groups, such as community action and tenants' organisations do from time to time achieve some kind of say in the political sphere. While not downgrading the importance of such participation and the need for its expansion, we must place it in a perspective which acknowledges its relevance for probably only a small minority of the great numbers of voluntary agencies that exist, and, within those agencies, only a minority of activist members. Being a voluntary worker or a member of a voluntary organisation and thus participating in matters outside one's personal or domestic concerns, does not, for the vast majority of such people, take them beyond participation in the very narrowest sense towards gaining access to influence in the wider society. It could even be an impediment to broader forms of participation through being diversionary of energies, time and awareness.

The simple form of participation – being a volunteer or joining an organisation – cannot be invested automatically with the significance of public or political participation. Is it, however, an important avenue to another form of participation – that of having a say in the affairs of the voluntary agency itself, in a way that the individual volunteer or member perhaps does not enjoy in the work environment or in any of the public sector services? The voluntary agency is frequently viewed as superior in this respect to any statutory equivalent, offering to individuals scope for influencing or determining some part of their environment and the agency's activities and policies. There is no doubt that some voluntary organisations do offer their members such opportunities, but is such participation an enduring characteristic of most voluntary agencies? Are they internally democratic, offering to their membership, staff or consumers rights of participation in the affairs, decisions and policies of the agency, from consultation to control? The general picture is not encouraging, nor is this surprising given the overwhelming bias in British society towards the values associated with authority, hierarchy and social control.

Even within those voluntary bodies formed around the principle of self-help, it is likely that empirical enquiry would find a high rate of non-participation on the part of the greater part of the membership, plus, possibly, a not insignificant dissatisfaction with the dominance of a small élite. Where voluntary agencies are small, they may retain all the advantages of an informal mode of operation, with the intimacy of face-to-face contact and the possibilities of horizontal or co-operative forms of management. Where they are large, however, as in the case of some of the most important social services agencies, forms of internal democracy have to be consciously provided for and worked at.[46]

Andrew Rowe, reviewing the participativeness of voluntary organisations against a set of criteria which included the power to direct or advise on the agency's goals or methods, came to pessimistic conclusions. 'It is a comparatively rare philanthropic organisation', he writes, 'which includes on its management committee a member of staff or a client. Even when this occurs, such committee members are always in a minority, outnumbered by the representatives of the various elitist groups whose support is thought to be indispensable to the success of the organisation.'[47] 'The present situation in the voluntary sector (viewed primarily from the social service angle) appears to be . . . one in which the vast majority of organisations are controlled by an elite whose members see themselves as accountable either to themselves and their consciences or to an "irresponsible" membership which seldom even tries to assert itself.'[48] It is among consumer-oriented bodies that the potential for participation has greatest promise, in Rowe's opinion, and he looks towards these to 'nudge the voluntary sector into setting the pace towards a more participatory society'.[49]

Participatory potential in the sense of scope for sharing in the internal decision-making of the organisation by members, staff or consumers, must be greater for the voluntary agency than for the statutory, but there is little convincing evidence that it is often actualised. The voluntary organisation is not subject to the constraints on direct participation that the public accountability framework imposes, for instance, on the statutory social services department.[50] There is all the same a distinct tendency within the voluntary sector, even for relatively new agencies, to adopt hierarchical and pyramidal forms of organisation and authoritarian styles of management – a pattern often fostered by statutory funding authorities partial to a mirror image of themselves. The closed circle of middle-class patronage and paternalism noted in an earlier chapter (Ch. 5) is a recognisable feature of many of the larger voluntary organisations in the social services sphere. Pressures for greater participative opportunities for this or that group do emerge from time to time, leading to internal crises or even to schisms by breakaway groups forming their own dissident organisations. The general pattern however, appears static and complacent and non-participative, perhaps unchallenged because of the strength and ubiquity of the voluntary sector's image as a rich source of participation by citizens.

THE ARGUMENTS

We have now reviewed three of the strongest and most enduring claims made on behalf of the voluntary sector and used by its partisans to support arguments for its transformation into the main line of personal social services provision alongside the informal sector. The preceding discussion has indicated that in no way can any of these claims be taken as given. That the voluntary sector is more innovative, cost-effective and participative than the statutory sector is not proven. That, in certain forms and under certain conditions, *some* voluntary organisations merit these attributions, and, under the same conditions, that *all* voluntary agencies may have the potential to do so, is not contradicted. The crucial question, one which relates directly to the points made earlier about acceptable standards of provision, is – even were these claims validated for the whole of the voluntary sector in its present social services roles, would they still be true of a voluntary sector which had expanded to carry a more total responsibility? In other words, if voluntary organisations had to shoulder the universal, comprehensive and mandatory responsibilities at present carried by the local authority social services departments, could they retain such advantages? Could they remain innovatory, cost-effective and participative? This point has been made elsewhere – Ann Shearer, having acknowledged the partial validity of such claims, writes:

> But the point about all this is that the voluntary sector has the edge precisely because it doesn't have to worry about the nuts and bolts of statutory care but can concentrate on the experimental edges. Once it started taking on the sheer weight of statutory care – and lost its present luxury of choosing its customers – it would not be long before innovation came pretty poor second to simply keeping the wheels turning. It would not be long before participation gave way to bureaucracy – and that without even a Town Hall gallery to shout from or a vote to cast. And once the costs were added up and like was compared with like, it would be surprising if there was much left of the cost-effectiveness argument either.[51]

If we return to the hypothetical models posed earlier, and relate the first, fully financed option – of a more or less total voluntary sector social service delivery system – to this supremely important point, what can we then say? We were to ask, you will remember, how feasible is the proposition of gradualist welfare pluralism that voluntary social action replace the statutory personal social services and become the main line provider? It is in fact the only one of the two hypothetical options that can be reasonably discussed, planned for and achieved, for a shift to reliance on the informal sector primarily, associated with a massive definancing of the statutory or voluntary services, would simply mean the disappearance into the realms of the invisible and unmeasurable of social services as we know them. Assuming, under our hypothesis, that such a transfer were fully financed, and assuming also that no less than present standards of provision were acceptable, is it practically possible for the voluntary sector to undertake such a task? Leaving aside the certainty that an instant expansion of the voluntary sector to the degree required would be out of the question, which no one would seriously dispute, could the substitution be effected gradually in a way that would leave the undoubted advantages of voluntary sector services intact while sustaining the 'nuts and bolts of statutory care'? We have already laid down the main principles and standards of provision currently operated at least theoretically by the statutory sector. What other characteristics of the voluntary sector can we retrieve from earlier chapters to help place the above questions in realistic perspective?

So far in this chapter we have conceded, with important reservations, the features of innovatoriness, cost-effectiveness and participativeness as, at the most, potential attributes of the voluntary sector. We know that voluntary agencies have a range of positive possibilities: they are able at times to detect new needs and develop new strategies for dealing with them; they can focus on minority and unpopular groups and causes in a way that public authorities find difficult; they can develop specialist expertise by concentrating their efforts in limited areas; they can often circumvent the bureaucracy that accompanies large-scale enterprise and public accountability; they can tap reserves of voluntary endeavour that add fresh resources to depleted social services reserves, and offer opportunities of altruism and need satisfactions to volunteers. They can and do offer, through their very multiplicity and 'purposive duplication'[52] a wide and perhaps competitive range of choices to the consumer. All these positive attributes are to be found, in varying degrees, within the voluntary sector as it is presently constituted, although not in ways that are either predictable or reliable, nor as generously distributed as is often claimed.

Any calculation of the effects of a statutory–voluntary sector replacement would also, however, have to take into account the negative features of the voluntary sector. These features, particularly relevant to any expansion of its role, are rarely accorded the prominence given to negative aspects of the public social services which have been so heavily criticised by pro-voluntarists. We know that the Wolfenden Committee regarded the uneven distribution and performance of the voluntary sector as one of its most serious weaknesses. We know, from the research findings discussed in Chapter 4, that voluntary organisations, which are self-generating by definition, do not emerge automatically where the need for them is greatest and that their spread is governed significantly by class factors. Particularly where voluntary agencies are heavily dependent upon private giving and fund raising, resource distribution is biased towards wealthier geographical areas and towards groups and causes with the most popular appeal. The multiplicity of agencies that exists, from some points of view a positive advantage, means that fragmentation of effort and coverage, and wasteful duplications as well as inter-organisational boundaries and rivalries, impede the integration and coordination of services. Although agencies can offer at times a greater 'whole-person' approach to certain categories of consumer than can the more multi-purpose statutory authorities, other facets of the voluntary sector such as the unevenness, variability and multiplicity of its agencies would militate against the attainment of a 'one-door' policy for multiple and complex problems and the achievement of one recognisable port of call. Voluntary agency specialisms, valuable in themselves as back-up to the statutory services, would fragment a generic approach.

One of the most serious problems affecting a voluntary sector expansion would be that of accountability, understood not just in financial terms but also in the wider, political sense. Voluntary groups and agencies, while evidence of a lively and articulate tradition of self-help, communal effort or protest, are relatively narrowly defined in terms of their interest groups and constituencies. While supplementing the representative democratic system in a way that is valuable and necessary, they can lay no claim to as great a public representativeness as democratically elected authorities – however imperfect the system is. The boards of management of voluntary agencies are neither democratically elected nor removable; they are not answerable to identifiable constituencies nor to consumers. Their public accountability for the use of resources and policies implemented is virtually non-existent, being limited to the simple accounting requirements attached to the legal status of a registered charity, friendly society or trust. Their services are available not as a matter of right but on the basis of charity. If all or a major part of the statutory social services were to be transferred to voluntary agencies, this transfer would amount to a radical depoliticisation of the social services, leaving the public authorities only the relatively indirect mode of control and oversight that is possible through the disbursement of finance.

It should also be remembered that, besides the relatively small range of sophisticated, well-financed and professionalised voluntary organisations which have, as we have seen, operated alongside statutory social services in child care, adoption, care of the elderly, etc. there exists a vast plethora of groups and agencies in the voluntary sector which are of the shoe-string variety. They are characterised by uncertain and sparse funding, perhaps ill-defined or constantly changing memberships, little formal structure and rudimentary forms of organisation, dependence upon voluntary effort and good-will and the employment of one or two permanent staff at most, who may or may not be trained for their jobs. The informality, structure-lessness and amateurism of such bodies may be viewed as part of the voluntary sector's strengths and general appeal in contradistinction to the bureaucratised statutory services, but the assignment of a sub-stantial and responsible social services role to such bodies raises serious questions. To devolve responsibility for the kind of social services we currently enjoy to a mass of informal, ill-organised groups and organisations would constitute as great a dismantling of the personal social services system as to leave its functions solely to hidden providers of informal care. Alternatively, such a devolution would have to recognise the lack of organisational capacity and require the formalisation of these bodies and their transformation into structures which could be held accountable for the use of public money and the performance of social services functions.

It might be argued that many of these more negative characteristics of the voluntary sector only appear as deficiencies when viewed from the perspective of the statutory sector's much more total and compre-hensive responsibility. Furthermore, it might be suggested that such deficiencies derive essentially from the small-scale and precarious nature of their resources, and from their need constantly to pour time and effort into raising charitable funds and processing grant appli-cations. Might not the major defects of lack of coverage responsibility and fragmentation, lack of public accountability and lack of organ-isational capacity be consciously redressed with the gradual assump-tion of a greater social service delivery role and the underpinning of this role by the availability of adequate public funds? Public funds were, for the welfare pluralists at least, to be the key to developing such a role. Gladstone, for example, sketches out ten possible modes of statutory support for voluntary social action, any combination of which might include direct financing, fiscal relief to charitable giving and fiscal incentives for donors, matching grants, contract-financing and the weighting of central government grants to local authorities who finance voluntary agencies. The enhanced availability of public funds, together with an augmented charitable income encouraged by statutory measures, might in due time serve to ensure that voluntary initiative springs up evenly through the land to preserve some notion of territorial justice. It might also be used to tighten up organisational structures and management, just as government subsidies are being linked to such conditions increasingly under the present system, and measures might then be devised to use public finance as a sanction to promote public accountability. How successful such a financial system – provided, sponsored or governed by the state – would be in achieving these goals and counteracting the deficiencies of a voluntary sector social services delivery system, is open to argument. Whether it would also bring in its wake serious repercussions for the voluntary, non-statutory identity of the groups and organisations concerned is also a matter for consideration. Whether, in counteracting the voluntary sector's deficiencies, such a statutory financial and regulatory role would also stifle many of its more positive aspects is another. In a qualified way, it is possible to gain insights on such questions from the experience of other countries which rely substantially on voluntary sector provision of social services. The two examples chosen here are the Netherlands and the United States.

INTERNATIONAL LESSONS

In choosing the Netherlands and the United States to illustrate the voluntary sector role as major social services deliverer, we are selecting two advanced industrial societies, one large and heterogeneous in composition, with a federal governmental system, the other small and homogeneous with a relatively simple and centralised governmental system. Both are high welfare spenders, even though the United States has been described as 'a reluctant welfare state'; both have a cultural tradition that is anti-government and pro-private enterprise, although this is stronger in the United States than in the Netherlands. Both have a strong historical tradition of church-based social services and social influence. Both depend to a great extent for the delivery of social services on the activities of voluntary agencies which receive substantial finance from public sources. There are also clear differences between the two countries and their voluntary sectors which will emerge as we look in detail at their social services systems. Either country represents, for our purposes, a kind of 'test-case' against which to measure the transfer from a statutory to a voluntary sector system which we have hypothesised in this book. In asking how a 'welfare pluralist' system works elsewhere, however, we must remain aware of a most singular distinction between Britain and the two countries under consideration – neither the Netherlands or the United States developed a statutory system of social services first and then dismantled it in favour of a voluntary sector system. The early history of voluntary social services, common to all three, was superseded for the personal social and community services by a statutory system only in Britain.

A brief overview of the Dutch social services system can only draw out its dominant characteristics and trends and point the reader in the direction of a wider literature.[54] Personal social and community services in the Netherlands are almost totally (and generously, by British standards) financed by government but are wholly, with a few minor exceptions, delivered by non-statutory agencies. These agencies, known by the Dutch as 'private initiative' organisations, owe their origins to the denominational and secular social welfare traditions of the nineteenth century which were expanded and built upon by government in the modern era of the welfare state. Like British voluntary agencies in that they are self-generating, self-governing, non-profit-distributing, of public benefit and constitutionally separate from government, Dutch social welfare agencies bear closest resemblance in their composition to British voluntary organisations at the most formal end of the range, such as Barnardo's or the Family Welfare Association. They are highly professionalised and bureaucratised, with paid staff and virtually 100 per cent of their funds comes from government. They do not therefore depend on fund raising nor on the efforts of volunteers, except for voluntary boards of management. Governmental subsidy has ensured not only their survival but also their institutionalisation, and their strong monopoly over social service provision has been and continues to be based upon a traditional antipathy in Dutch society, rooted in its religious history, to a direct governmental role in social service delivery. The multitude of 'private initiative' welfare agencies is seen as a necessary bulwark against the encroachments of the state, and supporters of the system claim that they are uniquely 'of the people' in a way that the cumbersome political system is not.

Here in the Dutch welfare system we find a useful, if perhaps idealised, prototype of the 'welfare pluralist' system we have hypothesised – one that is adequately financed through public funds. We can see right away that the effect of the availability of public subsidy has been to force Dutch voluntary agencies in the direction of formal, rational and bureaucratic organisation. Such developments have been a requirement of subsidy policies, along with all kinds of administrative controls designed to safeguard public investment and ensure high-quality services. The agencies are held in a much closer relationship with the state than is the case in Britain – so much so that they might even be defined as 'quasi-statutory' or as 'privately administered public institutions'.[55] They have in fact lost many of the features that still distinguish their British counterparts, even those which rely heavily on government funding. Not having to compete with a superior statutory provider, they have less recourse to arguments based on claims to greater innovatoriness, cost-effectiveness or participation, although these do surface from time to time when the agencies feel under threat of more government control. Such claims are heavily countered by the barrage of criticism aimed at the Dutch 'private initiative' welfare system in recent years as pressures on welfare expenditure have forced cutbacks. The agencies stand accused of all the defects and deficiencies held to be characteristic of the statutory social services in Britain and of any institutionalised welfare system.[56]

They are also held by their critics to be defective in ways peculiar to their status as 'private initiative' organisations, and in need of governmental reform and control. They are deemed to be expensive, inefficient and wasteful of public money, cooperating with each other only to form an over-powerful interest group continually pressurising for higher welfare expenditure, rigid and unresponsive to unmet social need or the demands of consumers, duplicating activities wastefully and leaving serious gaps in provision, over-professionalised and impersonal. Their fragmentation 'into a host of small, unifunctional agencies which can give little assurance of continuity of service, where people in need of their services wander from one office to another and get lost, and where even the information and advice services contribute to the general confusion'[57] has not so far been rectified through government financial or administrative controls, nor is there any guarantee that this is possible. Government subsidy has not achieved an even spread of agencies or activities either geographically or in relation to social need and deprivation. The mounting criticism of recent years, sharpened by the effects of economic recession, has led to calls for greater government controls over the 'private enterprise' welfare system and for the entry of municipal government into a financial and regulatory role for the first time in an effort to localise this control and integrate the social services through a local welfare planning system. There is little pressure for the municipalisation of service delivery, and, although the local government role is seen as a potential corrective to the dysfunctions of the 'private enterprise' system and the inability of central government to control it, the local authorities will remain heavily dependent on both the expertise and the resources of the private agencies. The experience of most local authorities is limited to the administration (by social workers) of the public assistance scheme. In the larger cities, this cash benefit service has, however, been stretched in recent years to give welfare services to the marginal and unpopular groups neglected by the private agencies.

In contrast, welfare services in the United States may be delivered directly by public agencies such as the local public welfare departments, by proprietary (profit-making) agencies or by private, non-profit-organisations (voluntary agencies), sometimes known in the United States as the 'Third Sector'. The historical predominance of voluntary service organisations has given way to a massive expansion of the public sector. 'During the last twenty-five years the growth rate of government has been at least four times that of the voluntary sector, with a ten-to-one spending ratio of government to nongovernmental organisations.'[58] Private philanthropy, a large and important source of Third Sector funding, and far more significant than its equivalent in Britain, has not kept pace with economic growth over the last ten years[59] and many of the non-profit service agencies have become increasingly dependent upon public funds. A major philanthropic trust, the United Way, coordinates fund raising, mainly through payroll deductions, to raise more than $2 billion yearly[60] for its affiliated voluntary agency members, but even so, contributes only about 20 per cent of their average income.[61] This form of federated fund raising is described by Kramer as seeking 'to reconcile the interests of donors, agencies and consumers by imposing a greater meaure of rationality and efficiency on fund raising'.[62]

This and other forms of American philanthropy have come under attack from women's and minority groups who have challenged its business and corporate connections, its orientation to established institutions, its neglect of marginal and minority groups and its resistance to innovation or controversy. 'We believe that instead of being the venture capital for social change, philanthropy has, for the most part, patterned itself after its corporate and governmental counterparts. Most of it has become bureaucratic, safe and more conservative and less willing to take risks than the government.'[63] About 40 per cent of voluntary agency income is supplied from public funds[64] and the availability of this source of income, which has escalated rapidly since the late 1960s, has given rise to what has been termed 'the new voluntarism'.[65]

This renaissance of interest in voluntarism, dating from the 1970s, has marked out the Third Sector as a 'distinctive institutional sector'[66] and provoked much fresh debate on the proper role of non-profit organisations in a changing American society. Fuelling this renaissance, a spate of social welfare legislation, from 1962 onwards, facilitated the development of an agency relationship between state and local welfare agencies and the proprietary and non-profit sectors. Federal policies, culminating in the well-known Title XX amendments to the Social Security Act in 1974, made possible the contractual arrangements known as 'Purchase of Service' (PoS) whereby state and local welfare departments were authorised to buy services from profit and non-profit agencies and other public bodies.[67] With a 75 per cent rate of reimbursement to states from the federal government, Title XX became the 'major Federal source of general social service provision'.

The social service agencies, required to tender competitively for funds, had to make written contracts with the states for their services. The states were required to plan welfare services, stipulating the form of non-governmental agency participation. What resulted was the 'qualitative transformation of social services', encouraging a trend towards universal provision, diversified services, a shift from public direct delivery to a mixed public/private system, and the decentralisation of services.[68] The necessity for the integration and co-ordination of social services was emphasised, together with the involvement of the public in the planning system. For the non-profit service agencies, now heavily reliant on government purchase and other sources of public funds, there have arisen with new force, problems labelled by Kramer[69] as 'vendorism, grantmanship and dependency'.

The complexity and uncertainty of the competitive, tendering relationship where agencies 'sell' their services, or where they invest time and resources on negotiating grants, are problems that remain secondary, and are, in fact, contained within, the third problem of dependency. Growing dependency on public finance carries with it, as we have noted earlier, the risk of loss of identity, and it is this loss and the intermingling of the public and private spheres which has marked out the resurgence of the 'new voluntarism' in the United States and has given rise to anxious debate. The new 'Quasi-Non-Governmental Organisation',[70] created as a result of federal legislation or official initiative, almost wholly reliant upon federal funds, monitored by federal agencies and heavily dependent on government whim, is seen by Pifer as having jeopardised its 'place in the tradition of voluntary associations in American life'.[71] It is seen to be contaminated by government funds and to have sacrificed its role in the 'revitalization of the democratic process'.[72] More neutral assessments remark 'the blurring of the line between public and private agencies' which 'produces ambiguities in placing the responsibility for policy making'.[73]

A number of writers see this interpenetration as a means whereby the demand for services is accommodated with the strong American tradition of minimal government. 'Effectively, the mixing of public and private activities masks or screens the growth of government interference with the private sector and thereby makes it more palatable to the average American. This illusion maintains the myth of less government while government actually whittles away at the essential substance of private autonomy.'[74] Smith comments: 'Americans have sought a high service society while preserving the appearance of a limited government role.'[75] The growth of the hybrid, 'the public/private sector',[76] where distinctions between governmental, profit-making and non-profit-making agencies are more and more difficult to make, requires new levels of policy analysis and policy visibility as well as the sifting of alternative strategies to ensure 'access, adequacy, accountability, effectiveness and efficiency'.[77]

Besides concern with the changing governmental/non-profit sector relationship and the potential loss to the latter of its role in the pluralist system, there exists a vigorous critique of the 'pathologies of voluntary associations'.[78] This critique bears a striking resemblance to the criticisms already cited in relation to Dutch 'private enterprise' agencies. Langton lists ten problems of voluntary organisations which could as well be applied to Dutch or British agencies. The welfare system itself, divided as it is between different levels of government and between public and private sectors, and also varying greatly between individual states, exhibits an incoherence and fragmentation that militates against the effective or equitable solution of social problems. Within this relatively chaotic range of provisions, fragmentation, lack of access and visibility and neglect of certain groups and problems are exacerbated by the sheer multiplicity of voluntary agencies, their narrow focus and self-interest. Kramer writes:

> The large number of categorical programs for favored groups developed under governmental auspices, together with the specialized interests of voluntary agencies, has resulted in some of the most complex and multiproblem cases falling to the overextended and poorly staffed public welfare departments in each county. Despite the inequities and lack of coherence in the system, there does not appear to be any resolution of ambiguous role relationships between governmental and voluntary agencies.[79]

Among those who call for reform of this state of affairs through the assertion of a clear public responsibility rather than a renewed emphasis on the autonomy of the non-profit agencies, Alfred Kahn advocates the organisation of personal social services on the basis of a principle of universalism. Only through a 'case-accountable, integrated *system*' can efficient, effective and humane services be achieved. Existing problems 'can and must be solved in the framework of a sound public system on a state level, with many state and local variations. For this there is no voluntary alternative: there is no way to achieve an accountable, comprehensive, universal, personal social service system without a strong, operating, public sector.'[80] Once this is established, relationships with the voluntary sector can be profitably explored and the positive advantages of the non-profit agencies can be utilised to greatest effect.

Unfortunately, events overtook any consideration of a rational realignment of public/private relationships in the United States welfare system in the way suggested by Kahn. The year 1980 saw the coming to power of Reagan and the Republican Party committed to reasserting 'frontier values', cutting public expenditure on welfare programmes, lowering taxes for the rich and escalating defence spending. The net result of such policies for welfare and particularly damaging for the voluntary sector, was a cut of 25 per cent in federal funding of health, welfare and education programmes, and abdication of the former active role of federal government in favour of block grants to the states to spend on any purpose.[81] Over ninety programmes were abolished and sixty-six laws were repealed, including Title XX of the 1974 Social Security Amendments, the 'turning back of forty years of social reform in social policy'.[82] The Right, traditionally in favour of voluntary enterprise, 'confronted with the new voluntarism with its advocacy, consumerism, greater involvement of women, ethnic and sexual minorities, and its extensive reliance on governmental grants and contracts'[83] withdrew its support in the anti-welfare backlash provoked by economic recession. In Kramer's view, the fate of the voluntary sector in the United States is inextricably linked with the future of the welfare state itself. This, after several years of 'Reaganomics', has suffered substantial attrition, while at the same time poverty and social deprivation have been increased.[84]

Both the Dutch and the American examples of a voluntary social services system demonstrate instructively the inherent disadvantages for a comprehensive, coherent, accessible and equitable system of personal social services, of reliance on voluntary agencies either as monopoly providers or as major co-providers. In both countries, the availability of funding has produced some very high quality voluntary provisions, and the volatile American tradition, particularly, has thrown up imaginative and creative initiatives such as advocacy or independent living centres for handicapped persons, which shine out for replication in Britain. Viewing the personal social services systems in global terms, however, and applying the criteria of universality, access, etc. set up earlier in this chapter, and, indeed, utilised in both Dutch and American assessments of their services, it becomes clear that non-statutory agencies, by definition separately and atomistically organised, are incapable of meeting these criteria. Where such agencies assume a monopoly or major role, they inevitably become heavily dependent upon public funds and subject to some degree of governmental oversight. The resulting institutionalisation negates many or most of the positive features they exhibit in a supplementary and minor role. Having sacrificed their positive attributes in this way, they are affected by over-expansion of their role and responsibilities and their negative features and incapacities are thrown into sharp relief, thus provoking demands for more extensive measures of government control or, as is the case in the United States now, helping to fuel the arguments for a radical dismantling of services and a return to the residual welfare state. Hugh Lanning, in his study of the American purchase of service system, concluded:

> I can find no solid evidence that would suggest that Britain has anything to gain from a substantial change in the method of social service provision . . . This is not to say that the British welfare state is perfect in all respects for clearly it has many inadequacies. However, it is my view that the voluntary sector would be more usefully employed in seeking to change the Government's policy objectives and advocating specific improvements in the current system, rather than seeking salvation in the illusory hope that a new method of provision will cure

many of the problems. The American experience does not show that a different method of provision can, of itself, bring about changes that are not already the mutual objectives of the funders, the providing agencies and the clients.[85]

For Britain to have developed its personal social services along similar lines to those which continued in the Netherlands and the United States, was perfectly feasible at one time. Chapter 3 explored some possible reasons for Britain's divergence in the direction of a main-line statutory system and we need not repeat them here. Probably the most important explanatory factor in a comparison between the three countries is the strength of societal resistance to direct government intervention. Neither the Netherlands nor the United States achieved the basic and universal framework of statutory services that was established in Britain – a framework which, even though never adequately financed, can offer coherence, potential integration, equity and a host of other positive advantages which those countries lack. To downgrade or dismantle this established system in order to give a greater role to the voluntary sector, is to try to roll history back on itself – with the added lunacy of replicating defects which the Dutch and American examples should properly caution us to avoid. A further point to stress in this comparison, moreover, is the virtual disappearance in those two countries of the volunteer as a central component in service delivery. The process of development of the voluntary sector to the role of monopoly or major provider, with the aid of state funds, seems inevitably to follow a path similar to that taken by our statutory services – the path towards professionalisation and bureaucracy. Parallel to this process is one whereby statutory social services are marginalised and left with a residue of unpopular, difficult or neglected social problems, a low-status service created by the 'creaming-off' operations of the non-statutory agencies. This process can be clearly seen in the Dutch and American examples.

CONCLUSION

This chapter has tried as far as possible to subject to critical scrutiny some of the main arguments for the Conservative minimalist and the welfare pluralist case. It has found that claims for the inherent superiority of the voluntary over the statutory sector in the provision of social services in its capacity for innovation, its cost-effectiveness and its scope for popular participation have to be treated with some considerable caution. They have also to be understood in the light of the very natural tendency to inflate claims to attributes and characteristics which are known to be favoured by governmental and non-governmental funding agencies as a means of justifying the allocation of funds where perhaps other criteria are lacking. Possibly the most telling assessment of arguments based on these claims is that which measures them against the current relatively marginal responsibilities of voluntary agencies and their projected future expansion to something near complete coverage responsibility. It can be concluded that even the very real attributes of the voluntary sector which distinguish it from the statutory would be hard put to survive a more major role, and the experience of other countries has helped to illustrate this.

NOTES AND REFERENCES

1. WOLFENDEN COMMITTEE, *The Future of Voluntary Organisations*. Croom Helm: London, 1978, pp. 46–7.
2. GLADSTONE, F., *Voluntary Action in a Changing World*. Bedford Square Press: London, 1979, p. 63.
3. BARCLAY COMMITTEE, *Social Workers: Their Roles and Tasks*. Bedford Square Press: London, 1983, section 5:33, p. 82.
4. HINTON, N., 'Opinion' *Voluntary Action*, NCVO, Autumn 1980, p. 5.
5. KRAMER, R., 'Voluntary agencies in the welfare state: an analysis of the vanguard role', *Journal of Social Policy*, Vol. 8, Part 4, Oct. 1979; KRAMER, R., *Voluntary Agencies in the Welfare State*. University of California Press: Berkeley, 1981.
6. KRAMER, *Voluntary Agencies*.
7. KRAMER, 'Voluntary agencies', 1979, p. 477.
8. Ibid.
9. Ibid., pp. 479–80.
10. Ibid., p. 481.
11. Ibid., p. 483.
12. WOLFENDEN COMMITTEE, op. cit., p. 47.
13. KRAMER, *Voluntary Agencies*, 1979. p. 487.
14. JOHNSON, N., *Voluntary Social Services*. Blackwell & Robertson: Oxford, 1981, p. 38.
15. KRAMER, *Voluntary Agencies*, p. 189.
16. WALKER, P. 'Institutions: a 19th Century answer to a 20th Century problem? *Community Care*, 26 Mar. 1981.
17. SMITH, J, *The Times*, 14 Apr. 1978.
18. BARCLAY COMMITTEE, op. cit., p. 81.
19. JOHNSON, op. cit.

20. KRAMER, *Voluntary Agencies*, p. 188.
21. HATCH, S., *Outside the State*. Croom Helm: London, 1980.
22. SMITH, J., 'The case against the voluntary sector . . . knocking the "sacred cow" ', *Social Work Today*, Vol. 9, No. 13, 22 Nov. 1977, pp. 8–9.
23. KRAMER, *Voluntary Agencies*, p. 189.
24. ENNALS, D., *Municipal Review*, August 1976.
25. DEPARTMENT OF HEALTH AND SOCIAL SECURITY, *Priorities for Health and Social Services: The Way Forward*. HMSO: London, 1976. Section 10:4, p. 72.
26. DAVIES, B., *The Cost Effectiveness Imperative, the Social Services and Volunteers*. Volunteer Centre Occasional Paper: Berkhamsted, 1980, p. 5.
27. HATCH, S. and MOCROFT, I., 'The relative costs of services provided by voluntary and statutory organizations' *Public Administration*, Winter 1979.
28. WOLFENDEN COMMITTEE, op. cit., p. 155.
29. HATCH, S., 'The voluntary sector: a larger role?', in E. M. Goldberg and S. Hatch, *A New Look at the Personal Social Services*. Policy Studies Institute: London, 1981, pp. 68–78.
30. Ibid., pp. 71–2.
31. HATCH and MOCROFT, op. cit.
32. DAVIES, B., 'Strategic goals and piecemeal innovations: adjusting to the new balance of needs and resources', in Goldberg and Hatch, op. cit., pp. 46–67.
33. DAVIES, *Cost Effectiveness Imperative*.
34. Ibid., p. 5.
35. HOLME, A. and MAIZELS, J., *Social Workers and Volunteers*. Allen & Unwin: London, 1978.
36. DAVIES, 'Strategic goals'.
37. Cited in HATCH and MOCROFT, op. cit., pp. 397–405.
38. KLEIN, R., 'The social policy man: priest or pragmatist?' *The Times Higher Education Supplement*, 15 Feb. 1980.
39. Ibid.
40. HATCH, 'Voluntary Sector', p. 69.
41. DAVIES. *Cost Effectiveness Imperative* p. 8.
42. *Guardian*, 4 Feb. 1984.
43. FINCH, J. and GROVES, D., *A Labour of Love*, Routledge & Kegan Paul: London, 1983.
44. RAISON, T., *The Voluntary Sector: Some Questions*. Assocation of Researchers into Voluntary Action and Community Involvement, Occasional Paper, No. 2, 1980, p. 9.

45. WEBB, A. and WISTOW, G., *Whither State Welfare?* RIPA: London, 1982, p. 65.
46. BRENTON, M., 'Worker participation and the social service agency', *British Journal of Social Work*, Vol. 8, Part 3 (1978), pp. 289–300.
47. ROWE, A., 'Participation and the voluntary sector: the independent contribution', *Journal of Social Policy*, Vol. 7, Part 1, Jan. 1978, p. 48.
48. Ibid., pp. 54–5.
49. Ibid., p. 56.
50. BRENTON, 'Worker participation'.
51. *Guardian*, 21 Nov. 1979.
52. WEBB and WISTOW, op. cit., p. 66.
53. GLADSTONE, op. cit.
    Journal of Social Policy, Vol. 11, Part 1, Jan. 1982, pp. 59–80; KRAMER, *Voluntary Agencies*, WOLFENDEN COMMITTEE, op. cit., appendix 7, pp. 275–8.
55. GILBERT, N. and SPECHT, H., *Dimensions of Social Welfare Policy*. Prentice-Hall: New Jersey, 1974.
56. BRENTON, 'Changing relationships'.
57. BRENTON, Ibid., p. 71.
58. KRAMER, *Voluntary Agencies*, p. 67.
59. FILER, J., *Giving in America: Toward a Stronger Voluntary Sector* (Filer Commission Report). Commission on Private Philanthropy and Public Need: Washington, DC, 1975.
60. NATIONAL COUNCIL OF VOLUNTARY ORGANISATIONS, *The Community Fund: United Way Feasibility Study*, NCVO: London 1983.
61. KRAMER, *Voluntary Agencies*, p. 135.
62. Ibid., p. 134.
63. DONEE GROUP REPORT, *Voluntary Action Leadership Journal*. Winter 1976.
64. KRAMER, *Voluntary Agencies*, p. 151.
65. LANGTON, S., *Journal of Voluntary Action Research*, Vol. 10, No. 1, pp. 7–20. Jan.–Mar. 1981.
66. Ibid.
67. LANNING, H., *Government and Voluntary Sector in the USA*. NCVO: London 1981.
68. GILBERT, N., 'The transformation of the social services', *Social Service Review*, No. 51, Dec. 1977, pp. 624–41.
69. KRAMER, p. 152.
70. PIFER, A., 'The Non-Governmental Organisation at Bay', in

D.C. Hague, (ed.) *Public Policy and Private Interests*. Macmillan: London, 1975, appendix II, pp. 395–408.

71. Ibid., p. 382.
72. BECK, B., 'The voluntary social welfare agency: a re-assessment', *Social Service Review*, Vol. 44, Part 2, June 1970, pp. 147–54.
73. BRILLIANT, E., 'Private or public: a model of ambiguities', *Social Service Review*, Vol. 47. 1973, pp. 384–96.
74. Ibid., p. 394.
75. SMITH, B., quoted in JACKSON, J., 'Voluntary Sector Research in the USA.' *ARVAC Bulletin* No. 17, Summer 1984. Association of Researchers into Voluntary Action and Community Involvement: Wivenhoe, Essex, p. 10.
76. KAMERMAN, S., *The New Mixed Economy of Welfare*. Social Work, Jan.–Feb. 1983, pp. 5–10.
77. Ibid., p. 9.
78. ADAMS, L., quoted in LANGTON, op. cit., p. 14.
79. KRAMER, *Voluntary Agencies*, p. 70.
80. KAHN, A., 'A framework for public–voluntary cooperation in the social services', *Social Welfare Forum 1976*. Columbia University Press: New York, 1977, p. 56.
81. KRAMER, R., 'Societal trends affecting the voluntary sector in the United States,' Speech to National Institute of Social Work Seminar, London, July 1981.
82. Ibid.
83. Ibid.
84. RAYNOR, G., 'Welfare in America'. *Voluntary Action*, NCVO, Winter 1983, pp. 6–7.
85. LANNING, op. cit., p. 46.

Chapter Ten
PRESENT AND FUTURE

The previous chapter has taken up some of the principal practical arguments put forward in support of a greater reliance upon voluntary sector social services and has tried to separate fact from myth in their use. At this pragmatic level, the case for a major substitution of the statutory social services is unconvincing even within its proponents' own terms. There is little point in replacing public social services, for all their undoubted faults, with voluntary services which, while equally or more expensive, do not offer very considerable advantages over the statutory sector. It is claimed that voluntary services are a better and more effective way of spending public money on social services, but, as we have seen, even where this argument goes beyond myth to demonstrable fact, the positive benefits of voluntarism cannot be sustained if what is wanted is a system of provision approximating to the one we have now in terms of standards and coverage responsibility. If an *equivalent* system of provision is not feasible, therefore, where does the logic of these arguments take us? It is not clear from the arguments of welfare pluralists what real losses might be expected alongside the real gains they promise, whether they balance each other out or whether the resulting downscaling of the social services might pass beyond what is acceptable for a society such as our own. The remaining roles and responsibilities of the statutory authorities are sketched in with only the broadest of brushes, with little attempt to examine the problems of financing and regulating an expanded and diffused collection of voluntary sector provisions.

The idealisation of voluntary social services and the promulgation of a rich mythology regarding their capacity to substitute for and improve on the statutory services is a strategy shared by welfare pluralists and New Right politicians alike. The latter's arguments, motivated by the desire to restrict government responsibility and cut welfare spending, are perhaps more transparent in their implications.

They are directed towards a substitution which offers substantial cost advantages, and are, therefore, only realisable in terms of volunteer rather than paid labour, and unpaid, informal care by women rather than collectively organised services. They envisage the return of responsibility for 'self-help' to individuals and communities, and imply the possibility of a radical dismantling of the personal social services through a gradual process of resource starvation. They are vague about the nature and precise level of the state's role in providing support services or a minimal system of provision.

AN IDEOLOGY OF VOLUNTARISM

It was suggested earlier that the two schools of thought share common ground in the manufacture of a climate of opinion which fuels and sustains the individualist and anti-welfare sentiments fostered in the economic recession by the New Right. It is perhaps at this level, the creation of an ideological climate through the steady attrition of the old orthodoxies and the constant reiteration of 'radical alternatives', that we have seen most actual change in recent years. As previous chapters indicate, the official policies in operation have not actively matched the policies enshrined in the rhetoric, and substantial moves towards privatisation and the dismantling of welfare services have not yet occurred. In cases like that of the NHS, this reticence is evidently based on a pragmatic assessment of the strength of popular attachment to this institution, and of working-class ambivalence towards market and statutory options in a range of social services.[1] A government looking forward to a further term renewal of its mandate has every motivation in proceeding slowly and cautiously building up popular receptivity to its radical agenda. Much has been written of the apparent susceptibility of the British working class to 'the revival of liberal political economy with the social market as its centrepiece, and a new "authoritarian populism" mobilised by issues of law and order, sexual permissiveness, strikes and scroungers'.[2] Where welfare services are concerned, such an appeal is fostered by bringing the welfare state into disrepute and offering a confirmatory ring to the legitimate dissatisfactions of those who are at the receiving end of unsatisfactory, stigmatising and sometimes openly contemptuous social services. Writing of the Thatcher period, Golding found its strength in 'its ability to ventriloquise the genuine anxieties of working-class experience'.[3] Consideration of the extent of popular support for anti-welfare policies has to take into account not only the direct recipients of the social services, but those who shoulder the main burden of financing them. The regressive impact of a taxation system which now begins at a threshold of 41 per cent of average male manual earnings for a two-child family compared with 179 per cent thirty years ago,[4] has paved the way for considerable resistance to the further expansion of social services. Add to this the 'ideological vacuum'[5] of the Labour Party and its tired statism predicated on economic growth and existing patterns of redistribution,[6] and it could be said that the New Right ventriloquists have had little need of the supportive eloquence of co-ventriloquists from the welfare pluralist camp.

The suggestion that welfare pluralists have contributed towards the legitimation of the New Right is a critique taken up by Beresford and Croft, who suggest that far from the New Right needing such legitimation, what we are seeing is a shift in the Fabian consensus: '. . . it is such an accommodation of Fabianism *to the right* rather than a smokescreen role *for the right* which has been the reason for welfare pluralism's development and present prominence'.[7] The welfare pluralists stand accused here of depoliticising welfare issues, neglecting the political and economic context of social policies, perpetuating acceptance of exploitative gender divisions, and preparing the way for the New Right's real locus of interest, the burgeoning of the market in social welfare. Additionally, their critics conclude, writers such as Hatch, Hadley, Gladstone, etc. have, in finding state welfare wanting, 'then argued for welfare pluralism without making any serious attempt to consider or explore the reform of existing state welfare'.[8]

In Chapter 1, we posed the question whether the collected positive aspirations and negative reactions of the proponents of a voluntary sector social service delivery system amount to 'an ideology of voluntarism'. Do we find, among the arguments of politicians and welfare pluralists, a coherent theory for the redistribution of personal social services responsibilities away from the state? In the era we have examined, in Chapter 7, of the Conservative Party's initial swing towards the voluntary sector, there is little to suggest a theory of voluntarism in its own right, with systematic reasoning, conclusions, proposals or a programme of action. The rhetoric of politicians has been shown to lack clarity and consistency, and, in the final analysis, their enthusiasm for voluntarism amounts to a refraction of the market ideology that has been given new fervour with the rightwards swing of politics. The voluntary sector, in all its forms, represents varying degrees of privatisation, and because the political arguments in support of it derive mainly from the economic and governmental philosophy inherent in New Right ideology, and not because of its own proven and intrinsic merits, this particular case for it cannot be described as a theory in itself. The lack of specificity is a failing in the welfare pluralists' case also, although there is much of substance and value in their critique of the welfare state as it is, and in their attempt to integrate lines of thought on such issues as community action, popular participation, etc. This study has endeavoured to highlight the essential defects in much of their argument, however, and to point to the unproven nature of some of their claims, and the romanticism of some of their proposals.

Alongside this lack of realism in practical terms lies a failure that is more serious – the welfare pluralists' neglect of the political and economic structures and relationships that condition social welfare. The welfare state's lack of success in transforming these structures and relationships and in eradicating some of the grossest forms of inequality in our society, are arguments used to good effect in the welfare pluralist critique, but its location of the roots of such failure in the characteristics of this or that statutory social service is an unsatisfactory and superficial diagnosis. Its proponents make the mistake, common among social policy writers, of focusing myopically on the formal structures of the welfare state only, ignoring the real determinants of poverty and inequality in the wider economic and political system. If their institutional diagnosis is faulty, it follows then that their alternative institutional remedies will fall seriously short of solving the real problems. Because of this superficiality, and because of the relative naïvety of the welfare pluralists in failing to perceive their own origins and popularity in terms not just of 'the crisis of the welfare state' but of the ideological swing towards the Right and against welfare born of the economic recession, their case cannot be viewed as an entirely separate and independent one from that of the Conservative politicians we have examined. Despite the differences in view that we have noted, the defects in their arguments may well mean that the end result of a switch to reliance on a voluntary system would be the minimal social services desired by the New Right. However, disregarding the possibility that the welfare pluralists' case might constitute a further push towards a market ideology, their arguments do represent, in their own terms, a serious attempt to rethink the formal structure of the social services and to put forward alternatives. Their ideas and proposals contribute to 'a theory of voluntarism' but fall short of the requirements of a credible alternative to the present system.

THE FUTURE

If this book has reached a negative verdict on the proposal for a major transfer of statutory social services responsibilities to the voluntary sector, what alternative future does it then see ahead? This can only be put forward as a possible option, rather than as a prediction, for it is highly unlikely that policy makers will ever bother to take stock and carefully work out a constructive division of labour between the two sectors which will capitalise on the strengths of each to minimise the weaknesses of both. The more likely scenario for the future is one of drift, possibly towards the run-down of services in the public sector and the hand-over of responsibilities to the voluntary sector and informal care. What are the assumptions on which we can build a picture for the future at least in ideal terms? The first premiss is one that is outside the scope of this study but crucial none the less – there will be and can be very little essential improvement in the contribution that provisions like the personal social services make to social justice, equality and the eradication of poverty, without a basic change in society's priorities and values. The latter depends to a considerable extent, not on economic growth, but on a redeployment of economic resources. The problem is thus circular, but to the extent that the actual workings of welfare state machinery have contributed to the support of anti-welfare strategies by much of the working class, there is scope for important reform in individual social services. Where the personal social services are concerned, this study would contend that the public sector delivery system is at least potentially better designed than the voluntary sector to guarantee services that are comprehensive, universal, accountable and effective. It offers greater scope as an instrument of equitable distribution, although this capacity could be vastly extended by radical measures to democratise and decentralise its services. This second assumption is followed by a third – that the voluntary sector has, in its various manifestations, a valuable contribution to make in this field and that this is maximised in a situation where it operates in special roles and is thus not responsible for the bulk of service provision.

What is envisaged then is a mixed system as now where statutory and voluntary sectors continue to coexist and where the former is emphatically assumed to provide not just a bare minimum level of services but a full and comprehensive range. What is required is a total vision accompanied by a whole strategy directed at the overriding goal of meeting social need, where each system would make the input it is best fitted to make. An essential part of this whole strategy would be a firmly articulated *political* commitment which, while acknowledging the salutary critique of those who censure the welfare state in its present forms, and the value of voluntary and informal systems of care as signalled by welfare pluralists, would fight to reinstate the public sector in the public mind. So far a war of attrition has been waged in the realm of ideas, paving the way, as we commented earlier, for the erosion and dismantling of the statutory services or, at the very least, for a halt in their further development. This destabilisation of the statutory principle needs to be thrown into reverse. A further message requiring definitive expression to counter the more fanciful assumptions of the Conservative minimalist line particularly, concerns the dependence of both voluntary and informal systems of care on a broad framework of statutory services for their effectiveness and development. This point has been reinforced by DHSS-commissioned research findings on neighbourhood care[9] which, its authors conclude, indicate that ' "informal caring networks", "care for carers" and so forth depend fundamentally on the prior existence of strong and well-financed professional services and are a realistic prospect for social policy only on that basis. What informal care needs is not a safety net but a springboard.'[10] Commenting on the failure of government efforts to encourage a voluntary care system for the elderly, Abrams concludes that 'governments have got it wrong. They will need to spend money to provide back-up services. If we want to go into neighbourhood care in a big way in urban areas, the evidence we have points to the conclusion that caring must be turned into a proper job with paid wages, and not rely on volunteer housewives who simply don't have the time or sufficient numbers to do the work.'[11]

Are we then advocating a return to the 'tired rhetoric of the Labour Party and the orthodox left'[12] in its uncriticial and unimaginative attachment to the existing patterns and institutions of the welfare state? Is a reassertion of the primacy of the statutory sector to mean just a reaffirmation of the traditional Left's defence of the welfare state which 'has failed to recognise its contradictory nature, that in its scientised, bureaucratised and masculinised form it has become largely indefensible'?[13]

A number of writers have taken up the challenge to the Left posed by the New Right's ability to tune in so accurately to the feelings of powerlessness and alienation engendered in recipients of the social services. They indict the traditional Left for its failure to move beyond incremental reforms and tinkerings with the system as it stands to an understanding that what is needed above all is a total and radical restructuring of the relations of production and their dependent patterns of distribution. Stanton writes that

> . . . the state, and state agencies are not simply things; an apparatus to be restructured. It is a process of social relations. Without understanding that this is the problem, and how the structures reflect and mediate these social relations, there is the likelihood that simple restructuring (decentralising as such, for example) may simply reproduce the same sets of relations in miniature. The important issue is therefore relations between worker and worker, and workers and users.[14]

Rose and Rose talk of the 'transformative understanding of need' which will acknowledge the alienation of social and productive relations as the starting-point for radical change in the welfare state. In his analysis of the 'limits of welfare-statism', Walker comments, 'Labour's approach to social policy reflects a belief that the structure and operation of the welfare state is basically sound . . . Labour's social plans do *not* start from the position that a fundamental change is required in the structure of the welfare state, in particular between clients and claimants and those who administer benefits and services.'[15]

It is in the acknowledgement of the unequal power relationships upon which all other relationships in society are predicated and in the call for their transformation that we become most aware of the lack of such an analysis in the arguments of welfare pluralism and its essential orientation towards the status quo. The New Left's evaluation of the failures of the welfare state has stemmed from its understanding of 'our role as bearers of capital's social relations'[16] whereby alienation permeates relationships at every level of society, not least in the experience of workers and consumers of the state's welfare services. Structural change in economic and social relationships at a macro-level thus has to be replicated in a transformation of the social relations of welfare services which redresses the imbalance of power between consumers and professionals, administrators and political decision-makers who currently dominate. 'It is not simply a matter of planning to restore Tory cuts and reverse the privatisation of social services', writes Walker. 'What is required is the *socialisation* of social services, giving clients and claimants and other local citizens a significant role in their management and operation.'[17]

It is in the case made for community control of the social services and in the handing over of power and resources[18] that a defence of the public sector's role is rooted. The welfare state's critics who propose substitution of the statutory services by the voluntary sector are pinpointing as a central and cogent justification, the dichotomising into 'them and us' of service providers and decision-makers on the one hand, and the general public and consumers on the other that is characteristic of the public sector. Their proposed resolution of this dichotomy, to repatriate the services to 'the people' through privatisation, fails to resolve it because it assumes an irreconcilable divide between government and the governed. Alternatively, socialist proposals for transformation of public institutions like the social services, face the dichotomy head on in asserting that we, the people, have a right to control the services we pay for, to demand accountability from those who purport to represent us. To set out to transform the social relations within the statutory social services and make them reflect social need is both to mirror and to reinforce the wider struggle.

Where in all this do we see the future role of the voluntary sector? What are the special functions that its various organisations and groups may perform to best effect with or alongside the mainstream statutory services responsible for universal and comprehensive coverage? We have documented many of the positive roles, real or exaggerated, of the voluntary sector earlier in this study and have noted their origins for the most part in the scope, challenge, uncertainty and freedom of a comparatively marginal status within the welfare state. In projecting an ideal role for the voluntary sector, where it may maximise its best capabilities in meeting social need, a number of caveats must be borne in mind. There is an existing historical distribution of roles and functions within it which will determine the limits of change. There is also, in the absence of any overall regulatory authority, a limit to the positive direction of its activities one way or another. However, in discussing the future role of the voluntary sector, we are speaking, from a public policy perspective, only of those parts of it which have a direct relationship of some kind with the statutory sector, in that their activities fall within its sphere of responsibility either designedly on the part of the public authorities or by default, and possibly depend to some degree on public finance or sanction. A significant measure of direction is thus within the scope of the public policy process. Statutory authorities can choose to make a comprehensive provision themselves which will make voluntary action redundant, or they can neglect a certain field or consciously delegate it elsewhere. The availability of finance from public and charitable sources is, as we have seen, a crucial determinant of the direction in which voluntary agencies develop. Redirection also becomes possible through the spontaneous decisions of voluntary organisations and groups themselves. In line with the socialisation of the main-line services advocated above, it should be possible to identify cooperatively certain parts of the total strategy geared to meeting social need which are best entrusted to special-purpose or special-interest agencies. This identification should, where public money is involved, be a publicly accountable exercise. It follows too, that public subsidy could be used to redress existing bias in funding policies and consciously to redirect funds, in the way that the Greater London Council used to good effect, away from traditionally favoured agencies and functions towards neglected areas and groups, particularly those with a working-class orientation. Additionally, public and other funds could be used constructively to encourage voluntary bodies to transform their own social relations, and maintain both internal democracy and external accountability.

In his book *Voluntary Agencies and the Welfare State*[19], one of the best studies of this area in recent years, Ralph Kramer assigns a selection of five possible roles to the voluntary agency. It may be regarded as 'a bulwark against, an alternative to, a substitute for, or a complement or supplement for, government, or as an obstacle to a more universal and comprehensive system of personal social services'.[20] In carving out an ideal role for the voluntary sector in relation to the statutory we can incorporate some of these elements, linking them with the functions categorised in Chapter 1 – service provision, mutual aid and pressurising. The service-giving functions of voluntary agencies and groups which come within the ambit of public policy, financially or otherwise, should be seen in line with our analysis so far, as complementary to the statutory sector rather more than as a substitute for it. The major thrust of public encouragement of voluntary sector participation ought to be in the direction of special needs and minority groups for whom special-purpose or specialist strategies are clearly more appropriate than the general orientation of the statutory services. Funding should be withdrawn from those agencies which cannot meet these criteria and which operate in parallel to the statutory social services for no very good reason but historical inertia. Voluntary organisations should concentrate on doing things that they can genuinely do better than governmental agencies or which the latter cannot do at all. In recommending such a concentration and economy of effort, Jef Smith comments,

Voluntary organisations are the corner shops of the social services. By developing specialised lines, by watching keenly for gaps in the market, by offering a more personalised or more dedicated service, by simply trying harder, the better managed groups may stay somewhat precariously in business. But they cannot any longer offer a realistic alternative system to the state-run social service supermarkets and they should not aim to compete with the professional statutory organisations which will increasingly have to carry the load of mainstream provision.[21]

Where voluntary action does not involve substantial sums of public money of course, it is free to flourish as it will. Where there is substantial donation of volunteer time and energy, directed at a social purpose which fits in with the aims of social policies, then statutory authorities should actively encourage it and help to finance its organisation. It should be no part of public policy to off-load functions and services which are best systematically organised and guaranteed within formal structures and with a paid labour force. The main thrust again should be in the direction of a category of activities which either cannot or should not be provided within the public sector.

It is in the areas of mutual aid, self-help, community and neighbourhood action, information and advice services, etc. that the voluntary sector comes into its own. Such functions belong uniquely to voluntary initiative, even when fostered within a statutory environment, and may variously serve as an alternative to, a complement to government, in Kramer's typology, or at times as a bulwark against it. These are areas where statutory encouragement and finance should be readily available, so long as this subsidy is not made the excuse for resource starvation and under-provision in the main-line social services system. The two sectors could work together, each supporting the other in ways special to its own competences. We have noted earlier in this book the burgeoning of these forms of voluntary action over the last two decades – they are areas where the voluntary sector can demonstrate strengths and special claims, and where future development should be encouraged.

If there is one direction in which the voluntary sector could make a significant and valuable contribution to the overall goal of meeting social need, it is that of mounting a watchdog role over the main-line provisions of the welfare state. What Kramer calls the 'improver role or advocacy' is a role which, within a system dominated by a socialised system of statutory services, could perform a function that is both essential and requires a separate, detached status. A system of social services that is controlled in formal, political terms by the community for which it exists, still has need of an extra, external monitoring capacity. Chapter 5 in this book has discussed the important developments of the last twenty years in the field of pressure-group activity. Voluntary action and voluntary organisations should adopt this role above all others and perform a very real public service in criticising the main-line provisions of the state, in demanding adequate levels of service and attention to neglected areas, and in campaigning in the public sphere for the redistribution of social resources according to social need. Such an advocacy function needs to operate at the level of neighbourhood community action, advice and information services, as well as at the national level where the interests of minority, unpopular or neglected groups and causes require social policy and legislative response.

In urging the concentration of voluntary sector activity that is aided or influenced by the state into certain, restricted categories of activity where it may realise its unique potential and make its most forceful contribution to a whole strategy of meeting social need, we are advocating a division of labour which could reflect economic realities better than the present system which is *ad hoc*, ill-organised, duplicatory and fragmented. Local authories should have clear policies with regard to their subsidy and delegation to the voluntary sector, and the consumers and clients of their social services should have the possibility of controlling and influencing such policies. It is arguable,[22] that some voluntary sector functions and not others should be financed from the public purse. Specialist service provision and selfhelp should be fostered by public subsidy, and those voluntary agencies which accept public money should be accountable for it – although there will always be a need for flexible, risk or venture finance, over which local authorities should not exercise tight controls. Generally, such sums are small and represent potential investments on which a local authority could afford to gamble imaginatively. It might be suggested that the type of voluntary sector activity which should not be financed from public funds is the third and most important function that we have identified – that of the watchdog or bulwark, the critic of government. We have noted in Chapter 5 the dangers of political control and the muzzling of its critic by the governmental or charitable trust that feeds it, and the smothering of protest and campaigning which is not acceptable to the government of the day by the use of an obsolete Charity Law. In response to this suggestion, it has to be remembered that certain less popular or orthodox causes find it hard to attract alternative funds, particularly from the general public. There might be great value in a stronger commitment to the principle already established to a limited extent in government, of financing its opposition for the general health of the public good. When all is said and done, voluntary organisations will have to continue, if they value their separate identity and autonomy, to solicit their funds from a variety of sources in order to avoid the kind of dependence and incorporation that has become evident in the relationship between such agencies as the MSC and the voluntary sector that was discussed in Chapter 5.

CONCLUSION

In this chapter, a brief sketch has been attempted of the future options open to the statutory and voluntary sectors in their relation to one another. The arguments have drawn on the findings of earlier chapters concerning the historical development of this relationship before, and throughout the era of, the welfare state. These have been placed, as far as possible in this study, within the context of economic realities and political ideologies. The state and the voluntary sector are seen as essential but separate components of a total system for meeting social need, each of which has its own contribution to make. This division of responsibilities derives from an honest assessment of the attributes and capacities of both, an assessment which has been somewhat distorted in the arguments and rhetoric of Conservative minimalists and welfare pluralists. Future developments lie, of course, within the fortunes of the economy and the continuation or not of the rightwards swing of the political system. This study represents an attempt to counter the disinformation and detractions spawned within the present economic and political climate, and to defend the statutory social services against attack, in terms which look, not backwards to established and failed forms of welfare provision, but forwards to new systems of socialised response to social need where voluntary organisations and groups can play a new, clear and reinvigorated role.

NOTES AND REFERENCES

1. JUDGE, K., SMITH, J. and TAYLOR-GOOBY, P., 'Public opinion and the privatisation of welfare: some theoretical implications', *Journal of Social Policy*, Vol. 12, Part 4, Oct. 1983, pp. 469–89; TAYLOR-GOOBY, P., 'Two cheers for the welfare state: public opinion and private welfare', *Journal of Public Policy*, Vol. 2, Part 4, 1982, pp. 319–46.

2. ROSE, H. and ROSE, S., 'Moving right out of welfare and the way back', *Critical Social Policy*, Vol. 2, No. 1, Summer 1982, pp. 7–18.

3. GOLDING, P., 'Rethinking commonsense about social policy', in D. Bull and P. Wilding, (eds), *Thatcherism and the Poor*. CPAG Poverty Pamphlet 59, April 1983, p. 10.

4. WALKER, A., WINYARD, S. and POND, C., 'Conservative economic policy: the social consequences', in Bull and Wilding, op. cit., p. 19.

5. ROSE and ROSE, op. cit., p. 16.

6. WALKER, A., 'Labour's social plans: the limits of welfare statism', *Critical Social Policy*, Issue 8, Autumn 1983, pp. 45–65.
7. BERESFORD, P. and CROFT, S., 'Welfare pluralism: the new face of Fabianism', *Critical Social Policy*, Issue 9, Spring 1984., pp. 19–39.
8. Ibid., p. 23.
9. ABRAMS, P., *Patterns of Neighbourhood Care*. ARVAC Volunteer Centre: Berkhamsted, 1979; ABRAMS, P., 'Social change, social networks and neighbourhood care', *Social Work Service*, 22 Feb. 1980, pp. 12–23.
10. ABRAMS, P. *et al.*, *Guardian*, 4 Feb. 1981.
11. ABRAMS, P., *Guardian*, 16 Nov. 1981.
12. ROSE and ROSE, op. cit., p. 14.
13. Ibid., p. 16.
14. STANTON, A., 'Collective working in the personal social services: a study with nine agencies', MSc. Thesis, Cranfield Institute of Technology, quoted in BERESFORD and CROFT, op. cit., p. 34.
15. WALKER, 'Labour's social plans', pp. 50–1.
16. LONDON–EDINBURGH WEEKEND RETURN GROUP, *In and Against the State*. Pluto Press: London, 1979, p. 80.
17. WALKER, 'Labour's social plans', p. 62.
18. BERESFORD, P., *Community Control of Social Services Departments*. Battersea Community Action: London, 1981; BERESFORD, P., 'Public participation and the redefinition of social policy', in C. Jones and J. Stevenson (eds), *The Year Book of Social Policy in Britain, 1980–81*. Routledge & Kegan Paul: London, 1982.
19. KRAMER, R., *Voluntary Agencies in the Welfare State*. University of California Press: Berkeley, 1981.
20. Ibid., p. 273.
21. SMITH, J., 'Reforming the corner shops of the social services', *The Times*, 14 Apr. 1978.
22. KAHN, A., 'A framework for public–voluntary cooperation in the social services', in *Social Welfare Forum 1976*. Columbia University Press: New York, 1977, pp. 47–62.

Part Six
DOCUMENTS

Document One
THE GOSCHEN MINUTE ON THE DOCTRINE OF MUTUALLY EXCLUSIVE SPHERES

626. From the Poor Law side, the same principle was laid down in a circular issued by the Poor Law Board in 1869 and based on a Minute written by Mr Goschen (afterwards Lord Goschen) the President of the Board. In effect, the circular laid down that:
(1) charitable organisations would find their most appropriate sphere in assisting those who had some but insufficient means and who, though on the verge of pauperism, were not actually paupers:
(2) the Guardians should deal with the wholly destitute:
(3) if the chariable organisations did consider it within their province to deal at all with the persons on the parish lists, they should do so not by affording additional means of income but by supplying once and for all such articles as did not clash with or overlap the relief administered by the Guardians.

From: *Report of the Committee on the Law and Practice relating to Charitable Trusts* (Nathan Committee Report), Cmd. 8710, HMSO (1952), pp. 157–8.

THE ROLE OF VOLUNTEERS AND VOLUNTARY ORGANISATIONS

495. Linked with the idea of the importance of the participation of consumers of the social services is the question of the role of the volunteer and of the voluntary organisation. Voluntary organisations pioneered social service reform in the past and we see them playing a major role in developing citizen participation in revealing new needs and in exposing shortcomings in the services. In certain circumstances, voluntary organisations may act as direct agents of the local authority in providing particular services, though such arrangements can present problems both to the local authority, which may be led to neglect its own responsibilities and to the voluntary organisation which may be prevented from developing its critical and pioneer role. Voluntary organisations will have an important part to play in social development areas especially by considering the redistribution of their resources to those areas of greatest need.

496. The social service department should play an important part in giving support, both financial and professional, to vigorous, outward-looking voluntary organisations which can demonstrate good standards of service, provide opportunities for appropriate training for their workers both professional and voluntary and show a flair for innovation. A really productive partnership between the local authority and voluntary organisation in the social service field will require modifications in the ideas of both. The day when voluntary organisations could act as vehicles for upper and middle class philanthropy appropriate to the social structure of Victorian Britain is now past. Remnants of old practices and attitudes remain in the condescension and social exclusiveness of a few voluntary organisations and in the suspicion and mistrust of some local authorities. On the whole, however, established voluntary organisations are reviewing and assessing critically their policies, and new types of voluntary organisation are emerging, often around self-help groups, and in-

creasingly characterised by the youthfulness of their members and the radical nature of their criticisms of the existing services. The local authority will need to tolerate and use the criticisms made by voluntary organisations and not expect the partnership to be without conflict. A certain level of mutual criticism between local authority and voluntary organisations may be essential if the needs of consumers are to be met more effectively and they are to be protected from the misuse of bureaucratic and professional power in either kind of organisation.

497. Our views about the importance of community involvement in the services point to the need to encourage informal 'good neighbourliness' and to a crucial role for volunteers in the more formal sense, both within and outside the social service department. We indicate here only some general suggestions of how the relationship of the social service department and volunteers should develop, for a committee set up by the National Council of Social Service and the National Institute for Social Work Training, under the chairmanship of Miss Geraldine Aves, is examining the role and preparation of voluntary workers and we look forward to its report.

498. It is not surprising that the reaction to the increased government responsibility for health, welfare and education is to assume that there is less need for voluntary service. This is not the case. With the continuing growth of the personal social services it will be more and more necessary for local authorities to enlist the services of large numbers of volunteers to complement the teams of professional workers, and the social service department must become a focal point to which those who wish to give voluntary help can offer their services. There is sometimes difficulty in obtaining an adequate supply of regular voluntary workers, not only to meet new demands but also to replace those who have served for many years. We have little doubt that there is a large untapped supply of such people who would willingly offer their services if the jobs were worthwhile, were clearly defined and shown to be relevant to present-day needs even though they might involve a very modest amount of time. Volunteers would be forthcoming if it were known that, without their continued help, many of the social services might find it impossible to do much more than help the known casualties, with little hope of extending preventive action. Volunteers have an important role to play in residential institutions, such as hospitals and old people's homes, though a different one from that of professionally trained residential care workers. The recent growth of young people's voluntary service

movements is among the developments which show a new response to demonstrated need.

499. We are not suggesting that volunteers can replace professional workers but they can assume, within the framework of the service and with some preparation, many of the duties that need not be carried by a qualified professional worker and which volunteers may even be better fitted to perform. The direct use of voluntary workers by local authority departments will involve a working-out of functions which may only come about gradually after experiment. Meanwhile, there are advantages in working through existing voluntary organisations which would recruit the volunteers. By using volunteers in this way, not only will it be possible to give more help to more people who need it but also to encourage citizen participation and associate a considerable cross-section of the community with the work of the social service department.

500. Responsibility for using voluntary help wisely must rest with the principal officer of the social service department and, indeed, fitness for this particular responsibility should be among the qualifications for this post. He must show that volunteers are wanted, that their contributions to the social well-being of others is an essential part of the social services and that the social services rely on them to play a part. This attitude can be fostered by members of local authorities who, in a sense, are themselves volunteers. It would be a grave error for anyone to regard the service of a voluntary worker as charity, in the worst sense of that word. Indeed, we have no doubt of the social value of voluntary work, not only in contributing to the resources available to help the community but in showing concern for neighbours and for helping people returning to the community from institutions such as prisons and mental hospitals and so demonstrating community acceptance of them. The department must include volunteers in its plans and it will have to show, in the training of new staff, the important role of volunteers.

From: Department of Health and Social Security, *Report of the Committee on Local Authority and Allied Personal Social Services (Seebohm Report)*, HMSO (1969), pp. 152–4.

Document Three
LEGISLATION FOR CENTRAL GOVERNMENT FUNDING OF THE VOLUNTARY SECTOR

The following Acts of Parliament give statutory power for government departments to make grants to various recipients including voluntary organisations:

Department of Education and Science
Education Act 1944

Section 100(1)(b): empowers the Secretary of State to make provision by regulation for the payment of grants towards expenses incurred (other than by local education authorites) in the provision of educational services or for the purposes of educational research.

Department of the Environment

Housing Act 1974

Sections 29 to 32: grants payable for housing projects approved by the Secretary of State. These are made to housing associations who provide housing for rents, and who must be registered as a charity or Friendly Society.

Department of Employment
Employment and Training Act 1973

Section 2: enables payments to be made to organisations providing facilities for people to select, train for, obtain and retain employment

Section 5: enables grants to be given, subject to Treasury approval, to organisations providing people with temporary employment, and to organisations undertaking research into matters relating to employment, unemployment or training.

Disabled Persons (Employment) Act 1944
Section 15:   enables payments to be made to organisations providing sheltered employment for severely disabled people.

Department of Health and Social Security

Children and Young Persons Act 1969
Section 65:   powers to give grants to voluntary organisations in connection with the establishment, maintenance or improvement of voluntary homes which are, or are becoming, assisted community homes under part II of the same Act.

Health Services and Public Health Act 1968
Section 64:   empowers the Secretary of State to help voluntary organisations in the health and social services field if they are providing a service similar to a relevant service – that is,aa service which she or a local authority must or may provide, or are promoting or publicising such a service or a similar one, or giving advice on how such a service or a similar one can best be provided. (In addition, since 1 April 1974, this power has been delegated to the regional and area health authorities set up under the National Health Service Reorganisation Act 1973.)

Supplementary Benefits Act 1976
Schedule 5:   powers to give grants to voluntary organisations, towards the cost of maintaining centres for purposes similar to those of the re-establishment centres or reception centres maintained by the Supplementary Benefits Commission.

Home Office

Criminal Courts Act 1973

Section 51(3)(c): enables funds to be paid to any society or person engaged in establishing or carrying on bail hostels or approved probation hostels or homes

Section 51(3)(f): enables grants to be paid to any society or person engaged in supervising or assisting persons convicted of offences with a view to their rehabilitation.

Section 51(3)(g): enables funds to be paid to any body or persons approved by the Secretary of State in the conduct of research into the causes of delinquency and the treatment of offenders.

Local Government Grants (Social Need) Act 1969

This is the statutory authority for the Urban Programme. The Act empowers the Secretary of State to pay grants to local authorities which in his opinion are required to incur expenditure by reason of the existence in any urban area of special social need. The ability to channel assistance to voluntary organisations through the Urban Programme derives from the various powers which local authorities have to pay grants to voluntary organisations, and from the fact that such expenditure by local authorities may be grant-aided by central government within the terms of the 1969 Act.

Race Relations Act 1976

Section 44: enables the Commission for Racial Equality to give financial or other assistance to any organisation appearing to the Commission to be concerned with the promotion of equality of opportunity and good relations between persons of different racial groups. Government money may not be used for this purpose without the consent of the Secretary of State.

From: The Wolfenden Committee, *The Future of Voluntary Organisations*, Croom Helm, London (1978), pp. 232–6.

LEGISLATION FOR LOCAL GOVERNMENT FUNDING OF THE VOLUNTARY SECTOR

Statutory powers of local authorities and powers delegated to area health authorities

Appendix 4A of the Wolfenden Report listed the statutory powers for central government to make grants or assist them in other ways. The following Acts of Parliament give statutory powers for local authorities (and health authorities) to make grants at their discretion to various recipients including voluntary organisations:

England
Children and Young Persons Act 1963
Section 1: empowers a local authority to make arrangements with voluntary organisations for the provision of such advice, guidance or assistance as may promote the welfare of children by diminishing the need to receive children into or keep them in care, or bring them before a juvenile court.

Health Services and Public Health Act 1968
Section 64: The powers of the Secretary of State to give grants to voluntary organisations were delegated on 1 April 1974 to the regional and area health authorities set up under the National Health Service Reorganisation Act 1973, for local voluntary projects in the health field.

Section 65(1): empowers a local authority to make grants to voluntary organisations in the health and social services field who are providing a service which a local authority must or may provide, or who are promoting or publicising such a service or similar one, or giving advice on how such a service or a similar one can best be provided.

Section 65(2):   empowers a local authority to assist a voluntary organisation providing a service as under Section 65(1), by permitting them to use local authority premises, and by making available furniture, vehicles or equipment and the services of any local authority staff related to these (whether by loan, gift or otherwise).

Local Authority (Goods and Services) Act 1970
Section 1:   empowers a local authority to provide goods and services to other local authorities and to public bodies designated by orders under the Act.
SI 1972 No. 853 and SI 1975 No. 193 define the other public bodies, which include voluntary organisations.

Local Government Act 1972
Section 111:   gives local authorities the power to do anything (whether or nt involving the expenditure, borrowing or lending of money, or the acquisition or disposal of any property or rights) which is calculated to facilitate, or is conducive or incidental to, the discharge of any of their functions.

Section 137:   gives local authorities power to incur expenditure in the interests of their area which is not otherwise authorised; in particular they may contribute to the funds of charitable bodies in furtherance of their work in the United Kingdom, or of bodies providing any public service in the United Kingdom other than for purposes of gain. Total expenditure under this section is limited to the product of a 2p rate.

Local Government (Miscellaneous Provisions) Act 1976
Section 19:   gives local authorities power to provide premises for the use of clubs or societies having athletic, social or recreational objects; to make recreational

facilities available free or at reduced charges to such people as they think fit; and to make grants or loans to help voluntary bodies provide recreational facilities of a kind which the local authorities themselves have power to provide.

National Health Service Act 1977

Section 21(3): empowers a local social services authority to provide (or improve, or furnish) residential accommodation for officers employed by a voluntary organisation in relation to the care of mothers and young children, prevention, care and aftercare of illness, and home help and laundry services.

Section 23: The powers of the Secretary of State to make available to voluntary organisations, eligible for assistance under section 64 or section 65 of the Health Services and Public Health Act 1968, any facilities (including goods or materials, or the use of any premises and the use of any vehicle, plant or apparatus) provided by him for any service now under the National Health Service Act were delegated on 1 April 1974 to the regional and area health authorities set up under the National Health Service Reorganisation Act 1973.

Housing (Homeless Persons) Act 1977

Section 13: gives a housing authority power to make grants or loans to voluntary organisations operating in the field of homelessness. They may also provide premises, goods and the services of staff.

Price Commission Act 1977

Section 18(1) allows for payments to be made in respect of expenditure incurred in connection with the collection and dissemination of information relating to prices and charges and associated information. (This provision applies to England, Scotland, Wales and Northern Ireland.)

| Transport Act | enables voluntary bodies to operate community bus and social car schemes and empowers non-metropolitan local authorities to make a contribution to such schemes. |

From: The Home Office, Voluntary Services Unit, *The Government and the Voluntary Sector: a Consultative Document,* Home Office (1978), Appendix 1, pp. 45–7.

Document Five

THE VOLUNTARY WORKER IN THE SOCIAL SERVICES

CONCLUSIONS AND RECOMMENDATIONS

THE ROLE OF THE VOLUNTARY WORKER

1. *The place of volunteers in the expanding social services.* Voluntary workers have an essential part to play in the provision of personal social services. The special contribution of volunteers, as representing community participation in the social services, and as complementing the work of paid staff, should be recognized. (117, 118, 123, 124, 281)

2. *Clarification of aims.* The place of voluntary workers in each service or area of need should be re-examined, in order that their roles may be clarified and greater purpose and direction given to their work. (125, 282)

3. *Review of tasks appropriate for voluntary workers.* The distinction between practical tasks appropriate for volunteers, and those for which paid staff are employed, should be kept under review. Except in an emergency, volunteers should not be used, in public services, to undertake manual or domestic tasks, for which paid workers are normally employed. (119, 120, 121, 283)

ORGANIZATION OF THE WORK OF VOLUNTEERS

4. *Organizers of voluntary service.* There should be a full-time or part-time organizer of the work of volunteers in every service in which they are employed: the post may be held by a paid or voluntary worker without professional qualifications; or in certain circumstances by a social worker. (127, 145, 146, 294, 295)

5. *Organization by statutory and voluntary bodies.* Voluntary bodies have important continuing functions in obtaining and organizing the help of volunteers, and we expect that these functions will also increasingly be exercised by statutory bodies. Agencies of both

kinds must ensure that there is an effective organization with adequate financial support. (128, 132–134, 285–293)

6. *Volunteer bureaux.* There should be a comprehensive network of volunteer bureaux, as centres of advice and information for volunteers and to assist statutory and voluntary bodies which need their help. Their functions would include recruitment and preliminary selection and the keeping of records of volunteers. (143, 163, 164, 179, 180, 296)

7. *Financing of bureaux.* Local authorities should bear the major responsibility for financing volunteer bureaux. (143, 297)

8. *The volunteers' need for memebership of an organization.* Volunteers who are not members of an organization which gives them a sense of corporate identity may wish to establish an organization of their own, and should be encouraged to do so. (151)

9. *Expenses of volunteers.* Statutory and voluntary agencies should expect to pay travelling and other out-of-pocket expenses of their voluntary workers. (155)

10. *Insurance.* The insurance of voluntary workers should be considered by every organization which uses them, and every volunteer should know what arrangements are made. (156)

11. *Identification.* Each voluntary worker should be provided with some authorization or other evidence of his identity and bona fides. (157)

RECRUITMENT AND SELECTION

12. *Extension of recruitment.* Active recruiting methods should be developed with a view to increasing the number of volunteers and widening the fields from which they are drawn. (165, 166, 298)

13. *Organization of recruitment.* In every agency using volunteers there should be some person responsible for the organisazation of recruitment. (171)

14. *Criteria for recruitment.* Agencies should formulate their requirements more precisely and specify more clearly what kinds of people are wanted for particular services or specific jobs. (167)

15. *Recruitment of older people.* Particular attention should be paid to the recruitment of older people and to ways of attracting the recently retired to work which is specially appropriate for them. (169, 170)

16. *Selection.* Every agency which needs to select volunteers should develop selection procedures applicable to their fields of work, and apply them. (183)

17. *Prearation.* All volunteers need preparation for their wok. (186, 187)
18. *General educational courses.* Courses on the social services should be provided more generally by educational bodies in order that people of all ages may be aware of social needs and services. (210)
19. *Mass media.* Radio and television have an important part to play in developing interest in voluntary service and disseminating information about it. (217)
20. *Schools.* Voluntary service by school children is to be encouraged, but participation in community service should not be made part of the curriculum and undertaken as a school subject. (211–214)
21. *Organization of training.* In each agency there should be a person who is responsible for the promotion of training for its voluntary workers, and for ensuring that they are able to obtain it. (251, 252)
22. *Content of training.* The content of training should be closely related to the volunteer's needs and the work which he will do. (218–226)
23. *Methods.* Methods of training should be informal and flexible to suit the needs of people of a wide age range, from varied backgrounds, and often not academically inclined. (227)
24. *Supervision.* Supervision, consultation and advice should always be available to volunteers, and are particularly important for those whose work involves close personal relationships with clients. (233–237)
25. *Further training.* Short courses, conferences, seminars and discussion groups should be available to volunteers who have had some training and have started work. (242)
26. *Training for special responsibilities.* Short courses should be provided for both paid and voluntary workers who undertake work as organizers, trainers or supervisors of volunteers. (159, 243)
27. *Local Joint Committees.* Training should be co-ordinated locally, resources pooled, and courses planned to meet the common needs of volunteers in a number of different services. To assist in co-ordination, and to provide a local focus for the discussion and provision of training, Joint Committees should be established. (248, 249, 300)
28. *Financing training.* Statutory and voluntary agencies should regard the cost of training for volunteers as an essential item of

expenditure and make provision for it: local authorities should take account of this in considering their grants to voluntary bodies. (254, 255)

SOCIAL WORKERS AND VOLUNTEERS

30. *The training of social workers.* Greater attention should be paid in both the theoretical and the field training of social workers, to increasing their understanding of the contribution of voluntary workers, both as individuals and as demonstrating the growing participation by the community in the provision of social services. (266–272, 284)

31. *Functions of social workers and volunteers.* In all the social services there is a place for volunteers, but they should not be expected to undertake work for which professional training is required. Agencies which undertake to help people with serious social or personal problems need professional staff as well as voluntary workers. (278, 279)

A NATIONAL BODY

32. *The Volunteer Foundation.* We recommend the setting up of a national body financed initially from public funds; to be called the Volunteer Foundation and be a focus for all aspects of the work of volunteers. (250, 301, 302)

From: The Aves Committee, *Report on the Voluntary Worker in the Social Services*, Bedford Square Press, London (1969), pp. 195–8.

In our view the informal and statutory systems, taken together, constitute the principal means of meeting social needs in our society. In most of the areas of need with which we are concerned the commercial system remains marginal for the large majority of the population. Although the voluntary system, as we have shown, was once the chief form of collective action outside the Poor Law, it can now best be seen in terms of the ways in which it complements, supplements, extends and influences the informal and statutory systems. Beyond its contribution in these ways, however, we believe it should be evaluated in its role as one of the institutions in a pluralistic system of government and social structure. In subsequent chapters we review such evidence as we have been able to assemble on the scope and performance of the voluntary sector. Here we attempt only to identify some of the principal ways in which it has been suggested that the voluntary system can interrelate constructively with the informal and statutory systems.

The relationship of the voluntary and statutory systems In relation to the statutory system it would seem that the voluntary system may have three kinds of contribution to make. First, it may be able to extend the scope of existing provision. Second, it may be able to improve the standards of statutory provision. Finally, it may be able to offer services where little or nothing is available through the state.

Extending provision The voluntary sector can extend in a number of ways the services provided by the State. Traditionally, the voluntary organisation has been the setting for innovation. New methods of treatment, for example, have been developed in work with families and with delinquents. A second important way in which statutory services can be extended by the voluntary sector is by the provision of alternatives to statutory services (e.g. residential care for children, the handicapped, the elderly, youth clubs, housing associations). These not only extend the quantity of provision but extend the choices available to users of the service. Thirdly, voluntary organisations can be said to extend the absolute amount of resources available to the social services by attracting people, ideas and material resources that would not have been attracted by statutory organisations. People are often more willing to give time, energy and money to a voluntary body devoted to a specific cause than to a statutory agency. Finally, voluntary organisations may offer direct support services to statutory bodies, as for example, does the WRVS in providing meals on wheels, hospital trolleys and so on, and as do the various organisations of 'friends' which have grown up to help residential homes, social service teams and hospitals.

Improving the quality of government provision. The quality of government provision may be improved by the voluntary sector's extension. Where an alternative can be offered to state provision, the statutory service is no longer in a monopoly position. Choice for the user means the right to turn down the statutory service, with implications for subsequent effort to improve the service and make it closer to what the user wants. A second way in which the monolothic aspects of statutory provision may be diluted by voluntary activity is where the voluntary organisation works closely with a statutory body and opportunities are afforded to members of the voluntary organisation to observe or infiltrate the statutory body (e.g. 'friends' in a hospital). The very presence of outsiders can prevent possible abuses of power and stimulate higher standards of provision. Thirdly, voluntary organisations, whether working with statutory services or not, are well placed to act as independent critics and pressure groups. Similarly they can become specialists in the range of statutory services available and offer disinterested advice to users on their rights.

Sole or principal provider. For various reasons some recognised social needs may attract little or no response from the state. For example, the need concerned may be rated as a low priority (as in the case of pre-school play) or as inappropriate for direct statutory involvement (as in the case of certain kinds of advice and counselling). In such fields the provision of service will depend mainly or exclusively on the voluntary sector.

From: The Wolfenden Committee, *The Future of Voluntary Organisations*, Croom Helm, London (1978), pp. 26–7.

Document Seven

THE GOVERNMENT AND THE VOLUNTARY SECTOR

The Government pays tribute to the valuable work of Lord Wolfenden and his Committee on the Future of Voluntary Organisations, and to the support given by the Joseph Rowntree Trust and the Carnegie United Kingdom Trust which made this possible. We welcome the Committee's report for its useful survey of voluntary organisations and for identifying a number of important issues for further discussion.

The voluntary organisations play an indispensable part in our society. They are the essential partners of the statutory authorities in the provision of such services of the Welfare State as education, health, social service and the protection of the environment. Whatever the scale of statutory provision, we cannot do without the extra contribution from the voluntary sector. Individual volunteers and voluntary organisations help to provide social care in many areas. They bring to light new needs and help to meet them. In doing so, they represent one of the essential elements of a healthy democratic society. To involve the people themselves in the development of social services is the best way of ensuring that real need is met.

The Government's recognition of the role of the voluntary sector is reflected in the financial support we provide in various ways. We make direct grants to voluntary organisations. Resources are made available to voluntary activity through the Urban Programme, the Inner City Partnership and the joint financial arrangements of health authorities. Tax relief is another source of help, as are Government-sponsored research projects. The local authorities, similarly, support voluntary effort in their areas. They make direct grants, afford rate relief, and contribute to particular projects. They may also use services provided by voluntary agencies on a fee-paying basis, and make their own services, facilities and professional support available to the voluntary sector.

The Government has also encouraged a closer collaboration

between voluntary bodies and the statutory services in the fields of health, social services and the like. The Voluntary Services Unit has played its part in promoting a co-ordinated approach among government departments and in seeking to develop fruitful contacts between voluntary organisations and central government. We now intend to strengthen the Unit so that it can play a more positive role in co-ordinating the activities of Government and the voluntary sector and in improving the flow of information and views from one sector to another.

The Government has also encouraged community involvement through, for instance, the Good Neighbour Campaign. This has identified many new and worthwhile ways in which individuals and small groups can help to improve the quality of life of their neighbours. The Government looks forward to an even wider development of community involvement in the future.

The Government has however decided that it is time to review, in collaboration with all concerned, its relationships with the voluntary sector, with a view to seeing how its support for the voluntary contribution to our society may be most effectively developed within the available resources.

The present consultative document is offered as part of this process. It provides a means of enabling everybody concerned with the voluntary sector to contribute their views and so take part in the review. Lord Wolfenden's Committee played a valuable part in setting the scene for this sort of fundamental examination of the ways in which our policies can be improved and the voluntary sector strengthened.

From: Home Office Voluntary Services Unit, *The Government and the Voluntary Sector. A Consultative Document*, (1978), pp. i-ii.

RELATIONS BETWEEN THE VOLUNTARY SECTOR AND
GOVERNMENTA CODE FOR VOLUNTARY
ORGANISATIONS

1 Each voluntary body must regard its freely-chosen aims and objectives as paramount under the law in determining its policy and conduct.

2 Each voluntary body should make a conscious strategic judgment of the maximum proportion of government finance in its total income which is compatible with its basic independence as a voluntary body.

3 Each voluntary body should seek, both in its fund-raising strategy and in its financial dealings with government, to ensure that at least in the medium-term it does not allow its dependence on government finance to exceed that prudential proportion.

4 In all financial dealings with government, voluntary bodies should make a distinction between 'arm's-length' support for voluntary activity as such (albeit in a particular sector) and contractual payments on a customer/supplier basis for specific services rendered or functions fulfilled.

5 In the case of 'arm's-length' support voluntary bodies should accept reasonable accountability to establish the propriety of the expenditure, but should not accept interferences in policy or measurement of specific effectiveness.

6 In the case of contractual payments for services rendered voluntary bodies should endeavour to ensure that agreements are clearly written to establish what forms of accountability will be expected and should make a judgment at that time, before the contract is signed, as to whether these are practical and reasonable.

7 In costing services to be rendered under contract with government, voluntary bodies should be careful to include realistic provision for overheads, including management time and skills.

8 If, notwithstanding 4 to 7 above, a voluntary body judges in a particular case that its best intersts require acceptance of govern-

ment financial support on terms which lie between the clear poles of 'arm's-length' grants and contractual payments, then they should do so with a full appreciation that this is a compromise and they should make special efforts to ensure that the forms and degrees of accountability expected are precisely defined from the outset.

9 Subject to 1 to 7 above, voluntary bodies should judge all offers of government financial support, whether 'arm's-length' or 'customer/supplier', by reference to that body's aims and objectives and without primary regard to the possibly different, but overlapping, aims of government policy in offering that funding.

10 Voluntary bodies with charitable status should take care at all times, with appropriate professional advice, to ensure that their activities do not jeopardise their charitable status.

11 Subject to 9 and to the specific aims and objectives of each body, voluntary bodies should assert and exercise their freedom to advocate changes or continuity in public policy, programmes and law to the extent that this is judged to serve the aims and objectives of the body.

12 Voluntary bodies with charitable status, should not overtly or covertly, deliberately or inadvertently, become involved or allow themselves to appear to become involved in influencing the electoral process for or against any person or party.

13 In dealings with local government, voluntary bodies should contrive to apply, as appropriate to their individual circumstance, the principles of the report 'Working Together' (Bedford Square Press, October 1981), bearing in mind the principle of comparative advantage, namely that voluntary bodies should mainly do what they typically are good at (including deployment of volunteer effort, speedy and sensitive response to new social and other needs, imaginative and flexible experimentation with new services and techniques of service delivery and real community involvement) and are not in business to take over or inherit those activities which are best provided by statutory bodies (including local authorities' responsibility for strategic social planning and the large-scale expensive permanent personal and social service).

14 Voluntary bodies should bring to NCVO's attention (directly or through their local membership organisations), to reinforce NCVO's existing representation to Whitehall, examples within their experience of lack of co-ordination between Whitehall departments of the impact of new departments programmes on the voluntary sector.

15 Any voluntary body which becomes aware of apparent discrimination by government on the grounds of the private political convictions or activities of its leaders or staff should record the facts of the case as precisely as possible at the time, afford an early opportunity for the matter to be discussed by the senior officers or trustees of that body and, if the evidence appears substantial, is invited to report the case to NCVO; and

16 Voluntary bodies should consider whether in fact the apparent problems of working in the environment of a government with, as some see it, strong ideological commitments are not fully met by applying the rules above, and, if they are not so satisfied, voluntary bodies would seek further discussion with NCVO.

From: National Council of Voluntary Organisations.

CLASSIFICATIONS

Morice v. Bishop of Durham is, however, deservedly famous for a different reason; while putting the case for the next of kin, Sir Samuel Romilly formulated a classification of charitable purposes which is still influential today:

> There are four objects within one of which all charity, to be administered in this court, must fall. First, relief of the indigent; in various ways: money: provisions: education: medical assistance; etc; Secondly, the advancement of learning; Thirdly the advancement of religion; and Fourthly, which is the most difficult, the advancement of objects of general public utility. [11]

In 1981, nearly a century later, Lord MacNaghten adapted Romilly's classification and gave it the seal of judicial approval:

> How far then, it may be asked, does the popular meaning of the word 'charity' correspond with its legal meaning? 'Charity' in the legal sense comprises four principal divisions: trusts for the relief of poverty; trusts for the advancement of education; trusts for the advancement of religion; and trusts for other purposes beneficial to the community not falling under any of the preceding heads. [12]

The phrasing of the fourth head – 'other purposes beneficial to the community' – does not, however, mean *all* other such purposes but only those established by precedent – i.e. *some* other purposes beneficial to the community.

The Romilly/MacNaghten classification is followed by most textbooks and other guides to the field although often with some criticism of its adequacy. But there is a growing tendency to expand the classification, accepting the first three heads of the Romilly/MacNaghten scheme:

1. *relief of poverty*
2. *advancement of education* (including research and the arts)
3. *advancement of religion*

but sub-dividing the fourth, 'other purposes' head as covering too large a multitude of charitable purposes. There are at least four other major categories which might be described as:

4. *promotion of health* (including relief of aged and disabled people)
5. *social rehabilitation* (including help for refugees and disaster victims; ex-prisoners and other ex-offenders; alcoholics and drug addicts)
6. *provision and maintenance of public amenities* (including roads, bridges etc; libraries, museums etc; parks, recreational facilities etc; preservation of historic monuments; etc.)
7. *protection of animals and the natural environment generally* as well as a number of other, miscellaneous purposes making up a residual category of
8. *other purposes 'beneficial to the community'* (including the promotion of agriculture, industry and commerce; the protection of human life and property; the preservation of public order; and the defence of the realm).

From: F. Gladstone, *Charity Law and Social Justice*, Bedford Square Press, London (1982)

To sum up: case law has defined political activity as either (1) advancement of party politics: or (2) advancement of a political doctrine; or (3) promoting to the public a particular view on a broad social question (e.g. racial harmony); or (4) seeking or opposing a change in the law or in administrative practice. Broadly, none of these categories can be a valid charitable purpose, as such. But (3) and (4) may be permissible as a *means* to a non-political purpose provided that

●means and ends are *directly* connected

●the charity's *constitution* explicitly contains the relevant purpose

●it is not the sole means to the end (the 'substantiality' issue).
The Charity Commission has provided guidelines for trustees, notably in its annual reports for 1969 and 1981. These go well beyond the legal precedents in at least one respect: they lay great emphasis on the *style* of political activity – a 'reasoned memorandum' is acceptable but a public demonstration is not. It should be done in a seemly way.

This leaves a number of grey areas. What exactly is *substantial* – 20%, 50% or what? Where does *seemly* blend into unseemly? Where is the boundary between *direct* and indirect connection of ends and means?

One way of getting round the problem is to find a suitable non-political charitable purpose to which political activity is ancillary. This would not seem to help with peace, race relations or human rights but, interestingly, the Charity Commissioners have registered as charities the Institute for Race Relations as well as various branches of the Community Relations Commission. All of these have carefully worded their objects to include the advancement of education and the provision of recreational facilities. Failing this, an alternative solution is to split your organisation into two or more bodies some charitable, some 'political'. Some voluntary organisations have done this, War on Want, for example, and the National Council for Civil Liberties (NCCL); but in practice there seems usually to be a fairly high administrative price to pay.

From: F. Gladstone, *Voluntary Action*, NCVO, Autumn 1982, p. 14.

Document Eleven

POLITICAL ACTIVITIES BY CHARITIES

21. Political Activities by Charities

I believe it is not only the right but in fact the duty of charities in many areas to act as political pressure groups, and that legislation must end the present uncertainty about this forthwith. The days of confining charities to pouring soup into faulty old bottles should be consigned to the past; such cosmetic philanthropy can in fact be capable of postponing the more fundamental reforms that may be needed. Campaigning for changes in laws is often not only the most cost-effective but virtually the only policy for organisations like the Disablement Income Group or the Finer Action Committee to adopt: they cannot hope to finance the needs of disabled people or of one-parent families themselves. To further illustrate this point, it is worth recalling that when the British government cut its overseas aid programme by £20m in 1966 it did so by a sum greater than the total of all Oxfam's spending since its inception in 1942. It could be argued that if, instead of financing projects abroad, Oxfam concentrated on education, propaganda and political pressure in Britian which resulted in the government increasing its present net aid budget by even 10 per cent, vastly more 'poverty, distress and suffering' would be relieved overseas.

22. Politics – as distinct from party politics – being a charity's responsibility, one important role for contemporary charities can be, for instance, to act as lobbies for the deprived, the unorganised, or the unpopular. They can exert pressure on behalf of the inarticulate and those most in need: to campaign, for example, to make state schools as good as some (at present) charitable private schools are, or public libraries as good as the (at present charitable) London Library. While declaring my own interest in a number of organisations concerned with human rights, I know that support for such causes is shared by people of all party politics and of none: concern for justice, freedom of expression, mercy, etc., is felt by members of widely differing political views. I therefore cannot share the dilemma expressed in

paragraph 102 of the Majority Report. It would be ironic if (as at present) the prevention of cruelty to animals continued to be encouraged with charitable status for the RSPCA, while the prevention of cruelty to humans is not because similar status is withheld from Amnesty. I was impressed by the evidence of the then Permanent Secretary at the Department of the Environment, Sir James Jones: 'In the formulation of Departmental policy we are very considerably influenced, both at ministerial and at official level, by the views of charitable organisations . . . I would not wish to claim that we always see eye to eye with these bodies, since they properly see it as part of their function to identify departmental shortcomings. But I think we would always be prepared to admit that our policy-thinking would be narrower and poorer in quality without the stimulus arising from our contact with pressure groups of this kind. We would not therefore favour any argument that charities should abjure lobbying and should be made to stick to their more limited role of direct action in providing housing or relieving distress'.

23. The current opaque position, in any event does allow some political activity – but only on an anomalous and unfairly selective basis. On many occasions tax-exempt Churches campaign and try to influence both the government and voters about laws concerning – for example – divorce, abortion, birth control and other questions which affect even those who are not their co-religionists. Furthermore the present restrictions, real or assumed, result in most charities having to support the status quo, which in itself is a political attitude. The campaigning of the Lord's Day Observance Society (a charity) which persistently lobbies Parliament, is one active example: others play a similar role passively. Of course charities existing to defend current policies must be treated equally with those seeking change.

From: Ben Whitaker, Minority Report, *Charity Law and Voluntary Organisations, Report of the Goodman Committee*, Bedford Square Press, London (1976), pp. 148–50.

INNER CITY PARTNERSHIPS AND THE VOLUNTARY SECTOR

35. Some things will be better done, or done more satisfyingly, if they are undertaken by voluntary groups and bodies. The improvement of the inner areas needs to harness the good will and energies of tenants' and residents' associations, local councils of social service, settlements and charities, and more informal groups such as pensioners' clubs. The interest of trades unions and chambers of commerce should also be engaged. Public policy should aim to stimulate voluntary effort and help voluntary bodies to play a constructive role. This may require both local and central government to apply procedures and standards more flexibly to meet local needs. In some places elected Neighbourhood Councils (in Scotland Community Councils) may have a role in representing the community's views and in mobilising voluntary effort.

103. The regeneration of the inner areas is not, however, a job for central or local government alone. A new and closer form of collaboration is required between government and the private sector, between government and the community including the various representative organisations in the cities and bigger towns, with the voluntary bodies, and above all with the people living in the inner areas. It is their welfare, immediate and longer term, which must be the ultimate touchstone for success.

From: *Policy For The Inner Cities*, Cmnd 6845, June 1977.

INNER CITY PARTNERSHIPS AND LOCAL INVOLVEMENT

'I think that we would all agree that it is very important to involve the people in our cities – certainly in our cities with the worst problems – in the programmes of revitalisation which all of them wish to undertake. I believe that most local authorities have a whole network of connections with voluntary bodies in their areas. They are aware of the contribution that voluntary bodies can make, and I believe that that contribution will be a growing one in the period ahead.'

'. . . I am particularly taking up with the new partnership authorities under the inner city programme the whole question of how they can bring into the picture in perhaps a more regular way the local bodies in their areas in order to help them play their part in the programme.'

From: *Secretary of State for the Environment*, Peter Shore, answering questions in the House of Commons, 27 July 1977 (Hansard, cols 609, 610).

THE BARCLAY COMMITTEE'S VIEW OF THE VOLUNTARY SECTOR

The future for partnership

5.64 In this section we list briefly some practical issues which need to be addressed if a partnership of the kind we envisage is to evolve. Behind all of them lies the assumption that both sectors need each other and that neither is automatically the main sector in any particular situation. Local authorities must accept that the services they provide are a drop in the bucket compared to the social caring that goes on day and night, week-ends and year by year everywhere, and we focus below on ways in which they might reorient and reorganise themselves in relation to this vast army of carers.

5.65 Partnership must start with joint planning and joint analysis of the needs which the services and networks are required to meet.

5.66 Consultative and collaborative machinery is required which will allow decision making to be at the very least fully informed by (and consideration given to how it might in some circumstances be shared by), not only formal voluntary organisations but also local self-help groups and other parts of the caring networks.

5.67 The grant-making process of local authorities is by no means always open or clear enough for it to be readily understood by the voluntary sector. This can pose particular problems for new organisations, who may be challenging old methods of working or exploring new needs, and who may be quite reliant in their early years on local authority grants.

5.68 The secondment of staff from local authority to voluntary organisations and vice versa may provide a means of promoting partnership. Where we saw this in practice it clearly had much to commend it.

5.69 Joint research endeavours should be more actively considered particularly in relation to matters concerning informal networks and volunteers where we still know comparatively little.

5.70 Some of the informal voluntary organisations might well be in a position to offer more training opportunities to the statutory services because of their specialist work or their particular methods of working.

5.71 Active consideration needs to be given to the appropriate use of volunteers in a particular area or with a particular type of problem. Joint work needs to be undertaken if volunteers are to be fully used and properly trained and supported.

5.72 A partnership is most critically needed in social work with ethnic minorities and we can only lend our voice to the growing number of reports that highlight that need.

5.73 Written agreements exist between some local authorities and some voluntary agencies and serve to clarify questions of accountability. More use could be made of this method of making the partnership explicit.

From: The Barclay Committee, *Social Workers: Their Role and Tasks*, Bedford Square Press, London (1982), pp. 90–1

Document Fifteen

THE BARCLAY COMMITTEE'S VIEW OF THE VOLUNTARY SECTOR

SUMMARY OF CONCLUSIONS

1. Without informal caring the social services would barely be viable: but it cannot be limitlessly increased (5.10–11).

2. Social workers need particular skills in developing relationships with informal carers (5.12).

3. The variety of mutual aid groups demonstrates the need felt for mutual support; we would encourage social workers to continue to be active in establishing and supporting such groups (5.13–16).

4. Engaging and using volunteers satisfactorily and within their familiar situations is a sensitive and skilled task; acceptable principles of accountability have to be agreed by social workers and management (5.17–22).

5. Clients are potential volunteers: segregation of client groups may mask their potential (5.21).

6. The role of social workers in formal voluntary organisations differs from that of their colleagues in statutory agencies in emphasis rather than activities: their independence enables them to adopt a watchdog role; they often specialise, sometimes in a narrow field, and have scope for preventive work; they should be encouraged to test out new ideas (5.25–35).

7. The voluntary sector provides an alternative to statutory agencies and is better placed to carry out certain functions, but cannot, and should not, replace them (5.36–37).

8. It is likely that new organisations are needed to develop voluntary sector social work with ethnic minorities; social services departments should establish appropriate links with such projects (5.38–39).

9. Statutory and voluntary services should be seen as complementary and a partnership should be developed between them allowing joint planning and agreed distribution of tasks (5.40–54, 62–78).

10. We recognise that accountability and equity are complex issues (5.55–61).

11. The grant-making process of local authorities should be open: mutual secondment of staff, joint research, and collaboration in developing use of volunteers are commended (5.67–72).
12. More use should be made of written agreements: 'purchase of service contracting' should be further explored (5.73–75).

From: The Barclay Committee, *Social Workers: Their Role and Tasks*, Bedford Square Press, London (1982), p. 93.

SELECT BIBLIOGRAPHY

HISTORICAL

BEVERIDGE, W., *Voluntary Action*. Allen & Unwin: London, 1948.

BEVERIDGE, W. and WELLS, A. F., *The Evidence for Voluntary Action*. Allen & Unwin: London, 1949.

BOURDILLON, A. F. C., *Voluntary Social Services*. Methuen: London, 1945.

BRASNETT, M., *Voluntary Social Action: A History of the National Council of Social Services*. NCSS, London, 1969.

CROSSMAN, R., 'The role of the volunteer in the modern social service', in A. H. Halsey, (ed.) *Tradition in Social Policy*. Blackwell: Oxford, 1976.

HMSO, *Report of the Committee on the Law and Practice relating to charitable trusts* (The Nathan Report). HMSO: London, 1952.

MORRIS, M., *Voluntary Organisations and Social Progress*. Gollancz: London, 1955.

OWEN, D., *English Philanthropy 1660–1960*. Harvard University Press: Cambridge, Mass., 1965.

ROOFF, M., *Voluntary Societies and Social Policy*. Routledge & Kegan Paul: London, 1959.

WEBB, B. and S., *The Prevention of Destitution*. Longman, London, 1912.

GENERAL

ABRAMS, P., *Patterns of Neighbourhood Care*. The Volunteer Centre: Berkhamsted, 1979.

AVES, G., *The Voluntary Worker in the Social Services*. Bedford Square Press: London, 1969.

BARCLAY COMMITTEE, *Social Workers – Their Role and Tasks*. Bedford Square Press: London, 1982.

BERESFORD, P. and CROFT, S., 'Welfare pluralism: the new face of

Fabianism', *Critical Social Policy*, Issue 9, Spring 1984.

BIRRELL, W. D. and WILLIAMSON, A. P., *Voluntary Organisations in the United Kingdom and their Role in Combating Poverty*. Social Administration Department, New University of Ulster, 1980.

BRENTON, M., 'Changing relationships in the Dutch social services', *Journal of Social Policy*, Vol. 11, Part 1, January 1982.

BRENTON, M., 'Privatisation and voluntary sector social services', in C. Jones and M. Brenton (eds), *The Year Book of Social Policy in Britain, 1984–85*. Routledge & Kegan Paul: London, 1985.

CHARITIES AID FOUNDATION, *Charities Statistics*. CAF: Tonbridge, 1984, 1985.

DAVIES, B., *The Cost-Effectiveness Imperative: the Social Services and Volunteers*. The Volunteer Centre: Berkhamsted, 1980.

DAVIES, B., 'Strategic goals and piecemeal innovations: adjusting to the new balance of needs and resources', in E. M. Goldberg and S. Hatch, (eds), *A New Look at the Personal Social Services*. Policy Studies Institute: London, 1981.

DONEE GROUP, *Private Philanthropy: Vital and Innovative or Passive and Irrelevant?* Center for Community Change: Washington DC, 1975.

FILER, J., *Giving in America: Toward a Stronger Voluntary Sector* (The Filer Commission Report on Private Philanthropy and Public Need). Washington DC, 1975.

GERARD, D., *Charities in Focus: Conservatism or Change?* Bedford Square Press: London, 1983.

GLADSTONE, F., *Voluntary Action in a Changing World*. Bedford Square Press: London, 1979.

GLADSTONE, F., *Charity Law and Social Justice*. Bedford Square Press: London, 1982.

GOODMAN, A., *Charity Law and Voluntary Organisations* (The Goodman Report). Bedford Square Press: London, 1976.

GRIFFITHS, H., *The Development of Local Voluntary Action*. The Volunteer Centre: Berkhamsted, 1981.

GRIFFITHS, H. *et al.*, *Yesterday's Heritage or Tomorrow's Resource: A Study of Voluntary Organisations Providing Social Services in Northern Ireland*. Social Administration Department, New University of Ulster, 1978.

HADLEY, R., and HATCH, S., *Social Welfare and the Failure of the State: Centralised Social Services and Participatory Alternatives*, Allen & Unwin: London, 1981.

HADLEY, R. and McGRATH, M., *Going Local: Neighbourhood Social Services*, NCVO Occasional Paper. Bedford Square Press:

London, 1980.

HADLEY, R., WEBB, A. and FARRELL, C., *Across the Generations*. Allen & Unwin: London, 1975.

HATCH, S., *Voluntary Work: A Report of a Survey*. The Volunteer Centre: Berkhamsted, 1978.

HATCH, S., 'The Wolfenden Report on voluntary organisations', in M. Brown and S. Baldwin (eds), *The Year Book of Social Policy in Britain 1978*. Routledge & Kegan Paul: London, 1979.

HATCH, S., *Outside the State: Voluntary Organisations in Three English Towns*. Croom Helm: London, 1980.

HATCH, S. (ed.), *Mutual Aid and Health Care*. Bedford Square Press: London, 1981.

HATCH, S., 'The voluntary sector: a larger role?', in E. M. Goldberg and S. Hatch (eds), *A New Look at the Personal Social Services*. Policy Studies Institute: London, 1981.

HATCH, S. and MOCROFT, I., 'Factors affecting the location of voluntary organisation branches', *Policy and Politics*, 6 (1977).

HATCH, S., and MOCROFT, I., 'The relative costs of services provided by voluntary and statutory organisations', *Public Administration*, Winter 1979.

HATCH, S. and MOCROFT, I., *Components of Welfare: Voluntary Organisations, Social Services and Politics in Two Local Authorities*. Bedford Square Press: London, 1983.

HINTON, N. and HYDE, M., 'The voluntary sector in a remodelled welfare state', in C. Jones and J. Stevenson (eds), *The Year Book of Social Policy in Britain, 1980-81*. Routledge & Kegan Paul: London, 1982.

HOLME, A., and MAIZELS, J., *Social Workers and Volunteers*. Allen & Unwin: London, 1978.

HOME OFFICE, VOLUNTARY SERVICES UNIT, *The Government and the Voluntary Sector: A Consultative Document*. 1978.

HOME OFFICE, VOLUNTARY SERVICES UNIT, *The Government and the Voluntary Sector: An Analysis of the Response to the Consultative Document*. 1981.

JOHNSON, N., *Voluntary Social Services*. Blackwell & Robertson: Oxford, 1981.

KRAMER, R., 'Public fiscal policy and voluntary agencies in welfare states', *Social Services Review*, March 1979.

KRAMER, R., 'Voluntary agencies in the welfare state: an analysis of the vanguard role', *Journal of Social Policy*, 8: 4 October 1979.

KRAMER, R., *Voluntary Agencies in the Welfare State*. University of California Press: Berkeley, Calif., 1981.

LANNING, H., *Government and the Voluntary Sector in the USA*. NCVO: London, 1981.

LAWRENCE, R., 'Voluntary action: a stalking horse for the Right?', *Critical Social Policy*, 2:3, Spring 1983.

LEAT, D., SMOLKA, G. and UNELL, J., *Voluntary and Statutory Collaboration: Rhetoric or Reality?* Bedford Square Press: London, 1981.

NEWTON, K., *Second-City Politics: Democratic Processes and Decision-making in Birmingham*. Clarendon Press: Oxford, 1976.

NIGHTINGALE, B., *Charities*. Allen Lane: London, 1973.

RAISON, T., *The Voluntary Sector: Some Questions*. Association of Researchers into Voluntary Action and Community Involvement (ARVAC): London 1980.

RICHARDSON, A. and GOODMAN, M., *Self-Help and Social Care: Mutual Aid Organisations in Practice*. Policy Studies Institute: London, 1983.

ROWE, A., 'The Voluntary Services Unit', in K. Jones (ed.), *The Year Book of Social Policy in Britain, 1973*. Routledge & Kegan Paul: London, 1974.

SCOTT, D. and WILDING, P., *Beyond Welfare Pluralism*. Manchester Council of Voluntary Service, 1984.

SMITH, C. and FREEDMAN, A., *Voluntary Associations: Perspectives on the Literature*. Harvard University Press: Cambridge, Mass., 1972.

UNELL, J., *Voluntary Social Services: Financial Resources*. Bedford Square Press: London, 1979.

UTTING, B., 'Personal care by government purchase: lessons from the American experience', *Social Work Service*, 31, Autumn 1982.

WALKER, A., *Community Care – the Family, the State and Social Policy*. Blackwell & Robertson: Oxford, 1982.

WEBB, A. *et al.*, *Voluntary Social Services: Manpower Resources*. Personal Social Services Council: London 1976.

WEBB, A. and WISTOW, G., *Whither State Welfare? Policy and Implementation in the Personal Social Services*. RIPA: London, 1982.

WEISBROD, B., *The Voluntary Non-Profit Sector*. Lexington Books: Lexington, Mass., 1977.

WHITAKER, B., *The Foundations*. Eyre Methuen: London, 1974.

WILLIAMS, G., *Inner City Policy: A Partnership with the Voluntary Sector?* NCVO Occasional Paper. Bedford Square Press: London, 1983.

INDEX

Index